The Best of
"The Spirit of Medjugorje"

Volume I
1988-1997

Compiled by
June Klins

authorHOUSE™

1663 LIBERTY DRIVE, SUITE 200
BLOOMINGTON, INDIANA 47403
(800) 839-8640
WWW.AUTHORHOUSE.COM

First published by AuthorHouse 06/24/05

ISBN: 1-4208-4103-3 (sc)

Printed in the United States of America
Bloomington, Indiana

This book is printed on acid-free paper.

Editors declaration:
The decree of the Congregation for the Propagation of the Faith, A.A.S., 58,1186 (approved by Pope Paul VI on October 14, 1966) states that the Nihil Obstat and Imprimatur are no longer required on publications that deal with private revelations, provided they contain nothing contrary to faith and morals. The events of Medjugorje are presently under investigation. The editor and writers of the following works wish to affirm our readiness to accept the final judgment of the magisterium of the Church. A final decree of the Church will be made known once the apparitions cease.
Although the editor of this book and the previous editor of "The Spirit of Medjugorje" have made every effort to ensure the accuracy of information contained in this book, we assume no responsibility for errors, inaccuracies, omissions, or any inconsistency herein.

About the Cover

Designing a cover was the hardest part of creating this work. I wanted the cover to reflect exactly what the "spirit" of Medjugorje is all about. It was on my way home from a Eucharistic Holy Hour where we had prayed 15 decades of the Rosary that the idea popped into my head: The "spirit" of Medjugorje is a spirit of peace, love and joy, and the way to peace, love and joy is to **live the messages** of Our Lady. The cover should be a collage representing the 5 things Our Lady is asking us to do – Pray with the heart, Bible, Eucharist, Confession, and Fasting. These are known as the "five stones" or weapons against Goliath. More on this in Chapters 2 and 4.

All of the pictures on the cover were taken in Medjugorje. Thanks to Bernard Gallagher for the photo of Fr. Jozo with the Bible and to Diana Stillwell for the picture of the Mass celebration in St. James. And a big thanks to Helen Bell for her pictures on the cover as well as most of the pictures in this book.

This book is dedicated to Our Lady,
Queen of Peace, and to Her faithful daughter,
Joan Wieszczyk,
my predecessor, mentor and friend, whose work is
showcased in this book.

Table of Contents

Acknowledgments

I am very grateful to the Holy Spirit for the inspiration to compile this book, to Our Lady, for Her loving guidance through this project, and to all the people who prayed for this book to become a reality.

I am thankful to Joan Wieszczyk for her sixteen years of loving service as editor of "The Spirit of Medjugorje," and for her blessing and support in the publishing of this book. I am very grateful to Carolanne Kilichowski and also to Joan for their help with the arduous job of proofreading. I would like to acknowledge Helen Bell for the photographs of her pilgrimages to Medjugorje and Medjugorje conferences and events. With the exception of a few photographs, all the pictures contained in this book were taken by Helen. And, last but not least, I would like to thank all of those who consented to the re-publishing of their works in this book. I would like to pay tribute in a special way to both Msgr. James Peterson, the spiritual director of "The Spirit of Medjugorje" newsletter, and Sr. Emmanuel of "Children of Medjugorje," for their numerous and outstanding contributions.

Foreword

A short time ago, I gave several copies of the Message of Medjugorje to a man recently out of prison. When he finished reading them, he said, "Why didn't anyone ever tell me about this? Wow! What a difference it makes!"

This volume is a gold mine. It contains many messages from Mary – for individuals and for the whole world. It contains the testimony of sincere, simple, honest visionaries, of people earnest about their locutions.

It contains many beautiful and impressive testimonies from pilgrims whose lives have been enriched by their own visits to Medjugorje. It has some powerful excerpts of talks given by the spiritual directors of the witnesses and of the pilgrims.

You would be a rare person if you took the volume and read it through in a day or two. In fact, if you did it that way, you might lose some of its greatest value.

Take them one at a time or a few at a time, and savor them. They will speak to your heart and renew some of its happiest memories. They will also help you to put away some of the annoyances that depress you, when you let these articles lift you. You will understand why we call Mary the "Cause of Our Joy."

My gratitude to the editors and writers and publishers who have shared so generously in making the book possible.

Msgr. James Peterson

Introduction

The Birth of a Book

In 1998, after my first pilgrimage to Medjugorje, I became involved with "The Spirit of Medjugorje" newsletter when someone suggested that I send my testimony to the editor, Joan Wieszczyk. I was impressed with the newsletter from the very beginning, and continued to write at Joan's invitation, and eventually became co-editor. In June of 2002, Joan suffered a heart attack and the newsletter was thrown into my lap. A friend who had been a subscriber since it was founded in 1988 gave me all the newsletters she had saved over the years because she thought they might help me with ideas.

In March of 2004, I was looking through the old newsletters for something, and I began setting aside articles that I found especially interesting and inspiring. It wasn't long before I had a big stack. I stayed up late that night reading. I did not want to stop. The next morning, the inspiration came to me to compile these articles into a book. I had a good feeling about this, but prayed to discern whether this was God's will or just an idea of my own. (In my heart I thought it was God's will, because on one of my pilgrimages to Medjugorje while I was climbing Apparition Hill all by myself one day, I felt the call to publish a book about Medjugorje.) I went to Mass and Adoration and asked God to let me know if compiling a book was what He really wanted me to do, and asked God for a sign to let me know if this was indeed His will. I got it within a few hours. (See the Epilogue for more on this.)

When this book finally goes to print it will have been more than a year since the idea first germinated. This project turned out to be much more involved than I ever expected. First I presented the idea to Joan, who was excited about the idea of this new way for us to spread Our Lady's messages. Then I went through all the old newsletters to choose the best articles. When I discovered there were too many articles for one book, I decided to limit this book to the first ten years, and call it "Volume One," with the idea that there would eventually be a "Volume Two." Then I talked to our lawyer about the legalities of this, because we are a non-profit organization. He said we could not sell the book, but only ask for donations. This meant we could not put the book in bookstores, and it would only be available for a small fraction of people. I wanted this book to be available for EVERYONE. Our Lady's messages are for EVERYONE. I took all the articles I had chosen to Msgr. James Peterson, the spiritual adviser of "The Spirit of Medjugorje" and asked for his blessing on this project and on me. Msgr. Peterson told me to put the book in my own name so it could be sold. Although I was reluctant at first because it troubled me to put my name on what was ten years of Joan's work, I submitted for the sake of spreading Our Lady's messages.

The next step involved tracking down all the original authors and organizations whose works I had chosen to use. I enjoyed playing "detective," but I met with some disappointments when I was not able to locate some of the people, who had either moved or passed away. So there are a few articles that I chose that do not appear in this volume simply because I was unable to obtain permission to reprint the articles. Most of the people responded enthusiastically with encouragement and prayers.

My Objective

My objective for publishing this book remains the same as the objective of our monthly newsletter – to **instruct** people about Our Lady's messages and to **inspire** them to live and spread the messages. I hope, with the profits, to be able to donate copies of this book to prisons, schools, libraries, etc. My dream is to make enough money for postage to send the books to foreign countries. I want to help spread Our Lady's messages to the whole world.

Who Should Read This Book?

This book is for everyone. For those who do not know much about Medjugorje, it serves as an "extended beginner's guide." (We also publish a "beginner's guide" newsletter for those who know little or nothing about Medjugorje.) For those who have followed Medjugorje, it will serve as a "shot in the arm" to stir up that fire again.

How To Read This Book

This book should not be read in one sitting, but should be read a little at a time so to digest all that Our Lady is telling us. This is especially true for Chapter Two on the visionaries. The talks of the visionaries are very similar - as well they should be, as a sign of the authenticity of the apparitions. This is also true for Chapter Four, which focuses on how to live the messages.

The date at the top of each article is the issue in which the article was originally published. The articles are not in chronological order. I prayed to the Holy Spirit to help me compile and order all of the articles. As I do with the monthly newsletters, I took the book to Mass and Adoration with me for a week and offered it up and asked if there needed to be any changes. Just as there are always changes to the monthly newsletter, so too there were a number of changes with this book.

Please note that the articles that do not have a by-line were either transcribed from a tape or written by a member of the staff at the time. Joan originally had two partners who founded the newsletter with her, Bob Nietupski and Dr. Charles Jackson.

My Prayer

I hope and pray that every person who reads this book will be inspired to live and spread the messages of Our Lady - messages of peace, love and joy. I will pray every day of my life for everyone who reads this book. Thank you for responding to Her call.

Chapter 1:

About Medjugorje

Statue of Our Lady in St. James Church

(6/91)
Anniversary Prayer
By Lee Paolella

It's been ten long years since You first appeared
To six frightened children, chosen by God, Your secrets to hear.
The miracle on Earth touching many hearts,
A mystery divine from the very start.
Appearing each night to save all mankind,
Telling each soul how Heaven they'll find.
You're giving each visionary ten secrets to keep,
As each is unfolded, they want to weep.
They preach, they pray with penance and fast,
So man can overcome evil and gain Heaven at last.
Thousands climb that mountain to watch and stand by,
Amidst a trillion stars in that far away sky.
The sun twirls, bursting with colors galore,
Amazed, they kneel in prayer to the Lord they adore.
There's a light on the hillside moving from place to place,
It is Our Lady saying Her Stations, full of Heavenly grace.
They tell of Her beauty, none can compare
With deep blue eyes and curly dark hair.
Oh, beautiful Mother, You were chosen to lead
All mankind to gain Heaven by prayers and good deeds.
These messages You've given many years have shown
How close a place of glory you have near God's throne.

(1/95)
MARY IS CALLING YOU
By Joan Wieszczyk

On June 24, 1981, in Medjugorje, Our Lady appeared to six children. She identified Herself as the Blessed Virgin, Queen of Peace, and has continued to appear daily. Her message is PEACE, peace with God and man. Her words to the visionaries, "I have come to tell the world that God exists. He is the fullness of life, and to enjoy the fullness and obtain peace, you must return to God."

Today, all but two of the visionaries have daily apparitions of the Blessed Mother. During the apparitions, the visionaries do not react to light, don't hear any sound or react to being touched. They feel that they are outside of time and space. All the visionaries declare to see the Blessed Virgin as they see other people – in three dimensions. They pray and speak with Her.

The Blessed Mother said, "Peace in the world is in a state of crisis." She continually invites us to RECONCILIATION and CONVERSION.

The Blessed Mother is confiding ten secrets to each visionary (some are chastisements for the world) and promises to leave a visible sign at the place of the apparitions in Medjugorje for all humanity. This time, this period of grace, is for CONVERSION and DEEPENING OF FAITH. After the visible sign, those living will have little time for conversion.

The Blessed Mother invites us to PRAYER and FASTING and PEACE. "You have forgotten that with prayer and fasting you can stop a war from happening. You can suspend natural laws."

The reason that the apparitions have continued daily for these many years is because they are the last apparitions of this kind (or this many) of the Blessed Mother on earth.

Editor's update: When this was originally written, 4 of the visionaries were still receiving daily apparitions. Since September 12, 1998, when Jakov Colo had his last daily apparition, only 3 visionaries- Vicka, Ivan and Marija- continue to see Our Lady daily.

Mirjana, Ivanka left of center and Fr. Petar Ljubicic, Ivan, right, at the National Conference on Medjugorje at Notre Dame University, 1993
Photo credit: Carolanne Kilichowski

(9/92)
Official Letter to Pope John Paul II

The following letter was written by Fr. Tomislav Vlasic to Pope John Paul II on December 2, 1983. Fr. Tomislav Vlasic's letter was the fulfillment of Our Lady's urgent request of him. It is the official letter of the former pastor of St. James Church in Medjugorje to Pope John Paul II about the events in Medjugorje. It reports on the revelations that Mirjana received in 1982 and entrusted to Fr. Vlasic on November 5, 1983. The letter reads as follows:

After the apparition of the Blessed Virgin on November 30, 1983, Maria Pavlovic came to me and said, 'The Madonna says that the Supreme Pontiff and the Bishop must be advised immediately of the urgency and great importance of the message of Medjugorje.' This letter seeks to fulfill that duty.

1. Five young people (Vicka Ivankovic, Maria Pavlovic, Ivanka Ivankovic, Ivan Dragicevic, and Jakov Colo) see an apparition of the

5

Blessed Virgin every day. The experience in which they see her is a fact that can be checked by direct observation. It has been filmed. During the apparitions, the youngsters do not react to light, they do not hear sounds, they do not react if someone touches them, they feel that they are beyond time and space. All of the youngsters basically agree that:

"We see the Blessed Virgin just as we see anyone else. We pray with her, we speak to her, and we can touch her."

"The Blessed Virgin says that world peace is at a critical stage. She repeatedly calls for reconciliation and conversion."

"She has promised to leave a visible sign for all humanity at the site of the apparitions of Medjugorje."

"The period preceding this visible sign is a time of grace for conversion and deepening the faith."

"The Blessed Virgin has promised to disclose ten secrets to us. So far, Vicka Ivankovic has received eight. Marija Pavlovic received the ninth one on December 8, 1983. Jakov Colo, Ivan Dragicevic and Ivanka Ivankovic have each received nine. Only Mirjana Dragicevic has received all ten."

"These apparitions are the last apparitions of the Blessed Virgin on earth. That is why they are lasting so long and occurring so frequently."

2. The Blessed Virgin no longer appears to Mirjana Dragicevic. The last time she saw one of the daily apparitions was Christmas 1982. Since then the apparitions have ceased for her, except on her birthday (March 18, 1983). Mirjana knew that this would occur. According to Mirjana, the Madonna confided the tenth and last secret to her during the apparition on December 25, 1982. She also disclosed the dates on which the different secrets will come to pass. The Blessed Virgin has revealed to Mirjana many things about the future, more than to any of the other youngsters so far. For that reason I am reporting below what Mirjana told me during our conversation on November 5, 1983. I am summarizing the substance of her account, without word-for-word quotations: Mirjana said that before the visible sign is given to humanity, there will be three

warnings to the world. The warnings will be in the form of events on earth. Mirjana will be a witness to them. Three days before one of the admonitions, Mirjana will notify a priest of her choice. The witness of Mirjana will be a confirmation of the apparitions and a stimulus for the conversion of the world. After the admonitions, the visible sign will appear on the site of the apparitions in Medjugorje for all the world to see. The sign will be given as a testimony to the apparitions and in order to call the people back to the faith.

The ninth and tenth secrets are serious. They concern chastisement for the sins of the world. Punishment is inevitable, for we cannot expect the whole world to be converted. The punishment can be diminished by prayer and penance, but it cannot be eliminated. Mirjana says that one of the evils that threatened the world, the one contained in the seventh secret, has been averted, thanks to prayer and fasting. That is why the Blessed Virgin continues to encourage prayer and fasting: 'You have forgotten that through prayer and fasting you can avert war and suspend the laws of nature.' After the first admonition, the others will follow in a rather short time. Thus, people will have some time for conversion. That interval will be a period of grace and conversion. After the visible sign appears, those who are still alive will have little time for conversion. For that reason, the Blessed Virgin invites us to urgent conversion and reconciliation. The invitation to prayer and penance is meant to avert evil and war, but most of all to save souls. According to Mirjana, the events predicted by the Blessed Virgin are near. By virtue of this experience, Mirjana proclaims to the world: 'Hurry, be converted; open your hearts to God.'

In addition to this basic message, Mirjana related an apparition she had in 1982, which we believe sheds some light on some aspects of Church history. She spoke of an apparition in which Satan appeared to her disguised as the Blessed Virgin. Satan asked Mirjana to renounce the Madonna and follow him. That way she could be happy in love and in life. He said that following the Virgin, on the contrary, would only lead to suffering. Mirjana rejected him, and immediately the Virgin arrived and Satan disappeared. Then the Blessed Virgin gave her the following message in substance: *'Excuse me for this, but you must realize that Satan exists. One day he appeared before the throne of God and asked permission to submit the Church to a period of trial. God gave him permission to try the Church for one century. This century is under the power of the devil; but when the secrets confided to you come to pass, his power will be destroyed. Even now he is beginning to lose his power and has become aggressive. He is destroying marriages, creating divisions among priests and is responsible for obsessions and murder. You must protect yourselves against these things through fasting and prayer, especially community prayer. Carry blessed objects with you. Put them in your house, and restore the use of holy water.'*

According to certain Catholic experts who have studied these apparitions, this message of Mirjana may shed light on the vision Pope Leo XIII had. According to them, it was after having had an apocalyptic vision of the future of the Church that Leo XIII introduced the prayer to Saint Michael which priests used to recite after Mass up to the time of the Second Vatican Council. These experts say that the century of trials foreseen by Leo XIII is about to end.

Holy Father, I do not want to be responsible for the ruin of anyone. I am doing my best. The world is being called to conversion and reconciliation. In writing to you, Holy Father, I am only doing my duty. After drafting this letter, I gave it to the youngsters so that they might ask the Blessed Virgin whether its contents are accurate. Ivan Dragicevic relayed the following answer: 'Yes, the contents of the letter are the truth. You must notify first the Supreme Pontiff and then the Bishop.' This letter is accompanied by fasting and prayers that the Holy Spirit will guide your mind and your heart during this important moment in history.

Yours, in the Sacred Hearts of Jesus and Mary,
Father Tomislav Vlasic
Medjugorje, December 2, 1983

Editor's update: As of this writing (8/19/04), two of the other visionaries have received the tenth secrets. Ivanka received her last daily apparition on May 7, 1988. Our Lady told Her she would have an apparition once a year on June 25, the anniversary of the apparitions. Jakov received his last daily apparition on September

12, 1998. Our Lady told him he would receive an apparition every year on Christmas Day. Also, Our Lady visits Mirjana every second of the month to pray with her for the conversion of non-believers.

(6/93)
The Visionaries
Mirjana

Mirjana Dragicevic was a teenager of 16 years old when Our Lady first began to appear in Medjugorje in June, 1981.

Mirjana lived in Sarajevo with her Mom, Dad, and brother. As a student at the University of Sarajevo, she studied economics. During the summer months, she would visit and live with her grandmother in Bijakovici, a village adjacent to Medjugorje. This explains her presence when the apparitions began in the summer of 1981.

Mirjana was one of the first visionaries to have apparitions. It was to her that all 10 secrets were revealed. Therefore, she no longer sees Our Lady on a daily basis. The Blessed Mother continues to appear to her every year on her birthday, March 18, and at times of great difficulty.

When the first secret was revealed to Mirjana, it was like a film running before her eyes. She became sad and asked the Madonna if it had to take place that way. Mary said, "Yes." At a later apparition, Mary asked Mirjana, "How many people come to God's house with reverence, strong faith, and love for their Father?" Mirjana could not give Her an answer. Mary answered for her, "Very few."

The secrets revealed to Mirjana contain 3 chastisements for the world because of sin. They will be revealed through Father Petar Ljubicic, whom Mirjana had chosen for this task.

Mirjana is now married. This came as a surprise to many... thinking that she would have entered the convent since she was a visionary. Her Christian marriage was an example to the world at a time when many marriages entered into difficulties and ended in divorce.

She had married Marco Soldo on September 16, 1989 at 2:00 PM at St. James Church in Medjugorje. Their marriage was performed by an American priest, Fr. Milan Mikulich from Portland, Oregon. Mirjana and Marco Soldo are now a family. They have a daughter whom they named Marian.

Our Lady not only appears to Mirjana on her yearly birthday, but She now appears to her on the second day of the month. This usually occurs around 11 o'clock at night.

Mirjana has released the following information about her apparition on March 18, 1993:

"We all began to pray around 5 PM. Several of my relatives and friends were present as well as some pilgrims. Our Lady came at 5:20. The meeting with Her lasted seven minutes. It was the first time that Our Lady had not mentioned anything about the "secrets." During the apparition, we prayed one Our Father and the Glory Be for unbelievers. (We never pray the Hail Mary with Our Lady.) We also prayed for our own inner peace so that we may be able to offer it to others. She blessed all who were present and gave the following message: **'Dear Children! My desire is that you give Me your hands, that I may, as Mother, lead you on the right path, that I may lead you to the Father. Open your hearts. Allow Me to enter. Pray, because in prayer I am with you. Pray and allow Me to lead you. I will lead you to peace and happiness.'**"

Editor's update: Mirjana has two daughters now.

Ivan

Ivan Dragicevic was born on May 25, 1965. He is the oldest of the two male visionaries. During the early days of the apparitions, his personality was one of a quiet disposition. He was very shy. Despite this, he continued to greet pilgrims. Today, Ivan truly is an ambassador for Our Lady, traveling throughout many lands delivering the message of Medjugorje both to the people and to political figures.

Our Lady has shown Ivan his future until his death. Ivan therefore discourages personal questions concerning his life.

In June, 1987, Ivan completed his mandatory years of military service. While in the military, off duty, he received apparitions at a friend's house. He still has regular visions of the Madonna daily. Our Lady has revealed nine secrets to him.

In the spring and summer of 1988, he was the sole visionary present for the daily apparitions in the choir loft at St. James Church. Marija was with her prayer group in Italy, while Jakov was attending high school outside of Medjugorje. Vicka at that time was too ill to attend.

On Monday and on some Friday nights, Ivan led a prayer group which usually met on either Apparition Hill or the Hill of the Cross.

Today Ivan speaks mostly about the youth and the need for prayer groups, especially family prayer. When asked about the nine secrets revealed to him, Ivan replies, "A secret is a secret."

Editor's update: Ivan and his wife Laureen have three children now.

Ivanka

Ivanka Ivankovic was born on June 21, 1966. She was the first visionary to see Our Lady. She no longer sees Mary on a daily basis.

11

A special vision is given to her once a year on the anniversary of the apparitions, June 25th. Her last daily vision occurred on May 6, 1985. During that vision, she was given the 10th and final secret which Our Lady revealed to her.

At a special apparition in her home on May 7, 1985, Mary asked Ivanka what she would wish. Ivanka asked to see her earthly mother who had died several years before. Her mother appeared and was smiling. She embraced and kissed her daughter and said, "My child, I am so proud of you." She then disappeared. In the same vision, Our Lady told Ivanka, "Dear child, tell all your friends that My Son and I are always with them when they ask us and call on us." Later, Ivanka asked to kiss Our Lady. Mary nodded Her head. The visionary kissed Mary and received Her blessing. "Go in God's peace." Our Lady departed slowly with two angels.

On December 28, 1986, Ivanka married Rajko Branko Elez, and on November 10, 1987, they had a baby girl named Kristina. Then on June 14, 1990, a boy was born. They call him Joseph. Ivanka is a busy mother who radiates love and respect to both her husband and children.

Editor's update: Ivanka and Rajko now have three children.

Vicka

Vicka Ivankovic is the oldest of all 6 visionaries. Her birthday is September 3, 1964. She lived in the village close to Marija.

Vicka is a vivacious person. She is the most outgoing. Pilgrims remember her by her smiling face. It radiates peace and joy. Though appearing cheerful, she has suffered physically. She had a serious medical condition, and inoperable cyst. She suffered many headaches. Vicka was healed from all this on September 25, 1988.

One difference between Vicka and the other visionaries is that she was asked by the Blessed Mother to forgo her daily apparitions for a while. It was during 1986, on 3 occurrences, that she did not have the apparitions (for almost 2 months each time). Vicka willingly gave them up as she offered this for Mary's specified intentions. During these times, she was relieved of her physical pain but greatly missed seeing the "Gospa."

During a two-year period, Mary revealed Her life to Vicka. Many pilgrims ask her when this will be released to the public. She said, "Only when Mary gives Her permission."

Since 1985 Vicka has been given messages about the future of the world. So far, Vicka has received 9 secrets from the Mother of God.

When at home, Vicka still meets with and greets the pilgrims that come to Medjugorje. At times, she even prays over them.

Vicka reminds the pilgrims how important the Rosary is in our daily life. She says that Our Lady recommends it as family prayer. It is in this prayer that the family can be united together. Vicka also says that we should be examples to all our neighbors and friends. We can give that example by the way we pray.

Editor's update: Vicka married Mario Mijatovic in January, 2002. They have a son and a daughter.

Marija

Marija Pavlovic was born on April 1, 1965, in the hamlet of Bijakovici. Of all the visionaries, she seems the most prayerful. Her attitude is one of humility and joy. She asks the pilgrims to please not take any photos of her. She avoids them. Yet, she would spend many hours of the day answering questions and praying with groups of pilgrims that visited outside her house.

Marija seems gifted, for she can speak several languages. Although she still uses an interpreter, she has a heart of gold when it comes to giving of herself. She proved this by her love for one of her family members, her 31 year-old brother. She donated one of her kidneys to him. The successful transplant surgery occurred in the United States on Friday, December 16, 1988.

Blessed Mother has entrusted Marija with 9 secrets. Marija is the one who is responsible for writing the 25th monthly messages given for her parish and for the whole world.

All of the visionaries were invited by the Madonna to enter the religious life. Marija was trained as a hairdresser. In the early days of the apparitions, it seemed that she would be the one to enter the convent as soon as the apparitions ended. Many were stunned when they found out that she is also heading towards matrimony. Marija is formally engaged to Paolo Lunetti from Milan, Italy. They plan to marry some time this year.

Editor's update: Marija and her husband Paulo and four children live in Italy.

Jakov

Jakov Colo is the youngest of the visionaries. He was born on March 6, 1971. When the apparitions first began, he was only 10 years old. Both his parents died since the apparitions began. He then went to live with his relatives near the other visionaries in Bijakovici.

He has been chosen as one of Mary's messengers, and one who has been kissed by Her. She has entrusted messages to him for the world. Since he is God's instrument, he must spread them. The Blessed Mother has revealed 9 of the secrets to Jakov. At present, he still has daily apparitions. Our Lady has explained the future of the Church and of the world to him. She has shown him Heaven, hell, and Purgatory.

About the messages, Jakov, in the earlier days had said, "I try more and more to fulfill the messages that Our Lady gives us. They are PEACE, PENITENCE, CONVERSION, FASTING, and PRAYER. I feel that I'm closer to God now. I believe that we have to pray that God's plans will be realized."

The sacrament of matrimony seems to have prevailed in the lives of the visionaries. This year, 1993, Jakov married a girl from Montova. He had met Annalisa during his lengthy stay in that area. Once again, the wedding took place in St. James Church in Medjugorje, the same church where Mary had appeared many times to Jakov and the other visionaries. He forever remains Her beloved child like each and every one of us.

Editor's update: Jakov and Annalisa and their three children live in Medjugorje. Jakov received his last daily apparition on September 12, 1998. Our Lady appears to him now once a year, on Christmas Day.

(10/88)
Jelena

Jelena Vasilj, born May 14, 1972, is frequently called the "seventh visionary." Since December 15, 1982, Jelena has experienced messages from the Blessed Virgin Mary by means of inner locutions, hearing Mary, in Jelena's words, "with her heart." She has no knowledge of the secrets given by Mary to the other youths. The messages given to Jelena are usually spiritual counsels and guidance for the interior life and growth in holiness for the prayer group she is involved with.

These prayer groups were started in March, 1983, as a result of Our Lady's request. Mary asked for young people, unattached, to commit their lives for four years to prayer and fasting. She requested at least 3 hours of daily prayer and strict fasting on bread and water on Wednesdays and Fridays. 56 boys and girls from Medjugorje came forward to follow this call.

Jelena states, "Our Lady likes it very much when young people pray. She often remarks that it's not right for young people to be always leaving the church immediately after Mass. They should stay to thank God. She wants to help young people to be saved.

"Recently, Our Lady cried, mostly on behalf of the young people who have drifted so far away from God. She said that prayer is necessary. It touched my heart deeply and, at the same time, it made me happy that I see Her as my mother, Jesus as my friend and brother, and God as my father. They're so close to me. They help me and make me happy. I'm glad God doesn't want me to leave my friends. He wants me to tell them, and show them by my prayer life, what God means to me."

The Blessed Mother also revealed the date of Her birthday to Jelena. She said, "The day of my two-thousandth birthday was on the fifth of August, 1984." (The church officially observes Her birthday on September 8th.)

One day Jelena asked the Madonna, "Why are you so beautiful?" She replied, "Because I love. If you want to become beautiful like me, you must love. But love is a grace of the Lord. It is a gift of the Spirit. You cannot buy it, nor can you give it to someone else. All those who open themselves to God can have it."

Editor's note: In March of 1983, Marijana Vasilj (no relation), age 11, began to also have inner locutions of Our Lady. Unfortunately there was nothing ever published in "The Spirit of Medjugorje" about Marijana.

(6/93)
St. James Church

One of the places of special devotion in Medjugorje is the parish church of St. James. It has been a focal point and plays an important role in bringing Christ to millions of pilgrims. It seems that Mary had chosen this parish to be a witness and a model to the whole world. She is the spiritual guide in the hearts of all those that visit there in that unique land.

When the apparitions first began, and because of the huge crowds, the visionaries were prohibited by the government to worship on the hills. It was then that the Gospa was asked by the seers if She would appear to them in the parish church.

The church, which was completed in 1969, was unusually large. It could seat 600 people. The village itself had only about 500 families. They wondered why the church was built so large. It was after the apparitions began when pilgrims from all over the world started to flock into Medjugorje, that one could see why. It was all in God's plan. With the villagers, the parishioners, and the pilgrims coming to Mass, it soon became too small to accommodate such a vast crowd.

St. James Church is recognizable by its huge twin steeples. One can tell time by looking at the clocks on them. Inside, on the balcony of the choir loft is an unusual painting. It depicts Our Lady standing over the village of Medjugorje. She seems to be protecting it and showering many invisible graces on the land which She has chosen to appear daily with messages for the world. The astonishing thing is that I was told by my guide on my first visit to Medjugorje that this painting was painted before the apparitions ever began! Who would have ever dreamed that the Mother of God would actually appear to the visionaries in this church and in this choir loft? (Of special note… the crucifix on the left side is where Our Lady would appear during the Sorrowful Mysteries of the Rosary.)

Cross built in 1933 on the top of Mt. Krizevac

(7/93)
Mount Krizevac

This year marks the 60th anniversary of the building of the cross on Mt. Krizevac. IN HOC SIGNO VINCES… "In This Sign You Will Conquer."

Medjugorje is surrounded by mountains, and behind the church of St. James is a high mountain called Mount Krizevac. Pilgrims know it as the Hill of the Cross.

In 1933, the parishioners of St. James built a 35 foot (in height from its base upward) cross, not only in celebration and thanksgiving to Jesus' death and resurrection, but as a prayer, begging God to protect them during violent hailstorms. These storms had often been so fierce that their crops of tobacco and grapes were badly damaged. Some villagers were struck and killed by lightning.

The whole village took part in the building of the cross. They dug up and broke the stones. They carried the cement and materials needed on their backs up to the top of that steep and rocky hill. It took them a while before their project was complete. Incredibly, a 15 ton cross was erected on top of a huge mountain without the help of modern technology.

Through the spirit of penance, the people labored and succeeded. The cross meant so much to them that they changed the name of the mountain from Sipovac to Krizevac. ("Kriz" means "cross" in Croatian.) Since the building of the cross, there has been no more crop damage and no one has been hit by lightning.

A visit to Medjugorje should include a walk up the Hill of the Cross. Stations of the Cross are along the path up the mountain, and allow pilgrims to rest and pray.

The hill is steep and treacherous with sharp, pointed rocks. Many people (including the villagers) go barefoot to make it a more difficult journey to the top. There are those that climb it in 45 to 60 minutes without any stops, and others take 2 ½ hours. Some go to the top in wheel chairs and stretchers carried by their families, friends or volunteers. Coming down the mountain is just as difficult, especially when it is wet.

It was a custom even before the apparitions started to celebrate Mass on Mt. Krizevac on the Feast of the Exaltation of the Holy Cross (September 14). Each year on the anniversary, the number of pilgrims grows and a huge crowd of the faithful gathers for this special celebration.

Signs are numerous and witnessed by many people. A most important sign was the word "MIR" meaning "PEACE" that was written in large bright letters in the sky above the cross. This occurred in the early days of the apparitions and was seen by the pastor and many people of the village. We all know the message of Medjugorje is simply PEACE.

Pilgrims have seen the cross on Mt. Krizevac spin. Many have seen it turn into a column of light. Local people and pilgrims have seen the cross change into a bright form of a lady which they claimed to be of the Virgin Mary. There were times when the cross would disappear and in its place stood a figure of a woman with her hands extended.

The seers were asked to question Our Lady of Medjugorje about the significance of this, and She told them She was "the one on the mountain." She has told them that many times She prays in front of the cross.

On Wednesday, October 22, 1986, Our Lady's message to those present on Mount Krizevac along with the prayer group was:

"I thank those who are here for their efforts, for having come so high, and for their prayers. May they be prepared for the giving of Peace."

The place where Our Lady first appeared on Podbrdo

(6/93)
Podbrdo

Podbrdo is the hill on which the first apparition of Our Lady occurred. It is the hill closest to where the visionaries lived. Pilgrims call it the Hill of Apparitions. It is also a very treacherous hill, very rocky and steep, but not as steep as Mt. Krizevac.

The full 15 decades can be prayed as one climbs Podbrdo. Huge bronze plaques of the mysteries are stationed along the path, making it easier to meditate. Also found at the top of the hill are various wooden crosses made and left by the pilgrims of different countries. But the most solemn spot is the place where Our Lady appeared and still appears on certain nights of the week. There, a feeling of peace fills the air. No doubt, it is holy ground. As you look over the view, you can see Mt. Krizevac, not far in the distance. And when you are on the top of Mt. Krizevac, you can see Mt. Podbrdo, the Hill of Apparitions. The path to the apparition site has formed the letter "P" in the mountainside. Could that stand for "PEACE?"

Editor's update: In 2001, the metal cross which marked the place where Our Lady first appeared was replaced with a statue of Our Lady.

(5/95)
Medjugorje Pilgrimage
By Msgr. James Peterson

For years even before I visited Medjugorje, I heard people who were returning from there speaking of the spirit of the place and the pilgrims. Many spoke of marvelous signs in the sky, in the healing of people, in the grace of conversion, but those things never seemed to dominate the conversation.

They spoke of a deeper spirit of the other-worldly. Many spoke of the very deep sense that Mary had arranged their trip and invited them there. Not for some "extra-terrestrial Disneyland," but for some new mission She wanted them to undertake – some new stage in their spiritual growth.

Certainly the visionaries reflect that spirit. Their own sincerity is a testimony that went beyond miracles. The pilgrimages that brought people laid the groundwork. But more was needed and is needed.

Luke in his Gospel shows us the marvelous prelude to the Incarnation. Israel, Zachariah and Anna, and Joseph and Mary were being prepared and brought to the moment of Nazareth. But the eternal did not happen until the Spirit came upon Mary. Then the Holy One was born.

Luke shows the same thing with the Church. Peter and Andrew and the other apostles had been prepared, so had Mary and the disciples. But nothing really happened until the Holy Spirit came upon them – and the Church was born.

It is the same with all who have been prepared by Mary's invitation, by pilgrimage, by some great moments of hope.

The Holy Spirit is the gift the Risen Christ sends to the Church on Pentecost. He is the gift that brings to life our love of all souls. Paul calls Him, "the bond of perfection." When we are bound to all, we need to pray and to offer hardship for all in a spirit of trust and love.

We need to pray – not in saying words at God, but in the prayer of the heart to the indwelling Spirit.

A visit to Medjugorje is not a theme park vacation; it is in some ways a filling station. More wonderfully it is a new opening – to an abiding Spirit.

Editor's note: Msgr. Peterson is the spiritual adviser of "The Spirit of Medjugorje." He is a priest in the Erie Diocese and works for the diocesan Office of Special Ministries and Maria House Projects. He has authored a number of books. He was named a monsignor in 1994. Articles written after that time reflect the change.

Pilgrims enjoying a few minutes of lunch and laughter at Columbo's Restaurant in Medjugorje

(7/88)
Medjugorje Pilgrims

Those coming to seek God in Medjugorje endure inconvenience and often frustration over travel delays. Arrival and life there for a week means accepting a cut-off from many modern conveniences. A visit is not a sight seeing tour, but rather, a walk on holy ground. Like previous apparition sites, this one is in mountainous terrain and is not easily accessible.

The atmosphere of Medjugorje is serene and subdued. The most familiar sounds are of sheep bells or are from other farm animals throughout the village. The townspeople are pleasant, hospitable and welcome visitors into modest homes.

This place has an open spirit of prayer and penance. It is commonplace to see people praying in public. Large groups line up for open air confessions every day at 9:30 AM outside St. James Church. Barefoot pilgrims and villagers climb the Hill of Apparitions and the Hill of the Cross in atonement for their sins. The most frequent comment from returning pilgrims is, "I have changed." After experiencing the message of Medjugorje, they return to live and spread the message and share their experiences.

Chapter 2:

The Visionaries

Ivan and his interpreter Mark Sporanivich

(10/96)
Ivan Dragicevic speaks in Ohio

The Servants of Mary Center for Peace in Windsor, Ohio, USA, held an anniversary celebration on September 8, 1996. Ivan Dragicevic, one of the six visionaries from Medjugorje, was the featured speaker. The interpreter for his talk was Mark Sporanivich. For those who were not there, "The Spirit of Medjugorje" has written the text of his speech.

Ivan: I am very happy to be with you today, to share with you those things that Our Lady has asked us for the past 15 years. As you see, I am a young man, like many other young people among us. I'm not perfect. I'm not holy. I'm trying to attempt to be better and to be more holy, like the rest of us.

Fifteen years ago, when I was 16 years of age, on a beautiful Wednesday, a holy day, the 24th of June, 1981, I went to Mass with my parents. I came home and had dinner with them. After that, I went to my friend's to play soccer. When we were all tired out and returning to our homes, we met Vicka, Mirjana and Ivanka. One of my friends who was with me, asked them where they were going. They said that they were going for a walk to look for their sheep.

Then I went home to change and to take some things with me. I was going to come back with him to his house to watch a soccer match on television. At the half time of the game, I asked him to come to my house to get some other things so that we could make a bet for the second half of the game. We took those things and started approaching towards his house. We started, but we never got there. To this day, we have never seen the second half. Something else happened.

From a distance we heard someone yelling to us. "Ivan, Ivan, come to see the Gospa." We didn't care to listen to that, but we were hearing that voice repeating louder and louder. Vicka was behind us yelling at us. "Come, come to see the Gospa." (Gospa is "Our Lady" in Croatian) I turned to my friend and said, "What is she telling us? What kind of Gospa? What does she mean?" But Vicka was so persistent that we finally decided to go back with her to see. When we came there, we saw Mirjana and Ivanka turned toward a hill and looking at something. When we came closer to the hill, Vicka was telling us, "Look up above." I looked up there about three times and I saw the face of Our Lady. When I saw that, I was so fearful.

I fled home so fast that I thought no one would catch me. I was 16 years old. I was young. No one ever told me about miracles or anything of such nature, and I was very, very afraid. When I came home, I spoke nothing to anyone, to my parents nor anyone else. All night long, I had so many questions coming to my mind. I was sleepless. I could not understand what was happening. In that shock and that surprise, my parents did sense something. They were asking me, "What happened?" It was 1981. In those days, it was a little different under Communism. My parents were very, very afraid of anything religious. We could not speak much about religion.

The second day, we all spontaneously went there to the location where we saw Our Lady. Before we came to that place, approximately 50 yards, Our Lady was already waiting for us and waving to us to come closer. Our feet were like dead. We could not move forward nor backward. Some extraordinary power got over us and we went over those sharp rocks closer to Her. When we came closer to Her, She was telling us that She was our Mother and not to be afraid of Her. Vicka questioned Her, "Who are you?"

"I am the Blessed Virgin Mary, the Queen of Peace. I'm coming to you, my children, because My Son is sending me to help you. Dear children, peace, peace, peace. Peace must come between God and man and among men. My children, the world is in a very difficult time, and there is a threat that the world will destroy itself. For this reason, My Son is sending me to help all of you, to show you the way that you should walk." That was the first message Our Lady gave us and the rest of the world.

I just wanted to describe the first two days to some of you who have not heard about the beginnings of Medjugorje.

Fifteen years is not a short time. That's a long time. For fifteen years every day, I've been talking to Her. Even if I took one minute a day, that's a lot of minutes. What would you give to be one minute with Her? That's a great gift! However, it's a great responsibility. Whoever receives much from God, God demands a lot from him. I'm conscious of this responsibility and I'm living with that responsibility. Even though in the beginning of the apparitions, I was thinking of running away from all of this. However, Our Lady pointed Her finger at me and I could not escape.

I would like to summarize only the important messages that should show us the way to lead our lives.

As I said, Our Lady is coming as Queen of Peace. She is coming from the King of Peace. She is showing us the way how to get to Peace. She's coming to lead us by the hand and to take us to Peace itself. She is telling us, "Dear children, if you don't have peace in your heart, there's no possibility of peace in the world."

Today people are talking about terrible things that will happen in the world, "the three days of darkness." I would like to have you understand one thing that I'm going to tell you. Our Lady did not come to us to bring us terror. She's not coming to bring us darkness. She's coming to us as a Mother of Light and the Mother of Hope. She's coming to bring us hope, to teach us. And She's coming to warn us of those things that are not good, so that we could accept the good.

It is hard to talk about the love of Our Lady. Every word I have is too short to describe the love that She has for us. She said in one message, " Dear children, if you knew how much I love you, you would cry from joy."

She's carrying us in Her heart and She has placed us all in Her heart. As you know, every message of Hers starts with, "My dear children." Our Lady has never said, "My dear Croatians, my dear Americans or my dear Italians." Dear children, She's the Mother of all of us. We are all important. We are all needed, the small and large, sick and healthy, schooled and uneducated. No one is turned away from Her. We are all important to Her. However, She is asking us to leave sin aside - that we should take evil aside, so that we can prepare our way toward God in our hearts; so that we can prepare peace in our heart; so that we can prepare peace for Her messages and God's messages. We see today that there is no real peace in the world, and we're asking ourselves, "Why all this unruliness in the world? Where is this unruliness manufactured?" That unruliness comes from man's heart. If the man's heart is not at peace with God and man, it is impossible to have peace within that person. The peace that God gives us is a gift to us. We always have to have an open heart for that peace, and pray for that peace for our own good. It is important that all of you understand that.

We are witnesses of great crisis in the world today, in the family, among the young and even within the Church. However, crisis does not indicate a blind street. Our Lady is telling us not to be afraid of the crisis. The crisis means not annihilation. Our Lady is constantly asking us, "Dear children, return to God. Put God in the first place in your lives." She's not asking us to know better what others need to do. She's telling us to do what *we* can do. Open up our hearts and do what we can do. Our Lady is not teaching us to criticize others, but to pray for others. Our Lady especially is calling us to the Holy Mass as the central point of our lives, monthly confession, to the Adoration of the Holy Sacrament, the reading of the Holy Bible. In the last message to us, Our Lady tells us that the Bible has to be in a visible place in the home. However, She is telling us that the Bible should not be there just to be looked at or that dust should be falling upon it. She would love to have us live the word of the Gospel.

Conversion is a process that lasts a whole life. We cannot be converted in 20 or 50 years. Our conversion is complete when we die.

It is a program for life. She especially asks to pray with the heart. What is that to pray with the heart? Many times we pray so fast, being so mechanized, fast, speedy, without meaning. She wishes that our prayer, from the heart, be a speaking to and with God. Our prayer should be spiritual food by which we can grow. Our prayer should be a happiness, a joy. Our prayer should be a force, a strength. A prayer is a school which we should be attending every day. And every day we should study. I would like to tell you one thing not to forget. In the school of prayer, there are no weekends! We have to study every day and this has to be a continuity of the individual, the family, and the community. Many times we ask ourselves, "How can we pray better?" The answer is not all that difficult. If we desire to pray better, then we have to pray more. How to pray better is always an individual decision. How to pray more is a grace. That grace is given to those who pray more. Especially Our Lady is asking us to return to prayer among our families. Whenever our family becomes a group, we should pray together, because praying together in the family is a well, getting well, among the family and our society. Especially today, the times and the way and the manner of the young in the families and in the manner they live. Many times parents would say nowadays… "But we don't have time. We work a lot. We have no time for our children." But, if we took away only 10 minutes from television, and 10 minutes from shopping, we would have easily 20 minutes a day to pray together. But that's not even the problem. What is the problem? Time is not the problem. The hours in the day are not the problem. Where is the problem? The problem is love. When a person loves something, they find time to do that which they love. And if you don't love something, you always find excuses not to do what you should be loving. Let our decision be today that it should be love that should dictate our lives. And then, you will realize that this is an enormous gift!

Our Lady is asking us for penance and fasting on bread and water. Those that are sick and unable to do so can do something else instead. For some people, fasting might be a losing of something. However, there is a gain for everyone, because with penance, we cleanse ourselves. We are strengthening our spirit. We strengthen our faith…and we are getting the assurance of peace. God is asking very little from us, but He is giving us many blessings. The devil gives us nothing, but takes away all.

Our Lady is coming to strengthen the faith in all of us, to strengthen the Church in its faith. She is telling us, "Dear children, if you are strong, the Church is strong. If you are weak, the Church is very weak. You are the Church." Many Christians who claim to believe have left prayers alone, because they have died spiritually. Many people are in a spiritual coma, and only at times do they open their spiritual eyes -maybe for Christmas, maybe at Easter time or some other festivity during the year. For the last 15 years, Our Lady is trying to show us the way to get us out of these doldrums of life. She is calling for the priests for simplicity in life to speak to us in a manner that we can understand and lead to proper lives - to preach the live Word of the Gospel.

The apparitions are happening every day. Four of us see them every day. We do not know how long they will last. We're only the instruments through which She speaks to us. I see Our Lady the same as I see you now. I speak with Her in the same manner as I speak to you now. After 15 years, I can tell you that I am more comfortable talking to Her than I am talking to you now! And I can touch Her. It is very difficult to describe the beauty of Our Lady. I can tell you that Our Lady has a gray gown, a white veil, blue eyes, rosy cheeks, dark hair, and She is upon a cloud and there is a crown of stars upon Her head.

I hope that we will respond to the questioning and asking of Our Lady...to take up Her messages: the message of peace, the message of conversion, the message of prayer, of penance and fasting, strong faith, love and hope; and that we will try to create a better world worthy of the children of God. Let our decision today be that we shall be better. Do not wait for tomorrow, but start today. Let's decide to give ourselves for peace, for the good, for God, and let it be that way! Thank you and God bless you!

(10/88)
A Recent Interview with Marija
Pavlovic, 9/13/88

Q: *Marija, can you describe Heaven, Hell, and Purgatory?*

A: Heaven is a large space and people were walking, singing, praying and were very happy and joyful. The women are dressed in dresses that looked alike and everyone had different faces and were not thin nor fat.

Hell is also a large place where there is a big fire in the middle of it, and I saw a lot of people. A young lady got into the fire; and when she came out of it, she looked like an animal and not human any more.

Purgatory is a large place but not as big as Heaven and is misty and dark where the people are not very happy...They now need our prayers to go to Heaven.

We visionaries did not ask to see Heaven, Hell, or Purgatory, but Our Lady said, "There are many people on earth that don't believe about life after death," so She just wanted to show us, so we can witness that there is life after death.

Q: *Will we be able to join our friends in Heaven?*

A: I did not recognize anyone in Heaven.

Q: *Does the Blessed Mother bless the pilgrims?*

A: The Blessed Mother blesses everyone in Medjugorje every day.

Q: *How does Our Lady appear?*

A: When Our Lady appears, there are three flashing lights.

Q: *Does She appear alone or with angels?*

A: Sometimes with angels.

Q: *Are the angels big or small?*

A: Appears with both, large angels and little angels.

Q: *Has Our Lady appeared elsewhere in the world?*
A: Our Lady did not tell us about other apparitions.

Q: *Our Lady's true birthday is when, September 8th or August 5th?*
A: Our Lady said, "My birthday is August 5th, but the Church celebrates it on September 8th," but then She added that we can celebrate our birthday only once, but Hers twice.

Q: *Does Our Lady ever laugh, touch, or kiss the visionaries?*
A: Yes, Our Lady laughs and touches and kisses the visionaries.

Q: *What is the true day that Jesus was born?*
A: On Christmas Day.

Q: *Will the secrets ever be revealed?*
A: Only when Our Lady wants them to be revealed.

Q: *When Our Lady gives the secrets to the visionaries, do they all hear at the same time or individually?*
A: Both ways.

Q: *When do the visionaries get the secrets?*
A: We get the secrets at different times, and some She told the same time, so there is no special rule how Our Lady does it.

Q: *Does Our Lady mind when we take pictures in church when She is appearing?*
A: Our Lady does not say anything, and it does not bother the visionaries, because we don't hear or see anything else, but it's not right to take pictures. We should pray and not take pictures. There is never, ever a message to take pictures, but to pray.

Q: *Why did Our Lady send you to Italy?*
A: Our Lady did not send me. The prayer group and I decided to go there to pray and then return back.

Q: *Tell us about the prayer group that went to Italy.*

A: It was twelve people from Ivan's prayer group that went to Italy from Medjugorje to pray with me. They are all back in Medjugorje.

Q: *Did Our Lady appear to you in Italy?*

A: Yes, at the same time as in Medjugorje.

Q: *Do you know Our Lady's life story?*

A: No, Vicka is writing about it.

Q: *Do you know your future life?*

A: Our Lady did not tell me about my future life.

Q: *Do you want to become a nun?*

A: Only if it is God's will.

Q: *How can we get peace inside?*

A: Our Lady is always calling us to pray for peace, first in our heart, then peace in our family, then we will be able to pray for peace in the world. So we must have peace in the heart first.

Vicka in St. Augustine

(1/94)
An "Angel" Named Vicka
By Sandy Tobin

Much has been written about this 28 year old woman who is probably the most widely recognized of all the six visionaries in Medjugorje. It is no wonder, because once you have been touched by her smile, you can never forget her face.

Although Vicka always spends a lot of time with us in Medjugorje, having her here (in Clearwater, Florida-October, 1993) for two weeks, was a blessing beyond words. She touched the hearts of many people and showed us how to live.

During her visit, we did many things. We spent three days in St. Augustine for the dedication of the St. Vincent de Paul Farm, the 19th Community formed by Sister Elvira Petrozzi for drug and alcohol rehabilitation. We visited shut-ins, prayed with many individuals, spoke in several churches, and Vicka taped Our Lady's messages for a future broadcast on our local Catholic radio station. The main event was in our own parish of St. Cecilia where we prayed the Rosary, crowned the statue of Our Lady, celebrated the Holy Sacrifice of the Mass, and Vicka spoke, giving Our Lady's most important messages. In between all of these activities, however, there was quiet time – time for prayer, for sharing and relaxing, especially during the first week before the word got around that Vicka was here. We also found plenty of time for fun and laughter!

If I had to choose the one thing that made the biggest impression on me, it would have to be that Vicka truly lives everything that she says. She showed us, by her own example, how easy it is to live the messages.

I always thought that it must be very easy to live the messages if one were to live in Medjugorje, where life is so much simpler than it is here. Vicka showed us otherwise. She lived our hectic lifestyle, without ever compromising her priorities, and she did it with grace. No matter where we were or what we were doing, there was always an opportunity to pray the Rosary. Even in the midst of seeing the sights, Vicka would suggest that we find a quiet place to pray, and no part of the Rosary was ever omitted in a day. At home, I would find her spending a few minutes curled up with the Bible, or on her knees in our chapel. Cooking dinner one night, she began to pray aloud while she was peeling potatoes and I was fixing the salad. When Mike came in, he joined us, and by the time the Rosary was finished, dinner was on the table. We never drove anywhere without praying, and when we weren't praying, we were singing! Of course, no matter where we were or how busy the day, the Mass always came first.

As Our Lady appears to the visionaries wherever they happen to be, we were again privileged to have Her appear to Vicka here, in our home, throughout Vicka's visit. She also appeared in St. Augustine, at the Shrine of Our Lady of La Leche. During those times, we placed at Our Lady's feet the prayer petitions that had been sent to us, as well as the names of all of our friends and benefactors who have supported the Pilgrimage of Love with their prayers and sacrifices. Vicka prayed for everyone and recommended each of you to Our Lady.

We give thanks to Almighty God for the example He has given us in this beautiful young woman, and we thank Our Lady for choosing such a worthy servant to be Her spokesperson. We also give thanks for the gift of Vicka's personal relationship with our family. Her friendship and love are blessings beyond measure.

Pilgrim's Peace Letter – December, 1993

Jakov and Mirjana

(5/97)
Visit and Interview with Visionaries Jakov and Mirjana, 3/12/97

Jakov: There are still four of us that have apparitions every day: Vicka, Marija, Ivan, and myself. The apparitions take place every evening at 5:40 (or 6:40, depending on the time of year). Before the apparitions, we prepare ourselves for prayer. Then we have some prayers for the apparitions. Every evening we pray together with the Blessed Mother. I recommend all pilgrims that come to Medjugorje and all their intentions. And particularly, Vicka and I pray for the sick ones and we recommend the sick ones to the Blessed Mother. Each one of the six visionaries has a special mission. Vicka and myself pray for the sick ones. Mirjana prays for the unbelievers.

Marija prays for the souls in Purgatory. Ivan prays for the young people. Ivanka prays for families.

When I think of recommending the sick to the Blessed Mother, I pray first for the healing in his or her own hearts, because everyone who is healed in the heart will endure any kind of sickness. And it will not stand as a punishment from God. That person will be able to carry his cross for God.

The Blessed Mother gave us the main messages fifteen years ago. She has been repeating these messages for the last fifteen years. The messages are the messages of prayer, conversion, peace, fasting, and the Holy Mass.

The Blessed Mother invites us to pray every day all three parts of the Rosary- Joyful, Sorrowful and Glorious; to pray every day seven Our Father's, Hail Mary's, Glory Be's.

When the Blessed Mother invites us to prayer, She wants us to pray with the heart.

And also She invites all of us to fast on bread and water on Wednesday and Friday. This should be done out of love for God. Today is Wednesday!?

The Blessed Mother appeared here as the Queen of Peace. On the third day of the apparitions She invited all of us to pray for this special intention - prayer for peace. She says it should be between man and God. And it really is the time that we should accept the messages of the Blessed Mother but not when something happens, because all of us have the opportunity to accept the messages of the Blessed Mother. No one on earth can say, "I didn't know anything about it."

This is all from my side. Now it's Mirjana's turn to talk to you.

Mirjana: As Jakov already mentioned, my special mission is for the unbelievers. She says that they are those that haven't yet felt or learned the love of God. She is asking for our help. When I say "our help," I am not speaking of just us six visionaries. I think every single person should feel the Blessed Mother is his or her own Mother, because through our prayers and our example, we can change the unbelievers. She wants us to pray in our every day prayer for unbelievers. All the bad things in the world, such as drugs, war, divorce, and abortion come from unbelievers. She says when you

38

pray for them, you pray for your future. Besides our prayer, She needs our example. She doesn't want us to go around and preach to the others. She wants us to talk with our own lives, so they can see God and His love in us. I would ask you all if you could pray for them, because if you could see, just once, the tears the Blessed Mother sheds for the unbelievers, I am sure you would pray from the heart immediately. She wants us all to be the most beautiful bouquet that She can give to Her Son.

The Blessed Mother says this is the time of great decisions. Everyone who feels they are God's children should feel a great responsibility! This is why I have the apparition on the second of each month. Then we pray for the unbelievers.

This is all from my side now, but I would be very pleased if we could answer some of your questions.

Q: Is there a message every second of the month?
A: The message that is on the second of every month you can get from the parish office.

Q: What do Marija and Ivan pray for?
A: Marija's special prayer is for the souls in Purgatory. Ivan's special prayer is for the young people and the priests.

Q: A lot of Americans have heard that Mirjana will be in the States in August, and if so, where will she be able to visit?
A: Right now she will be able to visit Modesto, California. Now, she would love to visit all your beautiful towns but it is impossible because of the family and the obligations at home. She has two children at home.

Q: Is Fr. Slavko still the spiritual advisor of the visionaries, and will he be going to Modesto with her?
A: Yes.

Q: Does the Blessed Mother let Mirjana know what time and where the apparitions will take place?

A: During the apparitions that Mirjana has on the second of the month, the Blessed Mother tells her what time the apparition will be, but She doesn't talk about the place because Mirjana is the one who chooses that.

Q: How does Mirjana choose?
A: It depends on the number of people who want to be there. The bigger the crowd, the bigger the place necessary to hold the apparition.

Q: Tell us about the significance of what the Blessed Mother told you this month.
A: I can only tell you what the Blessed Mother has said. I cannot comment on the significance of what She has said. Through our prayers we can understand the significance of the message.

Q: How can I contact the visionaries about a special project for a healing church I have planned in the Philippines so they can ask the Blessed Mother how I should go about it?
A: Jakov says we are not able to ask any questions. It is not because the Blessed Mother does not allow us, but is because there are so many people with different needs and wishes that it is almost impossible to answer special questions. Every evening we recommend to the Blessed Mother all of you and all of your intentions. The Blessed Mother knows what you need. The answer you will get, Mirjana says, through prayer. Mirjana says, that to the Blessed Mother we are all of the same importance, the visionaries, all of you. There are no privileged children for the Blessed Mother. Whatever we would like to get, we have to pray the same as you would. She wouldn't be a good mother if there were privileged children. If you have any questions from your heart for the Blessed Mother, just ask Her in prayer to give the answer. "Open your heart and invite Me and I will be with you." When we saw the Blessed Mother on the first day, we spent the whole night in prayer just to be able to understand what was happening. So the same for all of you. For all the things that you don't understand, you have to ask the Blessed Mother through prayer.

Q: When Mirjana prays and with the Blessed Mother they pray together, since they don't pray the Rosary especially the Hail Mary, how do they pray together?

A: There are some special prayers that Mirjana was taught by the Blessed Mother. It is something similar to the Rosary. It is prayer to Jesus. The Blessed Mother has been repeating so many times pray, so that I can pray to My Son for you. She never says, you pray, and it will be given to you.

Q: On the second of the month when you pray for the unbelievers, is there any special prayer that was suggested to be prayed for them or is it appropriate to pray the Rosary?

A: Any prayer that you say with your heart is the best prayer. I have to say too what the Blessed Mother asks us and this is to pray the Rosary, all three parts. But if we pray something else, I am sure She will not be upset.

Q: Has the Blessed Mother changed over the sixteen years since She has been coming for the apparitions?

A: The Blessed Mother always looks the same. She isn't getting older.

Q: This is a beautiful question for Jakov: When the Blessed Mother appears, does She come with music, angels, stars or something similar?

A: There is no music when the Blessed Mother appears. Her voice sounds like the most beautiful music. In the beginning of the apparitions, the Blessed Mother appeared with angels.

Q: Mirjana, because of the fact that I am blind, can I have a little hug from you today? I cannot see you.

A: Of course you can. And it is no wonder that you are not asking for a hug from Jakov!

Q: How was the Blessed Mother during the last apparition on March 2?

A: The Blessed Mother was crying during the apparition.

Q: When the Pope comes to Sarajevo, will any one of the visionaries be able to go there to meet with him, and is there anything we can do to support the Holy Father?

A: We are planning to go to Sarajevo to meet with the Holy Father. Mirjana says it is my hometown anyway. I already had an opportunity to personally meet the Holy Father in Italy at Castle Gandolfo. He told me at the time that if he weren't the Holy Father, he would have been in Medjugorje already. He asked me to ask all the pilgrims that come to pray for his special intention. We have to say great thanks to the Blessed Mother and the Father because they gave us such a beautiful Holy Father here on earth.

Q: Some people are storing food and water for the future. Should we?

A: No, of course not. Whoever believes in God should not be afraid. There is no fear. We have to trust in God's love with an open heart. We have to wait to see what the day will bring for us. Those who don't have peace in their own hearts, they are afraid. I cannot understand why we talk about the future when we don't know what can happen tonight to us. Is there anyone of us here that can say that they will live tomorrow? We have to be ready every moment to go to God and not to have the cellars full of food and water.

Ivanka and her daughter Kristina in Erie, PA

(7/96)
15th Anniversary
By Joan Wieszczyk

June 25, 1996, marks the 15th year that Our Lady (Gospa in Croatian) has been appearing daily in Medjugorje. The people of the Erie Diocese have been very blessed. Many of them cannot get to Medjugorje, so Medjugorje came to them.

Visionary Ivanka Elez and her daughter Kristina, along with their interpreter Helen Sarcevic, traveled to Erie, PA. On June 6, 1996, at 6:30 PM in St. George Church, a prayer service began with Ivanka leading the Joyful and Sorrowful Mysteries of the Rosary in Croatian. Just as in Medjugorje, the Holy Sacrifice of the Mass followed immediately. After Mass, Ivanka, through her interpreter, gave a short talk followed by a question and answer period.

The church that evening was filled to capacity with extra seating available in the tent outdoors. Many have asked for videos and cassettes of that inspiring spiritual talk. None are available. To please our readers, we are sharing that evening in this newsletter.

We begin with Ivanka who greeted us all with the greeting, "Praised be Jesus and Mary" (in Croatian, of course).

She thanked all of us for attending the Holy Sacrifice of the Mass. It was after Mass when Ivanka began to tell us about the messages that Our Lady is giving. She said Our Lady is calling us to prayer and giving us advice on how to live our lives.

In 1981, Ivanka was an ordinary teenager, 15 years old, when she first saw Our Lady on Podbrdo Hill on the 24th of June in the village of Bijakovici in Medjugorje.

Both Ivanka and Mirjana were taking a walk in this remote village, a village without running water. Ivanka saw Our Lady, which she calls "the Gospa." She saw Her on the hillside. She then told Mirjana to look up to the side of the hill. But Mirjana did not want to look up immediately, so they walked back to the village. They still couldn't get off their minds what it was they saw on the hill. So they returned to the hill to see. Ivanka was again the first one to see Our Lady and then Mirjana was looking up and she was able to see the image of Our Lady. At that moment, they both knelt down. Then Ivan, Vicka and Milka (Marija's sister) came along. They all saw the same image. At this moment, they didn't know what to make of all this, so they hurried back to the village and told some of the people what they saw. It was mixed emotions. Some believed and some did not believe. Ivanka's grandmother said not to talk about it because it has to be tested. The visions have to be proven. They had all night to think about what they saw and what was happening.

As it turned out, they wondered what would happen the next day. The following day all six visionaries (Ivanka, Mirjana, Vicka, Ivan, Marija, and Jakov) showed up at the same place. Ivanka said that as soon as they got to the place where they were standing, they saw the light three times. At this time, some of the villagers came with them. At the moment that they saw Our Lady, She motioned them to come closer. Ivanka's grandmother, who came along with them, told them not to go any closer. But she said that something like a magnet pulled them so fast up the hill. Suddenly, in a second, they found themselves in front of Our Lady. Two months previous to this, Ivanka's mother had died. She was still mourning her death. As soon as Ivanka got before Our Lady, she asked, "Where is my mother?" Our Lady immediately told her, "Your mother is with Me!" The next day when all the visionaries came back to the same place, Our Lady introduced Herself – "I am the Queen of Peace." She then invited all of them to pray for peace.

On the third day, many more people gathered on the hill. The following day, there were more and more people coming to the place to see for themselves what was going on. At that time, they were under the Communist rule. The Communist government thought that there was some kind of uprising going on, so they separated the visionaries so as to question them. They even got a psychiatrist to lock them up to interrogate them. But because they were under age, they couldn't keep them jailed. The visionaries went through much hardship and persecution simply because they told what they saw. The Communist police came with guns and dogs, preventing them from going up the hill. But Our Lady still came to them, meeting them in different places, even in their own homes. Finally, they went to the pastor of St. James Church, who invited them to come to the church.

Every day, in all these years, Our Lady constantly is repeating the same message. First of all, She wants all of humanity to experience peace. But to come to this peace, we need to pray for conversion. And we need to pray and fast. Be friends and love one another as the gospel said today. Our Lady is asking us to first have peace in our hearts; then we can have peace in our families. If our families are destroyed then the world cannot have peace.

Ivanka was meeting with Our Lady every day from 1981 until May, 1985. Our Lady also gave Ivanka 10 messages. They are called secret messages. These messages are not to be revealed at this time. They will be revealed when the time comes. In May, 1985, Our Lady came to Ivanka for one whole hour, explaining so much to her. She told her that from now on Ivanka will only see Her once a year. This is a gift to her, for she will see Her as long as she lives.

Regarding the secret messages, many people contemplate on them, thinking this is something that is going to be the wrath of God, punishment of God, apostasy. Our Lady's messages are messages of hope, and of right direction. She doesn't want to scare any of Her children. Her messages show us how to live so that we can be with God…then we have nothing to fear. Our Lady is a mother who loves every person on earth.

Ivanka, whose mother died before the apparitions began, was able to see her mother five times. In the last apparition, Our Lady showed Ivanka her mother. Her mother said to her, "My daughter, I'm so proud of you." Our Lady told Ivanka not to be upset because she no longer will see Our Lady on a daily basis. She need not be afraid because Ivanka had fulfilled everything that Her Son asked of her. Then she was able to see her mother in Heaven. Before her mother died, she was in and out of the hospital many times. She was suffering and was very sick. When she saw her mother in Heaven with Our Lady she was radiant in beauty, love and peace. Ivanka wanted us to know this, to testify that there is life after this short life on earth. And this life with God is something we should always prepare ourselves for while we are here on earth. Many people ask Ivanka to describe how Our Lady looks. This is something words cannot describe, because it is not only the way they see Our Lady, it is the feeling of the beauty, peace and love of a mother. When Our Lady appears, She never stands on the ground, but on something like a cloud.

There is so much Ivanka would like to share with you. Ivanka says that Our Lady told her that Satan wants to destroy families. What we should do is pray. Families should pray together, especially the Rosary. You can protect the family life and the family can stay together in unity. If we have strong families, then our communities will also be strong.

(4/97)
The Image of the Queen of Peace

Many have in different ways interrogated the visionaries about Our Lady's appearance, as they have in general about what is happening in the parish of Medjugorje. Fr. Janko Bubalo, author and member of the Herzegovina province, was the most successful at that. He followed the Medjugorje apparitions from the beginning. For years he was coming to Medjugorje to hear confessions and thus he had experiences of Medjugorje spirituality. A visible result of such work was his book *A Thousand Encounters with the Blessed Virgin Mary in Medjugorje* (1985). It met with world wide success and received an award. In the book Vicka the visionary talks about her experiences. But, besides this conversation Fr. Janko also spoke about the same things with the other visionaries. In the end he published only the conversation with Vicka because it seemed to him that she answered his questions the most comprehensively. All the other visionaries are not essentially different from her in anything. As he testifies, he spoke several times with all the visionaries and did not publish anything that they did not approve.

Time has passed and attempts at portraying Our Lady have multiplied. Many of those attempts have been contrary to what the visionaries have said. In order to bring order into all that, Fr. Janko, although up in years (born 1913), made another attempt. He sent a survey sheet to the visionaries in which he interrogates them about Our Lady's appearance. Most of the visionaries responded to Fr. Janko's attempt (Ivan Dragicevic, Vicka Ivankovic, Marija Pavlovic Lunetti, Ivanka Ivankovic Elez, and Mirjana Dragicevic Soldo). They testified to the survey number of their own answers by personal signatures at Humac in 1992. Jakov Colo did not fill out his survey sheet for justifiable reasons, but he agrees with what the others visionaries said and had nothing special to add.

We now present the questions in full and the results of the visionaries' brief answers.

1. As the first thing, tell me: how tall is the Madonna, that you regularly see?
About 165 cm - Like me (Vicka). [5 feet 5 inches]

2. Does She look rather "slender", slim or . . .?
She looks rather slender.

3. About how many kilograms do you think She weighs?
About 60 kilograms (132 pounds).

4. About how old do you think She is?
From 18 to 20 years old.

5. When She is with the Child Jesus does She look older?
She looks as usual - She looks the same.

6. When Our Lady is with you is She always standing or . . .
Always standing.

7. On what is She standing?
On some little cloud.

8. What color is that little cloud?
The cloud is a whitish color.

9. Have you ever seen Her kneel?
Never! (Vicka, Ivan, Ivanka. . .)

10. Naturally your Madonna also has Her own face. How does it look: round or rather long - oval?

It's rather long - oval - normal.

11. What color is Her face?

Normal - rather light - rosy cheeks

12. What color is Her brow?

Normal - mainly light like Her face.

13. What kind of lips does Our Lady have - rather thick or thin?

Normal - beautiful - they are more thin.

14. What color are they?

Reddish - natural color.

15. Does Our Lady have any dimples, as we people usually have?

Ordinarily She doesn't - perhaps a little, if She smiles (Mirjana).

16. Is there some pleasant smile ordinarily noticeable on Her countenance?

Maybe - more like some indescribable gentleness - there's a smile visible as if somehow under Her skin (Vicka).

17. What is the color of Our Lady's eyes?

Her eyes are wonderful! Clearly blue (all).

18. Are they rather big or . . .?

More normal - maybe a little bit bigger (Marija).

19. How are Her eye-lashes?

Delicate - normal.

20. What color are Her eye-lashes?

Normal - no special color.

21. Are they thinner or . . .?
Ordinary - normal.

22. Of course, Our Lady also has a nose. What is it like: sharp or . . .?
A nice, little nose (Mirjana) - normal, harmonizing with Her face (Marija).

23. And Our Lady's eyebrows?
Her eyebrows are thin - normal - more of a black color.

24. How is your Madonna dressed?
She is clothed in a simple woman's dress.

25. What color is Her dress?
Her dress is grey - maybe a little bluish-grey(Mirjana).

26. Is the dress pulled in around the body or does it fall freely?
It falls freely.

27. How far down does Her dress reach?
All the way down to the little cloud on which She's standing - it blends into the cloud.

28. How far up around the neck?
Normally - up to the beginning of Her neck.

29. Is a part of Our Lady's neck visible?
Her neck is visible, but nothing of Her bosom is visible.

30. How far do Her sleeves reach?
Up to Her palms.

31. Is Our Lady's dress hemmed with anything?
No, not with anything.

32. Is there anything pulled in or tied around Our Lady's waist?

No, there's nothing.

33. On the body of the Madonna that you see, is Her femininity noticeable?
Of course it's noticeable! But nothing specially (Vicka).

34. Is there anything else on Our Lady besides this dress described?
She has a veil on Her head.

35. What color is that veil?
The veil is a white color.

36. Pure white or . . .?
Pure white.

37. How much of Her does the veil cover?
It covers Her head, shoulders and complete body from the back and from the sides.

38. How far down does it reach?
It reaches down to the little cloud, also like Her dress.

39. How far does it cover in front?
It covers from the back and from the sides.

40. Does the veil look firmer, thicker than Our Lady's dress?
No it doesn't - it's similar to the dress.

41. Is there any kind of jewelry on Her?
There is no kind of jewelry.

42. Is it trimmed with anything at the ends?
Not with anything.

43. Does Our Lady have any kind of ornament at all?
She has no kind.

44. For example, on Her head or around the head?
Yes - She has a crown of stars on Her head.

45. Are there always stars around Her head?
Ordinarily there are - there always are (Vicka).

46. For example, when She appears with Jesus?
She's the same way.

47. How many stars are there?
There are twelve of them.

48. What color are they?
Golden - gold color

49. Are they in any way connected with each other?
They are connected with something - so that can stay up (Vicka)

50. Is a little bit of Our Lady's hair visible?
A little bit of Her hair is visible.

51. Where do you see it?
A little above Her forehead - from under the veil - from the left side.

52. What color is it?
It's black.

53. Is either of Our Lady's ears ever visible?
No, they are never visible.

54. How is that?
Well, the veil covers Her ears.

55. What is Our Lady usually looking at during the apparition?

Usually She is looking at us - sometimes at something else, at what She's showing.

56. How does Our Lady hold Her hands about Her?
Her hands are free, relaxed, extended.

57. When does She hold Her hands folded?
Almost never - maybe sometimes at the "Glory be."

58. Does She ever move, gesture with Her hands during the apparitions?
She does not gesture, except when She shows something.

59. Which way are Her palms turned when Her hands are extended?
Her palms are usually relaxed upwards - Her fingers are relaxed the same way.

60. Are Her fingernails then also visible?
They are partially visible.

61. How are they - which color are they?
Natural color - clean cut fingernails.

62. Have you ever seen Our Lady's legs?
No - never - Her dress always covers them.

63. Finally, is Our Lady really beautiful, as you have said?
Well, really we haven't told you anything about that - Her beauty cannot be described - it is not our kind of beauty - that is something ethereal - something heavenly - something that we'll only see in Paradise - and then only to a certain degree.
Information Centre "Mir" Medjugorje, www.medjugorje.hr

(12/96)
A Christmas Story

The following story is an exact account in its original form and simplicity given in the early days of the apparitions by Jelena Vasilj in Medjugorje. Since December of 1982, Jelena has received the gift of inner locutions. This means that she hears messages inside her and often sees images. "Jelena's gift," Fr. Slavko writes, "could be called the 'heart' of the events in Medjugorje. Especially through the prayer group, Jelena transmits the messages, visions and instructions to us very simply." This vision is one that we feel very blessed to share with you.

The Drama

Jelena: A few days before Christmas a movie, "Ben Hur," was playing in Citluk. They said that Jesus was mentioned in it, how He was born, and how He suffered. The movie was starting at 7 PM. Marijana and myself were going to church every evening because Our Lady has asked this of us, and the vision was after Mass. Because of that, my dad was saying to me that I couldn't see the movie. I was sad for that reason.

Then Our Lady said to me, "Don't be sad. At Christmas I shall show you how Jesus was born." (Those Christmas days an angel was appearing to me, as in the previous year.) This is how the vision went: I see an angel. Then he disappears and I see darkness. In that darkness I see St. Joseph. He holds a staff in his hands. At that place there was some grass and stones on the road and a few houses around. Mary is on a mule. She travels. It seems like She is crying, but She is not crying. She is sad. She said, "I would be glad if someone would take us in to spend this night, because. I am tired." Joseph said, "Here are the houses and we will ask." And they were knocking at doors. Mary was standing in front of the house. Joseph was knocking on the door. People were opening the door and when they saw Joseph and Mary, they closed them. They were sad traveling. Joseph said, "There is an old house. No one sleeps in it for sure." Inside there was one mule. Joseph gathered some pieces of wood and they made a fire. He also put some hay in it, but the fire consumed it immediately. So Mary was more heated by the mule. Mary was crying and She was very sad. Joseph was feeding the fire. Suddenly I see Jesus in front of Mary. He smiles as if he were one year old. He is joyful and it seems as if He is speaking. He waves His hands. Joseph comes to Mary and Mary says, "Joseph, this day of joy has come, but it would be better to pray, because there are people who do not want Jesus to be born." And they prayed.

Suddenly I see a little house only. It was lit up a little bit. And then suddenly it became completely lit up as in day, and the stars were in the skies. I see two angels above the stall. They hold a big banner and written on it was: "We glorify You, Lord!" Above it there was a big choir of angels. They were singing and glorifying God. Then I see the shepherds. They were weary, tired and some were already sleeping. Some were walking. The sheep and lambs were with them. One angel approached them and said, "Shepherds, hear the good news: God is born! You will find Him sleeping in a manger in the stall. Know that I am telling you the truth!" The stable was surrounded in the light. Suddenly a large choir of angels joined them and they were singing.

Then a quarrel began among the shepherds. Some wanted to go to the stall and some didn't. One group said, "Maybe it is true! Let us go and see what happened." Some weren't sure. "We will go, we will not go." But then the shepherds began on their way and with them one who wasn't sure. He said, "How can I leave my little lamb, because the wolves might come and eat him. I can't leave it!"

And he put it on his shoulders and they went. It was a long, long journey. Some kept changing their minds on their way saying, "This is a long journey, and maybe He is not born." Traveling that way, they suddenly see a little house illuminated with light as in the day. There were no angels. One shepherd exclaimed, "Yes, it is here, we found it!" And they entered inside. There was one light coming from Jesus. He extends His hands to them, smiles, looks at them. They give Jesus their lambs, putting them around the manger. They are joyful.

Then Mary said to them, "Shepherds! I know that the good news has come to you that the Savior is born. It would be good if we prayed, because there are those in the world who do not allow Jesus to be born in the world." They prayed for a long time. Mary looked as if She were crying. But She was happy. (Once in the vision I felt that She forgives through crying.) Then the shepherds left and they were very joyful. They were singing the songs of thanksgiving to God. I saw them returning to their flocks, and the angels were in the skies.

Suddenly I see a big house. In front of it there was standing a large man and some kings. Like it was said in the Bible, they were carrying golden dishes. The three kings were asking the man, "Where might Jesus be born? Where might the new King of the world be born? We saw His star. It proclaimed to us that the new King of the world was born somewhere here in this land." That man got scared and he thought, "How could a King of the world be born, when I'm the king here?" Therefore he called some people and told them to find out and see (probably in the books) where the King of the world is supposed to be born. Then these people went somewhere, and the man stayed with the kings. When they returned they said that the King is supposed to be born in the stall of Bethlehem. The prophet said, "You the land of Judah are by no means least among the cities." It is written something like this in the song of Bethlehem. Then the kings began on their way to Bethlehem. Suddenly, there appeared in front of them a big star. That star led them. They were thinking to themselves without talking to each other. Suddenly they caught sight of an illuminated light and they looked toward it, like the shepherds. Then one king said, "For sure, He is there!"

Then they entered the stall. Mary said to them, "Your gifts are great, but it is necessary to pray for all those who do not allow Jesus to be born." She said the same to them as to the others, and they prayed for a long, long time. Jesus was smiling. He looked like He was praying with them. He was filled with piety as they were praying.

I did not see what happened after. I only saw the kings in the stall, as if they were sleeping. Suddenly I saw an angel above them saying, "Take another road as you leave because the king does not want to pay homage to the Child Jesus, but he does want to kill the Child." And they went the other way. And everything disappeared.

Fr. Tomislav: Did you look at this as in a movie?

Jelena: It looked real. I looked at that as I look at Our Lady.

(2/88)
Visionary Marija Pavlovic Writes a Letter to the President of the United States

Dear President Reagan,

The Blessed Mother appears every day in this small village of Medjugorje in Yugoslavia. She sends us a message of peace. We know that you do your best to improve the peace in the world and we remember you everyday in our prayers. We want you to know that you can count on our prayers and sacrifices. In this way we want to help you in your difficult task. Our Holy Mother said that with prayers and fasting, even wars can be avoided. May this message help you and Mary's daily appearances be a sign to you also, that God loves His people. United in prayer, in the hearts of Jesus and Mary (The Queen of Peace), we express to you our love, and greet you with peace.

Marija Pavlovic

Marija received a picture of President Reagan on Christmas Day, 1987 with this message: "To Marija Pavlovic – with my heartfelt thanks and every good wish. God Bless You. Sincerely, Ronald Reagan."

Marija's letter arrived just prior to his meeting with Mikhail Gorbachev at the December Nuclear Arms Summit in Washington, D.C. The letter was carried by the American Ambassador to Middle Europe, Alfred H. Kingon, who was on a two week pilgrimage to Medjugorje to pray and fast for his sick son. He personally delivered the message to the White House. On December 8, 1987, the Ambassador called Marija from the White House to tell her that Mr. Reagan was delighted with the message and that after he had finished reading it, exclaimed, "Now, with a new spirit, I am going to the meeting with Mr. Gorbachev." Later the same night, the

White House tried to contact Marija, but could not get through. Mr. Kingon sent a letter to Marija to encourage her to also send a letter of peace to Mr. Gorbachev.

(4/89)
Vicka's Miracle of Suffering
By Fr. Joe Galic, O.F.M.

Medjugorje- the place of apparitions of the Blessed Mother; for over seven years and nine months now, not only the visionaries and the people of the immediate area, but also people from the whole world, more than 13 million, have gone there with prayers, problems, pain, and suffering.

Beginning about six years ago, one of the visionaries, Vicka Ivankovic, 24, was asked by the Blessed Mother to endure a special suffering. Vicka responded that she would accept it. Right after that, she had headaches, fainting, dizziness, and, in a very short time, inflammation of the joints. Not only did she suffer intense pain, but the people around her began talking about her, making up stories. The gossip was very hard for Vicka to cope with; maybe harder than the pain itself. Also, she had to endure many long and arduous medical examinations which produced no results. All this was a trial for Vicka.

Young and enthusiastic, she was unable to tell anyone of the true nature of her suffering because of her promise to the Blessed Mother not to talk about it. Instead, she covered everything with a big smile!

Those close to her were aware of her pains and tried to help her, taking her to doctors, and suggesting that she should ask the Blessed Mother to stop the suffering. Even her own mother told her, "My dear daughter, ask the Blessed Mother to shorten a little your suffering!" Vicka answered, "If you would know how many souls will benefit from it, you would not say a word!" Her mother replied, "If this is God's will, let it be."

Vicka never prayed to ease her suffering. She told those who offered to make it easier for her, that she would prefer to suffer for everyone instead, and keep the suffering to herself.

For six years, Vicka endured the pains. Then, on February 4, 1988, the Blessed Mother promised Vicka that her suffering would stop completely on September 25, 1988. Vicka informed the Bishop's commission that was studying the apparitions. On February 4, she wrote a testimony letter to them and Fr. Janko Bubalo, her spiritual director. The translation of the letter, taken directly from her stationery, reads:

Bijakovici, February 4, 1988

"Janko, what I promise is here. The suffering will stop on September 25, 1988. This is just for you, like a confessional statement. Greetings from the heart, your little sister, Vicka."

Then, on September 25, 1988, she contacted the commission again. Later, on the same day, in the presence of three witnesses, Fr. Janko Bubalo, Fr. Vinko Dragicevic, and Fr. Luka Susac, the letter of February 4 was opened. A joyous Vicka was able to report that she felt no more pain, and that her suffering had ended just as the Blessed Mother had said. She has also agreed to submit herself to a team of doctors for medical verification of her healing.

It was a miracle! On that day, everyone's heart was full of joy to hear her leading the Rosary in the church and to see her without pain and smiling graciously!

Editor's note: Fr. Joe Galic is a Croatian Franciscan priest who lives in the United States. When Fr. Jozo was imprisoned, Fr. Joe was blessed to have been able to visit him in prison. He frequently accompanies pilgrim groups to Medjugorje as the spiritual director.

(4/90)
Mirjana's February Message Emphasizes Family Prayer

It is a well known fact that Mirjana Dragicevic stopped having regular apparitions after eighteen months of daily visions. During Mirjana's last daily apparition on December 25, 1982, Our Lady promised to visit Mirjana every year on her birthday and when something very difficult happens. These visits have encouraged Mirjana's faith.

In 1985 and 1986, Mirjana received inner locutions in which Our Lady told her not to be afraid of the secrets. To the question, "Why have the apparitions been lasting so long?" Our Lady responded, "Because so many people are taking so long to convert. There have never been so many unbelievers." This prolongation is a merciful delay.

More recently, visionary Mirjana has been receiving apparitions from Our Lady on the second day of every month in addition to her birthday. On February 2, 1990, Mirjana received her monthly apparition from Our Lady while she was visiting in Portland, Oregon.

Mirjana and her husband, Marco Soldo, were invited to visit America by their friend Fr. Milan Mikulich. Fr. Milan performed their marriage ceremony in Medjugorje in September, 1989. He is pastor of St. Brigitta's parish in Portland, Oregon. And so they came to spend a honeymoon week from January 30 through February 5.

Mirjana's apparition on February 2nd, took place in a small chapel adjoining Fr. Milan's residence. In nearby St. Brigitta's Church, many faithful people were praying the Rosary during that time. The message Mirjana received from Our Lady is serious and includes a plea for us to help Her. Mirjana said Our Lady's message is for the world; therefore, we ask you to spread the messages especially in your family and to pray for unbelievers.

Message from Our Blessed Mother to
Mirjana Dragicevic Soldo
February 2, 1990

"I have been with you nine years. For nine years I wanted to tell you that God, your Father, is the only Way, Truth and Life. I wish to show you the way to eternal Life. I wish to be your life, your connection to the profound faith. Listen to me!

"Take your Rosary and get your children, your families with you. This is the way to come to salvation. Give your good example to those who do not believe. You will not have happiness on this earth, neither will you come to Heaven if you are not with pure

and humble hearts and do not fulfill the law of God. I am asking for your help to join me to pray for those who do not believe. You are helping me very little. You have little charity or love for your neighbor, and God gave you love and showed you how you should forgive and love others.

"For that reason, reconcile and purify your soul. Take your Rosary and pray it. All your sufferings take patiently. You should remember that Jesus was patiently suffering for you.

"Let me be your Mother and your tie to God, to Eternal Life. Do not impose your faith to the unbelievers. Show it to them by your example and pray for them.

"My children, pray!"

The message was translated by Fr. Milan. He said that Mirjana told him that Our Lady meant the sacrament of Holy Confession for Catholics when She said, "…reconcile and purify your soul."

The Medjugorje Star

(3/91)
Text of Ivan's Letter to President Bush

Excerpt from Question to Ivan Dragicevic at Panel discussion – Sunday, December 2, 1990.

Question posed to Ivan was about his travels in the United States and perhaps comment, if possible, about his meeting with the President.

"I also would like to mention that I did visit Washington, D.C., and I was talking mostly with senators and congressmen. The topic of conversation was mostly about the abortion problem in the United States. And also the meeting with President Bush. I would not spend too much time to explain about that because most of it was private. But it's not everything as to be publicized.

"At this time I would just like to read to you just a few words that I left for him in his own office so that you can share in these thoughts."

Letter from Ivan to President Bush:

Mr. President,

It is a great honor for me to be able to be with you here today. I am sincerely greeting you and all your people. I know that in your position, you meet with many people from all over the world who come in the name of their nation with their problems seeking help.

I do not come as a politician nor as a diplomat. I do not represent any party or nation, nor am I sent by any group of people. I am a simple, young man from a part of Herzegovina inhabited by Croatian people. I come from a place called Medjugorje – the village of Bijakovici.

Almost nine and a half years ago an unusual phenomenon occurred to me, which still continues. With five of my friends, I suddenly saw a beautiful, all-illuminated, motherly figure. From that time, I see Her every day. She introduced Herself as "The Queen of Peace." Many already call Her by this name and ask Her intercession.

I pray for peace every day with a multitude of believers, many of whom are from this land, America. I pray not only with them, but also, with the Queen of Peace, the Mother Virgin Mary.

To many people this sounds incredible. And neither I nor my friends, the other visionaries, could ever imagine or wish for something like this to happen – that every day we pray together with the Queen of Peace for the peace of the world.

Mr. President, I'm familiar with your efforts to guard peace in this world. Please do everything possible that true peace comes everywhere. Believe that whenever you do anything for peace, you perform the Will of God, which He has revealed to us in these times through Mary. I personally, as well as my friends the visionaries, are conscious of the fact that with prayers and fasting we can accomplish much for peace. This we are constantly conveying to all pilgrims. I know that many in the world pray and fast. Therefore, Mr. President, believe that we will continue to follow your efforts with our prayers and fasting. I will recommend you and your nation to the Queen of Peace. She is the Queen of Life, the Mother of All People. She has said to us, that we are all important to Her in Her plans of peace for all of us, large and small, healthy and sick, learned and simple. She's teaching us that everyone can contribute in making peace happen.

Allow me, through you, to invite your honorable citizens by guarding and honoring life, putting aside drugs and alcohol, accepting every child from conception, honoring every old and sick person, helping the poor, to help build and realize Our Lady's Plan. May God bless you and your family and all people.

The Mir Response

Mirjana

(8/97)
Mirjana & Marco Visit California
By Annemarie Bullum Shawl

I spent the last three days with Mirjana and her husband Marco and I just wanted to share some of the things I've learned this last weekend.

First of all, Mirjana is such a wonderful girl, mild and humble, with a wonderful sense of humor. I picked her and her husband up from the airport and went directly to the Hilton in Anaheim, right next to Disneyland. The next morning at 10:30 AM she gave her first lecture, I guess you could call it. Some of the things we've all probably heard before, such as how many secrets there are, and what the Blessed Mother looks like, but there are a few things that were new.

She says that the Blessed Mother or "Gospa" is a little taller than she is and Mirjana is about 5'4," and that She has a little curl of black hair always on the right side of Her cheek and you can see that Her hair is long because it comes at Her waist underneath Her veil.

Mirjana has an apparition with the Gospa on March 18th every year and she has a longer apparition with Gospa on the 2nd of every month. This second apparition is longer and different than the rest of the apparitions because Mirjana never knows when the Blessed Mother will come. She knows She will come, but not when. Therefore, Mirjana stays in prayer the WHOLE day. This started in 1987. When the Blessed Mother comes, they either talk about things or they just pray. This Saturday was the 2nd of the month, so everyone left her alone to pray. Marco, her husband, asked me if I could take him around so he could give Mirjana the privacy that she needs. I took him to Beverly Hills, Rodeo Drive, Hollywood Blvd. and I even showed him where the O.J. Simpson and Nicole tragedy took place. He wanted to see as much as we had time for. He couldn't get over the houses, of course, in Beverly Hills.

I asked him a couple of questions about his life with Mirjana and the happenings of Medjugorje. First I asked him how they met and was he scared to start dating Mirjana knowing who she was speaking to all the time. He laughed. He told me that they had known each other since they were children, and they always stayed in contact with each other. He was living in Sarajevo, and she was going back and forth from Medjugorje to Sarajevo where she went to school at the University after the Blessed Mother told her it would be good for her to go. Marco said then that he had heard that in Medjugorje the Gospa was coming to six children there, then he found out that Mirjana, his friend, was one of them. His eyes got really big. He asked Mirjana if this was true and she told him it was. Mirjana said that Marco was always a church going Catholic who prayed the Rosary daily, went to confession and just was a really good person to begin with, so he didn't have to go through a big conversion like most people would think. They started dating off and on.

I told him that a lot of people thought that the visionaries would probably become nuns and did Mirjana think she wanted to become a nun. Mirjana always said that the Blessed Mother would bless any decision that they made, and she would not force them to do anything, but if she got married, that it should be a marriage that would need to be an example for others on how a marriage should be. So a while later, they were married and now have 2 children (4yr old and 1 1/2yr old), and she wants to have more. She said the Blessed Mother says that it is wonderful to have children, and there is a reason for it too, the more children you have the better, but she didn't want to expand on why at the time. I also heard that some of the visionaries were thinking strongly about becoming nuns and Ivan a priest but their purpose in life right now is to welcome and speak with pilgrims and this is what the Blessed Mother wants them to do. They were told that if they became nuns, and were given orders to stay in seclusion, then they wouldn't be able to speak and spread the word to pilgrims like the Blessed Mother would like them to.

Marco, was a wonderful, gentle man who seems to me to be taking on a role similar to that of St. Joseph. He protects Mirjana, always is thinking of her and how she's getting along, doesn't want her to get too tired, wants her to have her privacy when she needs it (especially when it's time for her to be alone with Gospa). Mirjana has so many responsibilities and he never interferes with what she is doing because he knows it needs to be done. She speaks to pilgrims wherever she goes and he is usually taking care of the kids when they're at home and helps with the housework. Whatever she needs, he's there for her, and always seems to take the backseat to wherever she is and he loves it. He loves his wife with all his heart. They always pray together as a family. This impression of St. Joseph always sprang in my head whenever I saw them, and it was wonderful.

Like I said, Mirjana likes to joke around a little too. She didn't mention that she sees Gospa to her then two year old little girl because she thought she was too young. They still prayed together always, but she was waiting to tell her about the visions. One day, her little daughter was playing with a friend in the front room of their house and the girls started to have a little argument. The one girl said, "My mom's better than your mom because my mom can drive a car." Mirjana's little girl said, "Well that's nothing, my mom sees the Blessed Mother." Mirjana finally realized that it was about time to explain it to her because her daughter figured out what was going on.

Mirjana is the girl that was given the parchment containing the 10 secrets. It used to be with her in Sarajevo, but then when she moved it went with her back to Medjugorje. Many people wanted to know this because of the craziness that is going on there; 20 of Mirjana's relatives were massacred there, I'll find out more on this later. She doesn't have to hide the parchment because no one can read what is on it. She took it out once to show a couple of her cousins and one girl saw a prayer on it, another girl saw something else, and they were shown it at the same time, so Mirjana is not worried that anyone will break the code.

There is always speculation and a lot of other apparitions going around. Mirjana was asked to please ask the Blessed Mother about all these other apparitions and were they real. Mirjana said the Blessed Mother told her to "Please pray for these people." Mirjana also said that people are coming all the time and saying that the first secret of Medjugorje has come to pass. Mirjana says this is nonsense. She has to tell Fr. Petar Ljubicic in Medjugorje 10 days before the secret is to happen and then both she and the priest are supposed to fast and pray for 7 days, and then three days before the secret is supposed to happen, the priest will announce it to the whole world for all to see. Mirjana said, she has never told her priest that any secret happened yet and she has never spoken to any one about them. And that NO secrets have come to pass. She jokes and said that her confessor which is Father Petar, tells her to come to confession and just tell him one. She always laughs at this. The reason she chose Father Petar Ljubicic (if anyone has been to Medjugorje, he is the one with the big glasses) is because from the first time she met him, he always was kind to the very poor people and the orphans and she loves this about him.

Speaking of orphans, besides visiting with pilgrims, everyday when she is in Medjugorje, she also helps out and takes care of many children in the orphanage. She wants to build another orphanage there in Medjugorje because there are so many Croatian refugees from other villages, without a mother or a father or sometimes both. She would like to see 10 homes for the poor and the orphans there. Her life is dedicated to helping all the little ones she can besides her own. One thing is certain though, if the U.N. peace keepers can't get food and supplies to people throughout Croatia, Medjugorje has been able to do it for a long time. The people in Medjugorje, even Father Jozo, and the visionaries personally take medicine, food, clothing to all the poor they can find.

Mirjana asked me some questions that were cute like, how do the girls in America get such shiny hair, is there something they use. They also said that to live here you must really like to drive.

Marco works as an auto repair man in a body shop near Medjugorje and he works hard. Mirjana works mostly with the children and orphans and speaks with pilgrims and I know she said something else but I just can't think of it right now.

I asked her what she feels like before the Gospa comes, what are her emotions like. She said that she feels so excited, and nervous and full of anticipation because she knows that for however long the Blessed Mother is with her, she feels no pain, sorrow or fear, only happiness, love and she feels like she's in Heaven. She has never hugged the Blessed Mother or vice versa but she says that just being so close to Her like that you almost want to burst with love. You feel sooooo loved by Her.

Never has the Blessed Mother told her, "Come to me and I will give you....." It has always been, "Come to me and I will lead you to My Son and He will give you ...."

Well, that's all I can remember right now, but I prayed like crazy so that I wouldn't forget anything, or twist anything around, or say something that wasn't truthful. If I can remember something I'll let you all know. If you have any questions that might jog my memory more, feel free to ask. I love talking about this subject, as if you haven't already noticed.

Oh, one other thing. Mirjana asked me to come and stay with her when I went to Medjugorje; I know some people are going in October and I would really love to go. Maybe there are some of you who might want to make a pilgrimage. Just a thought. Mirjana says that now is the quietest time they have had there in a long time. Everything is peaceful there she said. So, what do you think? God bless everyone. Hvaljen Isus I Marija. (Praised be Jesus and Mary)

www.medjugorje.org

Editor's note: Annemarie Bullum Shawl heads the IIPG (International Internet Prayer Group), the internet Medjugorje prayer group associated with Ivan's prayer group. She and her husband Steve frequently lead pilgrimages to Medjugorje.

(9/90)
Dobro Jutro! An Encounter with Ivan
By Christine M. Kelly

"Let the children come to me, and do not stop them, because the Kingdom of God belongs to such as these. I assure you that whoever does not receive the Kingdom of God like a child will never enter it." (Mark 10:13-16)

In Jesus' own words we are called to be as children. How often we hear ourselves called the "Children of God." All men, all religions are one in God's family. The message is for men of all ages, but today especially, for the youth of the world.

On the 26th of May, 1990, Ivan Dragicevic held a special meeting with the young pilgrims present in Medjugorje. The gathering took place in a quiet wooded field near his home. The mere sight of our small group (about 35 or 40) gathered around Ivan was very touching. Our intimate gathering with this very blessed young man came together at eight o'clock in the morning. I will not attempt to recount word-for-word what Ivan had to say. I could not do him justice. I will, however, highlight the main topics discussed and attempt to explain clearly the impressions he made on me.

As always, we began with prayer. Ivan asked us to consider this an informal gathering and invited us to ask any question that might come into our heads. He began by stressing the importance of family and family prayer. This is Ivan's special mission from Our Lady. Families around the world are destroyed by greed, dishonesty, alcohol and drug abuse, the absence of religion, and finally, divorce. Although Ivan stressed the importance of family prayer, the need for individual prayer is even greater when family unity is not present. For those who are fortunate enough to be part of the traditional nuclear family, they should place God at its center and make time for daily family prayer. God should always be at the center of our lives. Ivan urged us to pray for the unbelievers in our families. For them we should pray most fervently.

A young boy in the group asked Ivan how he could convince his friends to go to church and to live the messages of Medjugorje. Ivan told us to be examples to our friends. He said that we should pray for all of our friends, especially the unbelievers. Jesus said to the Pharisees, "If you knew me, you would know my Father also" (John 8:19). In our own meager way, we must be representatives of Christ to all those whom we encounter. It is not so very important that men believe that our Blessed Mother is appearing in Medjugorje. It is important that men live the messages of Medjugorje. The messages of Medjugorje are that of the Gospel, and we must be witnesses to His Word. We are members, by His grace, of the living Gospel!!!

"When He (Christ) was insulted, He returned no insult. When He was made to suffer, He did not counter with threats." (1Peter 2:23) These words can serve as a source of strength when our faith is mocked by unbelievers. As humans, we long for acceptance from our family, friends, classmates, and co-workers. Ivan encouraged us to conform to God's will and not to society's. Jesus said, "Happy are those who are persecuted because they do what God requires; the Kingdom of Heaven belongs to them" (Matthew 5:10). Jesus also said, "I solemnly assure you, there is no one who has left home or wife or brothers, parents or children, for the sake of the Kingdom of God who will not receive a plentiful return in this age and life everlasting in the age to come" (Luke 18:29-30). If we accept God's plan and live it joyfully, it will be easier to stand up to ridicule. Accepting God's will also means accepting His love. In God's love all things are possible.

Ivan spoke of the superficiality of our lifestyles. He spoke of marriage and our lack of understanding for such a commitment. Most Americans measure a successful marriage on the potential income, the size of a home, and the number of cars and possessions foreseen. How true this is! Ivan is writing a book on family life and marriage, to be published when Our Lady grants him permission. He touched lightly on this subject because it would have taken him three days to express all his thoughts! Ivan did say that it is important for the parents of the couple to meet and get to know each other. He also said that many young people rush into marriages at too young an age. I could not help but notice the deep respect he showed for his family and for the girl he may one day take for his spouse.

Ivan then pleaded with us to stay out of bars. He said that on his visit to America last year he was very disappointed in the way young people spent their evenings. It is true that young people do spend entirely too much time in bars and clubs (discos). Drinking and "partying" have become top priorities for teen-agers and young adults. This does not promote healthy, spiritual relationships. Even the movies we see are filled with evil, un-Christian messages. This goes like-wise for prime-time television, and especially for day-time soap-operas. We live in a society that has been brainwashed into thinking pre-marital sex, drugs, alcohol, and greed are acceptable. These things are not acceptable. Ivan suggested we spend our evenings with our families and/or in prayer.

He emphasized the importance of prayer groups. Coming home is often difficult after spending such a spiritual week in Medjugorje. Support groups can help us to continue living our faith as we should. Ivan has his own prayer group which meets on Monday and Friday evenings. They come together to pray, sing, and talk. Ivan sometimes has a special visit from Our Lady during these prayer group gatherings. He stressed the importance of having a spiritual adviser for the group. We should have a priest whom we can turn to for guidance and Reconciliation. Ivan showed a deep respect for the Church. We should also respect the Church, its laws and its teachings.

Let us begin now to live the messages of our Blessed Mother: Peace, Penance, Prayer, Conversion, and Fasting. Let us convert now so that others may be graciously converted through us. In God's infinite wisdom and mercy, He has sent Mary, our Mother, to lead us back to the path of salvation.

We are called to live chaste, obedient lives in the service of Our Lord. Our Father in Heaven knows what is best for us. If we pray and lead pure lives, He will guide us on our way. Mary is the Mother of all, blessing us daily with Her presence on earth. She wants to bring us all to Her Son, but we must first accept Jesus and His way of truth.

Our Lady is calling us to prayer. The Rosary is our strongest weapon against Satan. If we pray faithfully the 15 decades of the Rosary each day, we will be strong against Satan's influence. Through confession, prayer, fasting, and Holy Eucharist, our hearts will be made pure. Within our hearts we can receive the Holy Spirit and His graces and guidance.

Ivan said he will be coming to the United States in November to speak with President Bush. Please pray that Ivan will be successful in his talks with our president. May the Good Lord bless him and the Spirit of God speak through him.

We are living in a time of grace. I feel blessed beyond description that I could be present at this youth gathering with Ivan. We are the future of the Church and of the world. Please keep the youth of the world in your prayers. Also pray for the success of this year's Medjugorje Youth Festival to take place July 30th- August 6th. May we always live for the greater glory of God the Father, the Son, and the Holy Spirit.

The visionaries are Our Lady's instruments. Through them She is speaking to the world. Their task is often difficult and their responsibilities great. On our pilgrimages to Medjugorje we should remember that they are each human – giving generously of themselves. Ivan asked us to pray for the villagers and their children. They give so much time and energy to us. Ivan asked that we pray that the children are not neglected for our sakes. Let us keep the visionaries, priests and nuns, the villagers and the tour leaders of Medjugorje in our prayers. May we continue to heed our Mother's call! God bless you all!!!

"God who is mighty has done great things for me, holy is His name" (Luke 1:49).

The Mir Response

Editor's note: "Dubro jutro" is Croatian for "Good morning."

70

Vicka speaking to pilgrims

(7/97)
Visit with Visionary Vicka

We begin with prayer after which Vicka speaks to us about the messages.

Vicka: The most important part of the messages concerns prayer, conversion, fasting, penance, and peace. Also, Our Lady recommends that we pray every day, all three parts of the Holy Rosary: Joyful, Sorrowful, and Glorious as well. She invites us to fast on Wednesday and Friday, bread and water only. But the most important thing She asks of us is a firm faith. When She says pray, it's not that She wants us to pray with words, with our lips. On the contrary, She wants us to open up our hearts from day to day, so that the prayer may become a real joy to us. She advises us that before you start your prayers, try to get rid of all disturbing thoughts you may have. Start your prayer with a simple prayer, one Our Father. We should pray to Him as the Great Father in Heaven who has this enormous love for all of us. The prayer should be the moment when we present Him all our problems and all our wishes. Let His will be done and not ours. Then the next day you will be praying the Hail Mary. We should be praying to Her as a great Mother that we may see with the eyes of our hearts, who is all the time close to us, who dwells upon us, and who loves us. The third day we will be praying the Glory Be, to glorify Our Father, to thank Him for everything He is granting us, for both good and bad things as well. This is in order that we may become able or capable of accepting everything equal. So this should be the way we are supposed to open up our hearts. Also we should think and ponder on every word that we pronounce in order that we can grasp the meaning of the prayers so we can live the meaning of those prayers. While speaking on this, Our Lady gave us a beautiful example. She said that all of you back home all have at least one sort of flower. If we water this flower every day, we put only a few drops of water each day. Very soon we should see it blossoming into a beautiful rose. The same happens to human hearts. If we put or plant just two words of prayer into it daily, then you'll see it growing and blossoming, the same as this beautiful flower. But then again, if we stop watering the flower, we will see it vanishing as if it never existed.

Our Lady, in a way, is teaching that it is human nature to find excuses often not to pray. Today, perhaps I am tired, the next day I don't have time. Unfortunately, this is the way that we are going away from prayer, making a distance between us and God and the prayer, and in this way opening our heart for all negative things. Our Lady wants to tell us that the same as this flower cannot be without water, it is the same with the human heart that cannot live without God's graces. She says that prayer with the heart is not something we can learn like we learn something in school by studying. Prayer with the heart is only something we can live and therefore advance spiritually day to day.

When She speaks of fasting, she refers to all these people who are sick, who cannot stand a day without food. She recommends that on that day, they give up something they really like that they enjoy. But then to all of us that find excuses, like I feel sick, I feel dizzy, She says that we should bear one thing in our mind, that fasting is something we should do out of love for Her and Jesus. All that we need is a firm will!

Our Lady has also been calling us to complete conversion. She says, "Dear children, whenever you find yourself in times of trouble or problems, somehow you think that both Jesus and I are away from you." But then again She says, "You are wrong. We are all the time with you, close to you." But we are the ones who should open up our hearts, that we may be able to know Them with our hearts and know the love They have for us.

Also, She wants us to give up something we like most. She Herself would prefer that we stop sinning. She says that I am giving you My love and My peace, that you can bring them back home with you and share them with your friends and family. That is why She is granting us Her blessings, and She has been praying for all of us. In a special way She emphasizes that She would like us to renew the prayer of the Holy Rosary in our families and our communities. Both parents and children could have a bond in prayer that they could spend time together praying, and that way to stop Satan from doing us any harm. She stresses how strong Satan is and how he wants to interfere with everything we are doing. That is why, in particular, She wants us to make our prayers even stronger. Our prayer becomes the means, the weapon against Satan so that he cannot do us harm. Our Lady also recommends to us to keep something with us always that is blessed, something little such as a cross or a medal, something for our protection.

She recommends that we put the Holy Eucharist in the first place in our lives. She is teaching us that the Holy Mass is the most important and most holy moment in our lives because in Holy Mass, Jesus is coming alive, and we are receiving Him into our hearts. Our Lady tells us that we should prepare ourselves properly for Jesus' coming, so that we can receive Him with love and dignity. Also, She recommends to us, at least once a month, to go to confession. Or when we feel like it. But then again, She warns that we shouldn't take Holy Confession as something that we go there, tell our sins, and get rid of them, and then lead the same old lives as before. On the contrary, we should be changing into new personalities. We should talk to our priests, and ask and seek advice from them so that we can advance spiritually.

Our Lady has been especially worried about youth in our world. She emphasizes constantly how bad the situation is, that young people are in real bad shape. Again, She teaches that we can help them only with our love and prayer of our hearts. Addressing the young people, She says, "Dear young people, all these things that are offered to you in the mortal world are of temporary nature. But also, you can realize through this the evil of the things offered to you and that Satan is trying to get hold of every moment and have it working for him. These days, in the entire world, he has been working mainly on young people and he wants to destroy families." But Our Lady also says, "Dear children this is the time of great graces." She wants us to renew all of Her messages and She wants us to live these messages with our hearts. She wants us to become carriers of Her own peace. She wants us to pray for peace in the world. But first of all, She requests from us to find peace in our own hearts, then for peace in our families, and our communities. At the end, finally, we pray for those two to pray for the peace in the world. She said that if we should pray for peace in the world and at the same time we have a restless heart, this prayer for peace in the world would be in vain.

In the past, the years were dedicated to youth, young people. But Our Lady wants this dedication to be prolonged to the year ahead of us to be the year dedicated to youth and to our families. In this moment, this very moment, She recommends us to make our prayers stronger. She Herself is in need of our prayers. She needs our prayers for some plans of Hers and God. She also recommends that we take a Holy Bible every day. Read a few lines from Holy Scripture and live those lines throughout the day. Then Our Lady invites us to pray for His Holiness, the Pope, for the bishops, the priest, for the whole of our Church. She says they are in need of our prayers. And again especially, She wants us to pray in particular for a plan of Hers that is about to be released. She Herself has been praying for peace. She invited us to join Her in this intention for peace and She wants us to help Her with our prayers. Vicka says, that tonight, at the time of the apparition, she will recommend all you here and all your intentions that you came with to Medjugorje. She says that at the time you spend time in prayer and open your hearts and present to Her your wishes and problems and anything that you wish to the Blessed Mother. And here at the end let us remain in a quiet prayer for a little while and later we shall finish this meeting with one Our Father, Hail Mary and Glory Be.

Ivanka and her interpreter at St. George Church in Erie

(7/96)
Ivanka's Question and Answer Period

A question and answer period followed Ivanka's talk at St. George Church in Erie, PA, on June 6, 1996.

Q: Has the Blessed Virgin said anything about chastisements or the Second Coming of Christ?
A: Our Lady never said anything about chastisements in Medjugorje. These signs will lead you to pray. Pray for conversion, and by praying for conversion for others, we also purify ourselves. By purifying ourselves, we are preparing ourselves to meet Christ.

Q: The evils of abortion in the USA...does Our Lady speak of it?

A: Our Lady is the Mother of Life, and God is the Father of Life, so whoever is with God will never kill any life. When Ivanka gave birth to her second child, Joseph, Our Lady told her, "Thank you for giving new life to give life." So, Our Lady is always for life.

Q: The millennium is 4 years away. Do you feel the visitations of the Blessed Virgin Mary are coming to an end?

A: Our Lady never said anything about dates. Only God knows when it is going to happen.

Q: Does Our Lady speak positive about the power of prayer we say?

A: Our Lady said, prayer, especially prayer and fasting together, there is tremendous power in this. We can even stop catastrophes, and even war.

Q: When you pray to Mary, how do you know She is answering you?

A: Our Lady always hears our prayers, even now. She is always present with us. She says when we are in any kind of suffering and pain, we think that Jesus and Mary are far from us, but be sure- She is always close to you. She not only hears your words, but also your thoughts. She will always answer your pleas and sometimes the answer will not always be what we want. In the long run, it will be good for you.

Q: Did Our Lady say why She chose to appear to you in Medjugorje?

A: In the beginning, the visionaries asked Her why She chose them and gave them the messages. Our Lady answered, "I didn't look for the best." Ivanka says she is sure that there are better people than she is. She considers herself a normal person. God gave her this gift, and with this gift comes great responsibility.

Q: Is it true the Holy Father is going to Medjugorje, and when?

A: Ivanka said that they would like for him to come visit. On one occasion the Holy Father said that he would like to visit Medjugorje, and he would only do it if he were not the Pope.

Q: Is that picture a likeness of the Blessed Virgin? (A painting of Mary was near the altar.)

A: All the visionaries say none of the artists are able to depict on canvas or in statues exactly what they see. They see Our Lady much more beautiful beyond description.

Q: Did Our Lady say anything about the war? Why it is going on and why its nation wasn't protected? (pertaining to the Bosnia-Herzegovina war)

A: From the very beginning, Our Lady was saying that Satan is strong and has plans to destroy humanity. She was inviting and calling for prayer for peace. With prayer and fasting you can avoid catastrophes. Wars are sometimes visible. Sometimes less visible. Someone mentioned abortion here. It is a war against life and this visible war in Bosnia–Herzegovina is a war against life. The aggressors were always targeting the churches first. Everywhere aggression…against God, against good. The bottom line is war between evil and good. The aggressor is the one who is trying to destroy the good. Our Lady wants us with prayer to have strong faith in God. To be on the side of God. To be on the side of good. This is why She wants conversion to happen. In the last message, She said, " I want people to convert." It means to walk back to God. To live according to God's commandments. If this happens, then we would not have any wars. We would not have any destruction. We would live in peace and we would have Heaven on earth.

Q: Has Our Lady said anything about Fr. Gobbi and his way and his beloved priests?

A: Our Lady has never said anything about any specific priest, but priests in general. They should be shepherds of their people and they should explain the Gospel in a simple way so that everyone can understand.

Q: As a wife and mother, how do you bring spirituality into your family?

A: Simply through prayer. They pray together in the morning, sing songs about faith, about Jesus and Mary. When the children go to bed, Ivanka tells them stories from the Bible. They also go to church together. Our Lady doesn't ask us to do any more than that. Just live the normal Christian life. If all families lived like that, there wouldn't be any problems and divorces.

Q: Have you ever touched or embraced Our Lady? Has Jesus ever appeared to you?

A: Only as a baby on the second day of the apparitions. Also on Christmas as a baby. In May of '85 when Ivanka was having daily apparitions, Our Lady embraced Ivanka. She hugged her. Ivanka said the touch of Our Lady is different than touching another person. She can see Her as she can see any other person, but to touch is quite different. The feeling is so much love and so much peace. It is simply not possible to describe.

Q: Did the Blessed Mother ever tell you why She appears only to those of the Catholic faith?

A: Ivanka says when they asked Her about different religions, Our Lady says there is only one God. We divided ourselves on earth, but to Her and to God, we are all the same.

Q: Mary asks us to fast and pray and do penance. How often does She recommend we do this? And to what degree should we fast and pray?

A: Our Lady suggests to us to fast on bread and water on Wednesdays and Fridays. When they asked what is the best fast, She said to fast on bread and water on Wednesdays and Fridays. First it was only Fridays, then She added Wednesdays. She also said to come to this further fast, you have to advance to that slowly, gradually. The same goes for praying. For instance, if you are not accustomed to pray in the family, all three Rosaries daily, then start with only one Our Father, Hail Mary, and Glory Be. Then advance to seven Our Father's, seven Hail Mary's, and seven Glory Be's. Then come to saying a Rosary, and then all three Rosaries, if you can. Then the fasting…first start with giving up something that is dear to you, then gradually give up something else. Someone who is addicted to smoking can put away cigarettes that day or television. Fasting does not mean only food, but anything we put in front of ourselves as dear, as idols.

Q: Ivanka, you saw Heaven, hell and Purgatory. Can you briefly describe them?

A: Ivanka only saw Heaven and Purgatory. She did not see hell. Other visionaries did, Vicka and Jakov. Our Lady showed her Heaven and Purgatory very fast, like a film strip. Even from those pictures, it was obvious to see the difference. When Our Lady showed her Heaven, you could feel so much peace, so much beauty and so much feeling of contentment. Everyone who was there was happy and very much at peace. But when she saw Purgatory, it was quite different. The pictures were very dark, and even from that, you could feel the tremendous need for prayers. They were calling and calling for prayers and help.

Q: Can you describe the peace in Medjugorje?

A: It would be best if you would come to Medjugorje and experience it for yourself.

Q: How does the Blessed Mother feel about the conversion of one who has lived a sinful life?

A: Our Lady said God will forgive everything. He is a good Father, especially when you read in the Scripture that God has sent His only Son because He wants to save the world. So Our Lady really says the same.

Q: Did Our Lady ask any of the visionaries to consider the religious vocations?

A: In the beginning of the apparitions, Our Lady said She would like them to follow the religious life, but whatever vocation they decide, She would bless their decision. Our Lady never wants to impose Her will on anyone. Ivanka wants to share her visit that she had this morning with the cloister nuns. (She was taken to the Carmelite Monastery directly from the airport.) There were seven nuns, and it was so touching to see these women consecrating their whole lives to prayer. One really has to decide to love as they did. To Ivanka, they remarked that they see in her so much peace. They asked Ivanka what she sees in them. She replied that she sees in them such blessedness that she feels she is far from that.

Q: What does your husband think about all this?
A: Ivanka wishes that he were here so that you could ask him.

Ivanka wants to thank you all, especially for your prayers and also for your support and help. Many of you help those families in and around Medjugorje in Bosnia-Herzegovina, the families that are without fathers due to the war. All of you that help, know that your help is very much appreciated. These mothers and godfathers would not be able to see their children if it weren't for you. Thank you from the bottom of my heart.

It will be 15 years on June 25th that Our Lady began to appear in Medjugorje. This is the day Ivanka is going to meet with Our Lady. She has waited all year for it. She will recommend all of you and your families and all your intentions to Our Lady. At that time, you also pray. Remember your families and remember the message of Our Lady that She wants. She wants each one of you "to be the light."

Fr. Jozo

(12/88)
Fr. Jozo's Talk
10/14/89 at St. Elijah's Parish in Tihaljina, Yugoslavia

Father Jozo was the children's protector and later their spiritual adviser. Because he would not comply with a government directive to squelch the activities surrounding the apparitions, he was sentenced to serve three years in prison. He served 1½ years.

Fr. Jozo began with the story of the children. He did not believe them initially about seeing the Blessed Mother, and tried to convince them that they were wrong. One day, as he was praying in St. James Church in Medjugorje, he heard a voice, "Go protect the children." He got up and went to the door of the church and saw the children running in from the vineyards. They were being pursued by the local police. He hid them in the nearby rectory.

Jakov told Fr. Jozo that Our Lady wants us all to pray the Rosary. The Blessed Mother appeared to Jakov and told him that he was very important and that She needed him! The Blessed Mother said She needs all of us and we are all important to Her. We should teach our own children how important they are to God.

Fr. Jozo informed us that there have been many conversions from other religions including Muslim and Jewish.

The children confessed to Fr. Jozo that they did not know how to pray the Rosary and that Our Lady taught them how. They were chosen by Our Lady because of their humility and purity of heart. Our Lady chose these children who did not know how to pray the Rosary – to teach the world how to pray!!!

Fr. Jozo said he once saw the Blessed Mother cry because we have forgotten the Bible. He said we should never put the Bible on a shelf with other books, nor should we treat it like an object. We should create an "altar" in our home with a Bible, blessed candle, holy water, and a crucifix. This should be placed where it is very visible so as to gain our attention daily to remind us to pray!

Fr. Jozo spent much time on the need for prayer. "A parish that does not pray for the priests is like a graveyard – because no priests can come from that parish..."

He emphasized that our prayer must come from the heart! We should pray the Rosary to keep Satan out of our lives and out of the lives of our children.

Fr. Jozo said that we should offer up to God that which pleases us the most or gets in between ourselves and God.

He told the people that everyone who comes to Medjugorje is called by the Blessed Mother. We do not come by chance or accident, but are called as an individual. We are responsible to respond to Her call...

Fr. Jozo blessed the pictures of Our Lady and passed them out to everyone. After his talk, many were said to be "slain in the spirit" following the blessing.

Fr. Jozo is no longer the pastor of St. Elijah Parish in Tihaljina. He now has more time to spend with the pilgrims, preaching the messages of Our Lady of Medjugorje.

Editor's note: Fr. Jozo's talk has been included in this chapter on the visionaries because Our Lady has also appeared to Fr. Jozo, and has been called by some, "the seventh visionary."

(11/93)
Words from Mirjana
By Sister Emmanuel

Let us honor Mary by an increase of love through our prayers and our fasting! This love from the heart is necessary, as Mirjana has reminded us through this very moving story:

"It was in '81, and on this particular evening all 6 of us were together in the church for the apparition. The church was full, and a large crowd stood outside as many pilgrims had come from other countries. On seeing such a crowd, we were very happy and when Gospa appeared, we said to Her, 'You must be very happy this evening!' But She replied, ' Children, there are as many praying at this moment as you have fingers on your hands.'"

May each one of us be one of those fingers that the Virgin perceives with Her eyes of light...

A great joy to have had Daniel-Ange with us for a few days, he who is becoming more and more a burning apostle of Medjugorje. He blessed the child that Mirjana is carrying, and among others, asked her about abortion in order to complete what Marija had already explained:

"When I was in Sarajevo, I discovered that many women around me had had abortions and I spoke about this with the Gospa. She asked me to help these women, above all in showing them much love, all the love that God and She herself had for them, She said that abortion was a great sin, as to abort was to kill; that it was also certain that God would pardon this sin as He loves us all. But for this sin, God asks the father and the mother of the child to make a big sacrifice (a big penance). This is necessary, Gospa told us."

About a question concerning the Pope, Mirjana confided to us that she was able in '87, to speak with him privately. He knows that she has received her 10 secrets, but she has not revealed them to him, nor to anyone, according to the request of the Virgin. Mirjana told us that she could not repeat to us the words of John Paul II, except, "If I were not Pope, I would be in Medjugorje!"

Children of Medjugorje, www.childrenofmedjugorje.com

Editor's note: Sr. Emmanuel is a member of the Community of the Beatitudes. She has been living in Medjugorje since 1989. She speaks around the world about Our Lady's messages. She has authored a number of books and recorded many tapes.

(8/91)
Vicka Talks to the Pilgrims

Before any of the visionaries begin their talks to the pilgrims, they pray. Vicka started with the Our Father, Hail Mary, and Glory Be, and "Our Lady, Queen of Peace, pray for us."

With a smile, she gives us the main messages of Our Lady. They are: prayer, conversion, fasting, penance, and peace. The Blessed Mother asks us to pray all 3 parts of the Rosary every day. Wednesdays and Fridays we are to fast on bread and water.

When you pray, pray not only with words, but with your heart. We must open our hearts from day to day so that prayer will become a joy. Before you start to pray, try to put away all thoughts, especially bad thoughts that you have, and start to pray. Start with praying the Our Father. He loves us very much. At that moment, share all your wishes, problems, and let it be His will, not ours. Next, you could begin the Hail Mary. One great Mother in Heaven, She also loves us very much. Then the Glory Be. Next, give glory to your Father and thank Him for what He gives you, good and bad, so that we can take everything that comes from Him. Day to day open your heart and think of every word you are saying in prayer. By doing this, we can see how much They mean to us, and really start to live the messages.

The Blessed Mother is asking us for total conversion. She says when we have a great problem, we think that Jesus and Mary are far away from us. But it is not so. "We are very close to you. Just open your hearts so that with your own hearts you can realize how much We love you."

She's asking us to give up something that is most dear to us. The most She would like us to give up is SIN. She's telling us how Satan is very strong. He wants to destroy everything. This is why the Blessed Mother is asking us to increase our prayers so that with our prayers we can keep Satan away from us. She says the best weapon is to have your rosary in your hand. She tells us, "I'm giving you My life, My peace, so that you can take it to your families, friends, and neighbors. That is why I'm giving you My blessing and I pray for all of you."

We should start praying in the family. Parents should start praying with their children. It is not good to do nothing with your family.

Put Mass in the first place. This is the most glorious time in your prayers. In Holy Mass, Jesus is coming alive and He is coming to our hearts. You should be prepared for that moment.

We should go to Confession at least once a month. Don't go to Confession just to get rid of your sins. You must change your life and become a new person. Ask the priest for some ideas (help) for your life (spiritual direction).

Lately, Our Lady is asking us to pray for the youngsters in the world. They are in very difficult situations. We can help them with our love, our prayer with the heart.

The Blessed Mother says, "This time is the time of glory and graces. I want you to know My messages and start to live them with your heart. I want you to be a carrier of My peace, and pray for peace on earth."

Vicka ends with: "I always recommend all of you when I have my apparitions."

Marija

(2/92)
The Marija Story
By Christine Kelly Baglow

How would you react if you were suddenly told that Jesus was about to pay you a visit? How would you feel? Would you prepare for His arrival in some special way? Would you put on your best dress or suit? The following story was relayed to me by a villager in Medjugorje. It is about the visionary Marija Pavlovic and the very question above.

As most of you know, Marija had surgery in 1988 in which she gave one of her kidneys to her brother. The surgery was a success, but as with anyone, it took some time before Marija was fully recovered. While Marija was convalescing, Our Lady suddenly appeared to her in her bedroom. Our Lady told Marija to quickly get up and put on her best dress because Jesus was coming to visit her. Just imagine the excitement that filled Marija's heart! Such expectation!

Like the good Mother that She is, Our Lady helped Marija to prepare for Jesus' arrival. When Marija was dressed and ready, Our Lady went back to Heaven. I can only imagine how Marija's heart must have been pounding as She waited to see the face of her Lord and Savior.

There was a knock on the door and Marija opened it. Standing in the opened doorway was Fr. Slavko Barbaric. In his hands he held the Eucharist. Jesus had truly come to visit Marija in the Blessed Sacrament. He had come to visit her just as He visits each one of us whenever we partake of His Eucharistic banquet.

Through this simple act of love by Our Lord and His Mother, the True Presence of Christ in the Eucharist was reconfirmed in Marija's heart and mind. I have shared this story in talks I've given and love to listen to the gasps and sighs as people recognize its meaning. Very often I notice teary-eyes and sniffles as people take this story to heart. Even the smallest children's eyes light up when they hear it.

We can prepare for Jesus' visits by cleansing our souls frequently in the confessional. Let's adorn our hearts with the graces of purity and love. Please feel free to share Marija's story about the Eucharist with others. I am sure you will think of it the next time you go to meet Jesus in the Blessed Sacrament.

Praised be to Jesus and Mary forever and ever!!!

The Mir Response

(4/88)
Vicka Describes Heaven, Purgatory and Hell

Our Lady once took Vicka (and Jakov) by the hand and took them to Heaven and Purgatory, and gave them a vision of hell. Vicka's description:

"Heaven is one big space, without limits. There is one big light in the middle. Our Lady says, '...see how happy, how full with joy are all the people who are in Heaven.'

"And Purgatory...you can't see, but can feel and hear the people trying to get out of Purgatory. It's very dark, a gray color. We must pray for these people. We must help them with our prayers; they cannot pray for themselves. We should be responsible, we should pray for the souls in Purgatory to help them get out and go to Heaven.

"In hell, there is one big space without limit. And in the middle is a big open fire. The people go into the fire and come out from the fire. They are not human any more, mostly like animals, as beasts. And Our Lady once said that today people are asking to get into hell. It's up to them. It's their fault. She said that it (their choice) does not belong to God. He loves all His people, but they decide to go there."

Question: *Vicka, were you afraid when you saw hell?*
Vicka: When Our Lady told us She would take us to Purgatory and hell, we were not at ease; we were very scared. But once Our Lady took us by the hand, we were not scared. She was with us all the time.

Question: *Did you feel the fire?*
Vicka: No, I saw it. Our Lady took us just to see hell; we weren't in hell. Once She showed us what Heaven was like, She wanted to show the difference – Heaven, Purgatory, hell.

The "Blue Letter," The Riehle Foundation

(4/88)
Interview with Marija about Heaven, Purgatory and Hell

Question: *Were you taken to Heaven?*

Marija: I had a vision of Heaven. It was like watching a movie or looking out the window. I have never seen such a picture before; no one can even begin to imagine how it looks.

Q: *You said earlier that you saw flowers. What else?*

M: A multitude of people; they were around the flowers. The people in Heaven were full of joy, and all of them were giving thanks for the gifts given to them of God. They realize how much love God has for them.

Q: *What can you tell us about Purgatory?*

M: It was very misty; I heard a lot of voices begging for our prayers…they are looking for our prayers to help them enter Heaven someday. The people in Purgatory know God exists, and they are looking for our prayers to help them enter Heaven and be with God. Our Lady told us to tell all people to pray very often for them to be released from Purgatory into Heaven.

Q: *Has Our Lady ever revealed to you if a soul already in Purgatory can be lost and go to hell?*

M: No, once you are in Purgatory, you can only go to Heaven.

Q: *When you saw hell, you said you saw a girl standing next to the flames.*

M: She was in the flames; she came out, and she had something of an animal (look) on her face, something wild.

Q: *Was she the only person you saw?*

M: No, there were a lot of people, but we noticed her because she was caught by the fire.

Q: *Was the girl feeling deep pain?*

M: The people in hell were all running away from the flame. They had a lot of pain.

The "Blue Letter," The Riehle Foundation

Vicka praying with pilgrims

(7/92)
Medjugorje Relief Flight
An Interview with Vicka

On Tuesday, March 17, 1992, our group met with the visionary, Vicka. After she prayed with us, she began in detail reminding us of the main messages of Our Lady, along with prayer of the Rosary and of fasting.

We were told that every day we should open up our hearts so that prayer can be our joy. The Blessed Mother calls us to complete conversion and says, "Dear Children,...All of you, when you have problems and difficulties, think that Jesus and I are away and very far from you. We are very close to you, but you have to open up your hearts because that is the only way – by your hearts, you will know how much We love you!"

Our Lady also asks us to give up something that is dear to us personally. She would be very pleased if we stopped committing sins. And She said, "I give you My peace and My love so that you can bring that love and peace to your family and friends." That's why She is giving us Her blessing and She is also praying for all of us. In a very special way, Our Lady would be pleased if we renewed the prayer of the Rosary in our families. In that way, the parents would pray with the children, and the children would pray with the parents. In this way, Satan cannot harm us. Our Lady does intercede for us. That's the reason She asks us for our prayers. It is by our prayers that we can put Satan away. He cannot harm us that way.

The best way to do that is HAVING THE ROSARY IN YOUR HAND. That is the STRONGEST WEAPON against Satan. That's the reason Our Lady always recommends to us to have something blessed with us...for instance, some medals...because that's the best way of being protected from Satan.

The Blessed Mother also recommends Holy Mass, putting it in the first place, because that is the most important and holiest moment in our life. It is in that moment that Jesus is coming alive and we are seeking Him in our hearts. That's the reason Our Lady asks us to prepare in a special way to receive Jesus with love and dignity in our hearts.

She also recommends monthly confession to each of us. Just how should you feel about confession? Don't be going to confession to confess your sins to the priest and come out and continue the same life. We should change and become a new person, and if it's necessary, ask your priest for advice. He should show you how to go ahead.

Our Lady is worried about the youth. They are in a very hard position. We can help the youth only with our prayers, prayers from the heart. Our Lady is reminding the youth that what today's world offers you is just temporary. You can see from that, that Satan is taking advantage of every moment. Satan especially would like to destroy our families. That's the way he is going to use people. Our Lady says, "Dear Children,...This is the time, the time of your great grace." She would like us to review Her messages and start to live the messages with our hearts. Our Lady wants us to be people and carriers of Her peace; also that we have to pray for the peace in the world. But first we must pray for peace in our heart, in our family, and together with that peace, with our inner peace, we can pray for peace in the world. Because Our Lady says, if you pray without that peace in your heart, then the prayers of the whole world is useless. Last year was the Year of the Youth. That's the reason why Our Lady asked to continue the Year of the Youth again also together with the families...thus making it the Year of the Youth and the Family.

She also is asking us to strengthen our prayers because She really needs our prayers. When we give up something that is dear to us, we should do it for the love of Jesus and Mary.

We should read the Bible every day. Read a few lines from the Bible and try to live those few lines daily.

Also, in the last few messages, Our Lady emphasizes how She prays for the peace in the world. She would like us to pray with Her and help Her with our prayers.

At the end of Vicka's speech, Vicka said that she would recommend all of us and our families along with our intentions to the Blessed Mother at the time of her daily apparition. Vicka then said she would pray for us.

Questions and answers followed:

Q: *Vicka, are we winning or losing with all our prayers we say today?*

A: We have to sense that by ourselves. The best answer is when you pray with the heart and when you become aware of those prayers. Then all the time you can only win, you cannot lose.

Q: *Vicka was asked about her travels.*

A: She was supposed to go to South America last month, but because of the whole situation of the country, she said that she is expected to stay in Medjugorje at this time. Later, she will see if Our Lady will let her leave.

Q: *(Confusion in the United States about the "Poem of the Man God") ...Vicka, is it true that at one time Our Lady said that was a good book to read?*

A: That's always a question which American groups ask. Our Lady told Marija that it is OK to read that book. There's nothing against reading those books.

After a few more questions and answers, we gave our petitions that we brought from home to Vicka. She then prayed aloud with us. Afterwards, we took a couple of group pictures with her. She ended our visit by praying individually over each and every one of us.

Thank you, Vicka!

Note: Vicka spent a week or so in Switzerland just before the outbreak of war in Bosnia-Herzegovina. She was in the village, at home, during the battle.

(2/94)
Christmas Apparition
By Sr. Emmanuel

Just after the apparition on Christmas Day, Marija came to us; she radiated a marvelous sweetness.

"This evening," she told us, "Gospa came with the little Jesus, and She was particularly happy." Then Marija noticed our wax Infant Jesus in His crib and exclaimed, "The Infant Jesus is better dressed than yours! He is completely clothed in a golden garment. It is in this way that Gospa envelops Him in Her own veil. His eyes? They seemed dark, but one could hardly see them. He was very serene, nestled against His Mother. I don't know how to tell you this, but…when one sees the little Jesus, one encounters God!

"On one of our first Christmases with Gospa, the Infant Jesus wanted to play with us. He caught the veil of His Mother and hid behind it, then reappeared shyly before hiding Himself again, as children do. He wanted to establish an intimacy with us. He made us laugh!"

Infant Jesus, in front of you… who could still be afraid of God?

Children of Medjugorje, www.childrenofmedjugorje.com

Ivan
Photo credit: Judy Olivas

(4/96)
Ivan Speaks

It was a brisk cold day in Medjugorje, April 1995, when this talk took place.

"Since it's so cold we're going to warm you up with Our Lady's messages."

Our Lady's messages give you goodness and warmth. You feel good about them, and that gives you more power for living. The problem is we ourselves get lukewarm fast. As you yourself know, the apparitions began in 1981. That's almost 14 years now. This is a long time Our Lady is appearing. In these years, Our Lady has been coming every day. She comes at 20 minutes to 7. Even if She comes for a few minutes or more, it adds up. So much time She has spent with us (visionaries) and She is still coming.

Ivan writes on paper all the meetings, and time he spends with Our Lady. Sometimes the questions come to his mind, "Maybe I should summarize all the minutes and hours I spend with Our Lady. But I never did that as of yet."

It's much more than counting minutes, time, hours or days that we visionaries spend with Our Lady. It's the motherly words that She wants to project to us -the words, the motherly words that She gave us to convey to all of you. It's always hard to convey the true feeling what we (visionaries) feel when we are with Her. This is most difficult because it's such a beautiful warm feeling, not only to see Her, but to hear Her words, the way She expresses Her care for all of Her children.

You know, when Our Lady in the beginning came, She said, "I am the Queen of Peace." This describes Her desire, the Queen of Peace. Her desire and the desire of Her Son who sent Her is to help all Her children realize this Peace. We know from experience, that there are children who will accept Her advice and advance to this Peace. But there are others that don't have their ears and eyes open. It's good to see the children that follow Our Lady's message and advice. Those children will create a basis which is Peace.

What's most important is not only to have Peace within yourself, but Peace between yourself and God. This is a precious gift to have harmony with yourself and God. You know yourself what kind of problems are in the world. The crisis humanity is going through today is the result of so much negativism, especially the people who are misled in their own area. They put in front of themselves something else, not God. They are called idols, idols of different forms. So Our Lady comes and asks us, and gives us a question to open our eyes. "Children, where is God in your life?" What place does God have in your life? Is it something material that you see as most important? Is that foremost in your life?

In the beginning, Our Lady stressed reading the Bible. The Holy Scriptures should be in a visible place in the family in our homes. With this, She tries to emphasize the importance of the Word, the Scriptures. What is written in the Bible is a summary of all the messages; God's message, God wants us to live that message.

Ivan hopes that all families have a Bible in a visible place in their homes. If it is not in a visible place, maybe in a corner full of dust, we need to return it to have it placed in a visible place of the home. Many don't even know what the Bible says when they read it. Together with your family, you should read a few lines in the Bible, and then implement these words into the life of the family to see what they mean for you now, because the Scriptures are written for each one of us.

There are many times people come here and ask the visionaries of what is coming. Is there some kind of darkness coming? Ivan says he doesn't know where this comes from. Who produces these stories of darkness coming? Our Lady comes as a Mother of Light. She comes to help the children, not to bring fear. What is important is to be able to put that fear aside. In order to do this, we must first remove all the negativism from our hearts, especially sin. It's the sin that is blocking our view and our deception. Once we get rid of the sin, then God can be part of us. He can dwell within us. All the unrest in the world is produced from the human heart which is full of darkness and sin. That is why we can't open to this gift of Peace. So if we think that Peace can be created without us, it is an illusion, because, we are part of the creation of Peace.

When Our Lady talks about the crises that are present in the world, it is not to make us fearful or to do anything else but simply to make us aware of what is happening so that we can change it. Some people say, "Oh, I'm all right. I don't have to go through conversion any more. I'm fine the way I am." Every person needs to walk the way of conversion. Nobody's perfect. That goes for the visionaries too, including Ivan himself. It's a process. Conversion is an all life process. There will be falls, but you need to stand up and walk again. If we were always happy, without falls, without problems, it would be already Heaven on earth. To fall and be able to get up again, you need to pray for strength. Our Lady is giving us the instructions in what to do. With prayer, we are fulfilling all the dark holes and vacuums that are created by the evil power. It traps us to fall into the hole, so to say, but with prayers everything will straighten the path to the Lord.

In the messages, Our Lady tells us to pray, pray. Each time She tells us to pray, it's a new invitation, not repetitious. We learn so much from our Mother.

Our Heavenly Mother is like your mother. She would pat you on the head and say, "Do not fall asleep." Our mother is waking up the children very gently. You all have children -maybe not your own, but someone else's or your relatives'. You know when the child is waking up. We need to persevere. We need to decide.

You know when Moses received the 10 Commandments, he gave them to the people, telling them how to live. The people were not patient, and they built a golden calf. They were having that as their god. They were paying homage to it. The world is constantly offering this golden calf, so to say, in different forms.

We need to pray every day of our life. We must live by prayer. It's a spiritual proof we cannot be without. Prayer is always a meeting and an encounter with Our Lady and our living God. To God and to Our Lady, every prayer is very dear. It's very important that prayer is not said mechanically. It needs to come from the whole being. We should concentrate and pray from our heart because there is so much distraction in the world. It is normal. It happens because the world is such. We must continue to learn to pray with the heart as conversion. It's so important to decide for prayer first. We must decide and persevere in our decision, so we can slowly advance to the prayer Our Lady wants of us, the prayer of the heart. Every prayer is an advancement. We come closer to God in our being. It's 14 years She's with us. She is leading us through this school of prayer. You are all a part of this school. You are enlisted in this school of prayer. Our Lady is teaching you. If you live by Her messages, you'll always want to hear what She says. Sometimes, She points to our mistakes. Our Lady never reprimands. She always teaches us. This is such a great value. It's a great virtue of a mother. Ivan says he doesn't have the words to describe how much care Our Lady has for each of us. Ivan says he himself is not perfect yet. Every day he tries to be better and better. He is conscious of the fact of how much responsibility he has because he wants to share what he can with you. He cannot keep anything to himself. Our Lady would not be happy. Whatever he does during the day, he's always conscious in his mind whether Our Lady will be happy with that for now. He knows he has a meeting with Our Lady at twenty to seven. From one day to another, he lives with that. So whatever he says, whatever he does during this 24 hours, he wonders if it will be pleasing to Our Lady, and what She is going to say about it. It became a part of him. It's not as if he's afraid. If he did something that was not really right and he realized it, then at the time of the apparition, he would think, "What is She going to say?"

Translated by Helen Sarcevic

Editor's note: As we can see, all the visionaries are as human as we are. They have a life to lead, and they too must follow the messages of Our Lady. They follow the same messages that you and I are called to follow. These messages are messages of HOPE, not of fear.

Sr. Emmanuel holding photo of the Pope and Fr. Jozo

(2/94)
Protect Medjugorje
By Sr. Emmanuel

Although she is 8 months pregnant, Marija gives us the surprise of coming for the Anniversary. She shared with the pilgrims her concern for Medjugorje prayer groups:

"We (the visionaries) have shared in depth with Fr. Jozo all the graces, struggles, and sufferings of these 13 years. And we found that we agreed on a very important point: it is very urgent to protect Medjugorje in the world, and not to allow its message to be mixed with other revelations or messages. In the groups that have mixed messages of Medjugorje with other messages, the spirit of Medjugorje has been diluted and many Medjugorje prayer groups have been divided and even destroyed! Many false prophets are circulating and distancing people from the specific grace of Medjugorje and its fundamental message. There is danger of becoming like butterflies seeking the extraordinary instead of converting." Marija has seen this in Italy, in America, etc.

The Holy Father recommended to Fr. Jozo: "Protect Medjugorje," and Our Lady Herself tells us today: "I call you ALL to decide to live my messages which I give you HERE…"

Children of Medjugorje, www.childrenofmedjugorje.com

Chapter 3:

Testimonies

(7/91)
Miracles
By Joan Wieszczyk

Miracles do happen and Medjugorje is proof of that. Each year, "The Spirit of Medjugorje" sponsors a pilgrimage to that holy place. Most pilgrims who travel along with us experienced some sort of inner feeling, even if it only occurred while in Medjugorje (a small miracle in itself). Many come back home with a clear conscience after having made a good confession. Many priests are available for each penitent on a one-to-one basis. For some, it felt like Christ was calling them back to the sacraments of Penance and Holy Communion, truly an inner feeling of "PEACE."

A young pilgrim lends a helping hand up Podbrdo

The walk up Mt. Podbrdo and Mt. Krizevac is tiresome and time consuming. For some, a miracle. Making it the path of holiness both going up and coming down is very rewarding. Many tears are shed on both of these mountains. Tears of joy, simply because one made it up to the top of the hill. Also, tears of repentance, for the sins one has committed against God. Once again, the pilgrim feels a cleansing of the soul.

Mass is the highlight of the pilgrimage. The evening Croatian Mass is filled with PEACE, LOVE and JOY, for it is preceded with the recitation of the Rosary and the visit (apparition) of our Heavenly Mother, the Queen of Peace, the Miracle of Medjugorje.

A joy, a bit of a treat to any of the pilgrims, is a visit with one or two of the visionaries.

Just praying along with them leaves a huge impact of love with the group.

Some say just being in Medjugorje is a miracle. Many never dreamed it could happen to them, either financially or physically.

Miracles such as the dancing sun, the scent of roses, Rosaries turning to gold, or the spinning cross are very common in Medjugorje.

Besides many spiritual healings, there are the physical miracles, many which have been recorded.

In October, 1990, our group made a pilgrimage to Medjugorje. One gentleman traveling with us was ill with prostate cancer. When he came back home, he went to the doctor for a check-up. He was told that his tumor was gone and his blood was back to normal again!

Another miracle we witnessed was on Mt. Krizevac. It was there that we got to photograph Mrs. Heather Duncan. She came to Medjugorje with a Scottish group. Accompanying them was a priest of Irish origin, Fr. Peter Rookey. It was during Fr. Rookey's healing service that she was healed.

Heather Duncan had been in a very bad automobile accident which left her paralyzed. She came to Medjugorje in a wheelchair. She had been in that wheelchair for 5 years, bound to it by belts around the upper part of her body. Her X-rays and medical diagnosis showed that she would never walk again. If she would ever walk, every movement would cause her immense pain. It was during Fr. Rookey's healing service..."In the name of Jesus, get up and walk." She got out of her wheelchair and walked. I took a picture of her on top of Mt. Podbrdo with a walking stick and a huge, joyous smile on her face. In fact, while on top of the mountain, she was able to help another pilgrim who was struggling with an illness come to the spot where Our Lady appeared. They both rejoiced on that mountain by crying tears of joy and praying the Rosary together for the miracle God granted them.

In March, 1991, Mrs. Heather Duncan once again came to Medjugorje. This time she came with a Scottish television crew who was filming a documentary. The real reason for her visit was to give thanks to the Lord for her healing. In fact, she brought along proof, a medical certificate claiming there was no reason to doubt she had been healed, enabling her to walk.

This one is for the record. Yes, many miracles happen in Medjugorje, and along with Heather Duncan, we thank and praise God for allowing us to be part of them.

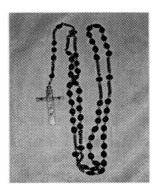

The mysterious Rosary

(10/93)
The Mysterious Rosary Beads

The Rosary played an inquisitive role in Vicka's life shortly BEFORE the apparitions began. During the early days of April, 1981, Vicka and her brother and sister were off on a chore picking branches for firewood. It was customary to use their tractor for this purpose. It was in this tractor trailer that some Rosary beads were found.

It was a different type of Rosary, one which they had never seen before. It had a large cross in place of the crucifix. On it were carved the 14 Stations.

Vicka's mother inquired in the village about the Rosary. No one had lost or claimed this Rosary.

Vicka was curious and asked Our Lady of Medjugorje about it. Mary told her that it was from God. It was a gift left by Our Lady.

(12/94)
The Fruits of Medjugorje
By Robert Panke

I recently spent some time visiting my Alma Mater, Catholic University, and as I saw the many new students arriving for their orientation to the University, full of expectations and hopes, I had some time to meditate and reflect as to how much my life has changed since I graduated in 1988. Without a shadow of a doubt, the most significant change in my life came following my first trip to Medjugorje.

One year following graduation from college, my parents approached me with the prospect of taking a trip (or "pilgrimage" as they called it) to a place where Our Lady was supposed to be appearing in a little town somewhere in Europe. At the time, my faith was wandering somewhere between apathy and confusion. I wasn't quite sure why the Church taught all that she did and I wasn't sure I cared. To be honest, the "pilgrimage" (whatever that was) was not the deciding factor for me to go to Medjugorje. The week we were to spend in Switzerland following Medjugorje was the real reason I went. As time passes, the mountains of Switzerland slowly fade from my memory, but I will never, ever forget that week in Medjugorje, which would subsequently change my life forever.

All of you who have experienced first hand the great love and beauty found in Medjugorje know that no words can adequately describe the tremendous graces given there. In retrospect, I can see that Mary had been trying and trying to introduce me to Her Son, and it was only in Medjugorje that I finally accepted the invitation. The Lord has since sent me on a journey I could never have anticipated.

Upon my return to the States, I found myself refusing jobs based on whether or not I could make daily Mass. I moved to Washington, D.C. in order to work in a more service-oriented field. Eventually, in 1991, just two short years after Medjugorje, I entered the seminary for the Archdiocese of Washington and was sent to do my studies in Rome. By the grace of God, I was ordained a deacon in Rome on the feast of Our Lady of the Rosary (10/7/94).

The three years I have spent in Rome have been fantastic. I have met with the Holy Father, and discovered the richness of that Holy City. I have also been able to see other areas of Europe, including Marian places of pilgrimage, such as Lourdes. However, the greatest gifts I have received since entering the seminary are the people I have met and the opportunity to develop a closer relationship with Our Lord.

St. Paul tells us that it is no longer his own life he leads, but the life of Christ within him. When we allow the Lord to enter into our own lives, when we truly die to ourselves and say "yes" to Jesus Christ, then our lives become filled with an unimaginable joy. We must continue to say "yes" to Jesus in the Eucharist in going to confession, in prayer, in fasting and in good works. With that "yes" to Jesus comes our peace.

Just a while ago the Church celebrated the feasts of two of my favorite saints: Augustine and Monica. We all know how diligently Monica prayed for the conversion of her son. Similarly, all of us here have a Mother in Heaven who intercedes for us and is desperately trying to lead us to Heaven. Many of us have felt a conversion like St. Augustine experienced. The reason why St. Augustine became a saint is that he took his conversion, and from that moment of grace, yielded much fruit. Our Lady brought us to Medjugorje, not only for our own spiritual peace and happiness, but also to ask us to help spread the message of the Gospel. We must all continue to pray for each other and the world. May God continue to fill all of you with many graces and love.

Editor's update: Fr. Panke is currently the Vocations Director for the Archdiocese of Washington.

(10/94)
A Present for Florence
By Sister Emmanuel

An avalanche of grace fell on the large crowd of pilgrims in Medjugorje on August 15th. One example: Little Florence Majurel from France, 16 years old, has Down Syndrome, and can hardly speak. She went to the Blue Cross at the foot of Podbrdo on the evening of August 15th with her mother for the apparition with Ivan's prayer group. At the very moment when Ivan went into ecstasy, the little girl began smiling at someone invisible near the cross, and said, "What is that, mother?" (She doesn't know how to say, "Who is that?") The mother sensed that something was happening and kept watching her. Florence nodded her head several times as if she was trying to imitate something that was being taught by someone in front of her, then she joined her hands together and gently interlocked her fingers, something which was impossible for her to do before. She was still smiling when she blew three kisses with the hand (as children do), just before the apparition finished. Then her mother asked her, "What did you see?" "Blessed Mother," Florence replied. "And how was She?" "Beautiful!"

The next day for the first time in her life, Florence spontaneously began to say, "Hail Mary, full of grace," (no more than this), when never before had she been able to pronounce any words in prayer. Now she prays most of the Hail Mary. A final test had to be done. As Florence does not know how to name the different colors, her mother put 6 sheets of different colored paper in front of her, asking her to point out which color looked like Our Lady's dress. Immediately Florence put her finger on the gold colored paper. To test her further, her mother pointed to the yellow sheet and said, "I rather think it's like that." But Florence replied angrily, "No, this one," once again pointing to the gold sheet. Then the mother was amazed; for on August 15th as at Easter or at Christmas, the Gospa always appears clothed in gold...

What a beautiful present for Florence and for all those whom the world so often holds in contempt – and a beautiful example of the inexpressible tenderness of God for the little ones, the most

107

vulnerable! A beautiful answer from Heaven to modern medicine, which so quickly programs their little unborn life towards abortion because they are handicapped – though they are so often making reparation for the sins of the very ones who exclude them!

Dear Gospa, everything you do is beautiful. Thank you, thank you!

Children of Medjugorje, www.childrenofmedjugorje.com

(6/97)
The Pope, Medjugorje and the Provincial of the Herzegovina Franciscans

The visit of Pope John Paul II to Bosnia-Herzegovina April 12-13, 1997, was a visit which many had hoped would end with a visit of the Pope to Medjugorje, since in several references he had expressed such a desire. Unfortunately, that did not happen. Nevertheless, the Pope did not forget Medjugorje.

At the Sarajevo airport April 12, the very first to await the Pope's arrival were the bishops and provincials of Bosnia-Herzegovina. When the provincial of the Sarajevo Province, Fr. Peter Andjelovic, as the first of the provincials approached the Pope to greet him, the Pope asked him the question, "Medjugorje?" He pointed to Dr. Fr. Tomislav Pervan, the provincial of Herzegovina, who said, "I am from Mostar and Medjugorje." The Pope nodded his head with satisfaction, and twice repeated, "Medjugorje, Medjugorje." All TV viewers who watched the presentation of the Pope's arrival also saw it.

While the Pope prayed with those gathered in the Sarajevo Cathedral, he prayed twice referring to the Queen of Peace for Bosnia-Herzegovina. Many of those present interpreted it as having recourse to the Queen of Peace from Medjugorje.

After supper, in the Sarajevo Catholic School of Theology, Fr. Tomislav took advantage of the occasion to personally present the Pope with the newest photo-monograph on Medjugorje, which the Franciscans who work in the parish of Medjugorje had sent to him. On that occasion, he spoke to him briefly about Medjugorje. The

Pope did not say anything, but by the expression on his face, he accepted both the former and the latter with satisfaction and interest. On the occasion of the Pope's departure from the Sarajevo airport, Fr. Tomislav Pervan by way of greeting said, "Holy Father, we are expecting you in Medjugorje." The Pope answered with a smile, "Medjugorje, Medjugorje" as was visible also on TV screens.

Information Centre "Mir" Medjugorje, <u>www.medjugorje.hr</u>.

(11/95)
A Miracle for Alice from Medjugorje
By Virginia Spaeder

It was October 13, and my husband and I were scheduled to ascend Mount Krizevac. We were up early so that we could be to the bottom of the hill by 7:30 AM. Our guide said that the climb would be less crowded if we went up early.

After picking out a nice walking stick from the assortment that was lying there, I was ready. It began to sprinkle lightly, so I donned my rain bonnet. As soon as all of our group had assembled, we began our ascent. The guide warned us that if any of us had back problems, a bad heart, breathing problems, or anything that would render us incapacitated, when the heart gets taxed to its limit, not to attempt this climb. This "Hill of the Cross" is one mile of steep climbing, very rocky, and it could be dangerous since a light rain had begun to fall, making the rocks very slippery. She did not want any "heroes" since the helpless victims would have to be carried down. One lady decided to bow out. It was probably a very wise decision.

We were now ready and eager to get to the top. We began our journey with Station I – Jesus is condemned to death. We meditated at each Station as we went. Whoever decided to put Stations of the Cross along the pathway was a very wise person. It was the only thing that provided an occasion to rest a bit and catch your breath. The climb at first did not seem to be too treacherous...until the Eighth Station. From this point to the top was very steep. I began to breathe heavier. At about 11:00 AM, we finally reached the top. We took group pictures and then began to pray the Sorrowful Mysteries of the Rosary. The guide said that we could lead a decade if we wanted to. I thought about this and decided that I would do the Third Mystery- the Crowning of Thorns – for my friend Alice.

Alice is a dear friend of mine who had gotten up one morning and fell. She discovered that her left side was not functioning properly. She could not navigate without some help from her husband. She was hospitalized twice with no improvement. Her husband decided to check her into a convalescent home for physical therapy. Alice spent a month there, but was unable to achieve any improvement in her motor skills because of the extreme pain she was in. Her body began to deteriorate – her left side was virtually paralyzed while the right side was almost completely non-functional. She had been reduced to living in a wheelchair, couldn't feed herself – just wasting away. The doctors ordered an MRI – a sophisticated X-ray scan. They discovered that Alice had two vertebrae in the neck area that were pressing on her spinal cord.

Surgery was scheduled, but first Alice had to be put in traction. They put a metal "halo" around her head which was secured by 4 metal screws – which were drilled into the skull- two in her forehead and two in the area behind her ears. From this contraption hung 20 pounds of weight. She could not turn her head or move in any direction without help from the nurses. To look at her, you would think "bride of Frankenstein." It was truly her "crown of thorns." I watched her suffer like this from last August through October and into November. She had to wear this "fashion statement" from the medical profession for three months.

Pilgrims praying the Rosary on Mt. Krizevac

Meanwhile, back on Mt. Krizevac, the third decade of the Rosary was fast approaching. When this decade was announced, I jumped in with the "Our Father." With each "Hail Mary" I thought about Alice and how much she had suffered with her surgery. By the third "Hail Mary," my emotions took over, my voice was cracking and coming out between sobs…the tears were streaming down my cheeks. I didn't think that I could go on. But I was determined to finish my decade for Alice. At this point, a lady standing next to me reached out, put her arm around my shoulder and reassuringly whispered, "You can do it…you can do it." She whispered these words of encouragement throughout the rest of the decade. When I turned to look at her when I had finished the tenth "Hail Mary," my eyes went to her name tag. Her name was "Alice." (Thank you, my dear Blessed Mother, for sending this woman to me when I needed her, I thought.)

When I returned home from Medjugorje, I found out that my friend Alice had had a tremendous improvement in her physical condition and would be able to go home sooner than expected. When I asked her husband when all this had happened, he told me that "it was about a week ago"…the same time that I had been praying on Mount Krizevac for her. When I visited Alice and related to her what happened to me on Mt. Krizevac, she told me that "her decade" (which was assigned to her by our Rosary Society) was the "Crowning of Thorns."

Today my friend is the Alice we all remembered. It is truly a miracle. Thank you again, my dear Blessed Mother.

Fr. James Peterson, affectionately known as "Fr. Pete"

(10/89)
Medjugorje Pilgrimage
By Father James Peterson

When I went on pilgrimage to Medjugorje in August of 1989, I had no special desire to be in or near the choir loft at the time of Mary's coming, or even on Apparition Hill at the time of a prayer meeting where She would speak to the seers.

Years before I had gone to the Holy Land with no special excitement, that when I was in Nazareth I could be thrilled to say, "Jesus was here," or that at the Sea of Galilee, "Jesus walked on this water."

I have such joy in the Holy Eucharist that I know "Jesus is here" in a presence that is palpable and a closeness that is intimate. I believe profoundly in the Communion of Saints. Mary is aware of me. That presence is there, whether I'm walking in a field or going to sleep at night.

For that reason, I like the emphasis I hear from those who are carrying the message of Medjugorje that "You don't have to go to Medjugorje to get the message or to benefit from its power." We don't need miracles, though they help. We don't need to travel to shrines, though a pilgrimage can be the occasion of a great awakening.

But we do need to change.

I felt drawn to Medjugorje to experience the effect of Our Lady's coming – as it was taken seriously by thousands of people. In America I find many people who call themselves Christians, who do not take God seriously. Many don't think the Incarnation has changed anything, except perhaps to make life harder. I know many who at Mass share a prayer in regard to "The saints on whose constant intercession we rely for help" who don't expect any help from the prayer of the saints, and who don't take Mary seriously.

The great joy of my visit was that Ivan and Vicka and the others – the whole parish- take Mary seriously. They are not fanatic or self-righteous or scrupulous. They are simple, honest and joyful.

The stress of conversion is not simply a series of sermons. It is obvious in the message as it is repeated by the seers, in the family life and the community life of the people of St. James Parish there.

The stress on fasting and on sacramental life is constant without being badgering.

And at the head of it all is the presence of Our Lady to Her people and of Her people to Our Lady.

I left the Holy Land years ago aware that every shrine had its own grace to bring me with new depth into the mysteries of Christ's life. I was renewed. My ministry and my preaching – which constantly merge- were renewed.

I left Medjugorje with the same awareness of renewal. The "prayer of the heart" strengthens me day by day. I know more fully Our Lady's presence as I go to a prayer meeting, or take up the Divine Office, or offer a Rosary.

Taking Mary's presence seriously is not a determined earnestness that is sad. It's cause for great joy and holy hope, and it's rejuvenating.

If you ever have a chance to be with Ivan or Vicka, you'll understand what I mean.

(4/96)
Croatian Customs
By Joan Wieszczyk

Last year I spent Palm Sunday in Medjugorje. It was one of many pilgrimages that I traveled to that holy place where Mary, our Heavenly Mother, is appearing daily. While there, I was able to stay in the home of the visionary Ivanka.

Ivanka is a seer that has been given the 10 secrets. She no longer gets daily visitations of Our Lady. She is able to see Mary only once a year- on the anniversary date, June 25th. She told us that this is a gift given to her by our Heavenly Mother. She was told that Mary will continue to appear to her every year while she is alive!

It was a pleasure being with Ivanka and her family. While we were at her house, our small group took part in two of the Croatian traditions or customs. They were both new to all of us.

The first custom took place late Saturday evening, the night before Palm Sunday. Ivanka had set a large blue bowl on the table. In it was an assortment of beautiful flower petals. These flowers were cut fresh that day from plants unfamiliar to me. Their custom is to cut whatever flower is in bloom at the time, remove the petals, and place them in a large bowl. During the night or early morning (before any of us were up), Ivanka came and poured plain water with a few drops of holy water in the bowl. The flower petals began floating to the top. We were told that the first thing in the morning on Palm Sunday we were to dip our hands into this mixture of water and petals and splash our faces with it. This is one of the Croatian customs symbolizing the washing of yourself clean. Palm Sunday in Croatia is not called Palm Sunday, but Flower Sunday.

We experienced another one of their customs which also took place on Palm Sunday. At home in our American churches, palms are blessed and distributed on that day. Palms to us are a sacramental. We assumed that we would be given palms at Mass while in Medjugorje. We wanted to bring them home as a spiritual souvenir, a holy remembrance. So our group went to Holy Mass

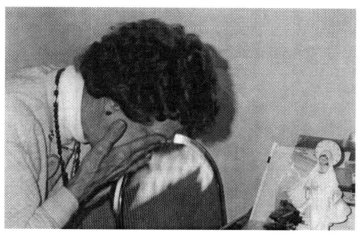

Pilgrim washing her face with "flower petal water" on Palm Sunday

hoping to march in procession. To our surprise, they did not distribute palms. Instead, we were all given a blessed olive branch. We all wondered, "Why an olive branch, not a blessed palm?" When we asked this question, they in turn answered, "Why a palm, not an olive branch?" We were told that it was an early Christian tradition. Olive branches were given because they were a sign of peace.

Croatia has many olive trees. You can see them along the coast. Every Croatian family has grown them. They cultivate them for oil. Years ago, wealth was measured by how many trees you owned.

This year Palm Sunday brings back these memories of our beautifully blessed time spent in Medjugorje last year. We will always treasure them.

And to all our readers, we wish you both an English and Croatian greeting... "Sretan Uskrs" - "Happy Easter."

(11/94)
Protestants in Medjugorje
By Sister Emmanuel

Sometimes it is the Protestants who confirm what is happening here (in Medjugorje)! A Protestant doctor, who is very prayerful and has been close to Jesus for a long time, came to Medjugorje to examine the phenomena of Mary's apparitions, alien to him. Like so many Protestants, he found devotion to Our Lady an obstacle to Jesus, and he arrived, therefore, with some unease. He had scarcely approached the church when Jesus spoke to his heart very clearly, and he began to cry like a child. The next day, he received the same words and told me with tears in his eyes, "I heard the voice of Jesus and He said to me, 'I have asked My Mother to come here. She draws all people here and brings them to Me. All generations shall call Her blessed.'" Since then, Mary has become for him a springboard for Jesus!

Another example – after 3 days in Medjugorje, a Swiss pastor confided to me: "There is nothing in my theology that opposes Mary's apparitions. Moses and Elijah appeared to Jesus on Tabor, so why not His own Mother!"

What Protestants are mostly touched by here is that Mary wept in saying, "You have forgotten the Bible." And they say to themselves, "Oh, if Catholics would only listen to Her!"

Children of Medjugorje, www.childrenofmedjugorje.com

(7/94)
Amber Pollard
By Joan Wieszczyk

It is over 13 years now since Our Lady first appeared in Medjugorje. Many miracles, both physical and spiritual, have occurred during these years. I remember in the early years when a little boy, Daniel, was cured after Mary told the visionary to tell his parents to fast and pray. They were also to believe that he would be cured. They did it all and Daniel was cured!

The message hasn't changed. Believe in God, fast and pray!

It was after my second pilgrimage that I began to spread the messages of Medjugorje wholeheartedly. Like many others, I started to hold presentations in my home, travel to other parish functions showing slides, pictures, videos, and sharing my experiences. In all ways that I could, I spoke about Medjugorje. It was during these days that I became a part of the newsletter, "The Spirit of Medjugorje."

My neighbor across the street became a grandparent for the first time. Such joy filled her heart. I was so happy for her. The joy did not last long…for her only granddaughter Amber was born a very sick child. It took 6 months before she was diagnosed with having cancer of the kidney. Amber was sent to Children's Hospital in Pittsburgh, PA. There she underwent surgery for the removal of the kidney, which at 6 months old had 7 tumors on it. She was then put on chemotherapy for 6 months. This didn't sound too good. They were very worried. The child needed prayers and so did the family.

I remembered the story of Daniel. I told her grandmother to fast and pray. Now I was beginning to spread the messages of Medjugorje to my neighbor. I was going there (Medjugorje) again, and I, too, would ask for a miracle for Amber.

When I returned, I brought back a medal and I gave it to Amber. That medal was hung on the child's bed. I asked her grandmother to promise to tell me if she ever was healed.

The other day while shopping, I saw my neighbor. We've seen each other many times in church. But we never discussed thoroughly about Amber. So I asked about her. She is 7 years old now, a beautiful fun-loving child. Amber is in the first grade doing exceptionally well scholastically. She is in the gifted reading class, is in advanced math, and is learning Spanish. She has taken dancing lessons for the past 4 years.

The cancer that Amber had is in remission for the past 6 years. To quote my neighbor… "Our many prayers to Our Lady of Medjugorje have been answered."

I wonder as I ask, "Just what do you have in store for this innocent child, dear Mother?"

Thank you, Jesus and Mary!

Amber, age 7

Editor's update: Amber is now a senior in high school and has been accepted by Ohio State in their pre-med program. She continues to dance.

(8/95)
Fruits
Spiritual Vocations

On June 18, 1995, Fr. Peter Dugandzic celebrated his first Mass in Medjugorje. Here is what he said on that occasion: "My name is Peter Dugandzic. I am from New York, I was born on Long Island in New York and grew up there. I came to Medjugorje for the first time in 1986. My family background is from the area of Medjugorje. I have a degree in Psychology. At first I worked with computers, and then with people as a psychologist, and now I work as a priest.

"Before coming to Medjugorje, I was not faithful to going to church. I was happy in my work. I earned a lot of money and because of my work, I traveled all through America. One time, my aunt told me they were going to the old country. I wanted to go too. After that, she told me about Medjugorje, that a group of six children were seeing Our Lady. At that time, I reacted like a psychologist: "Well good! Just let them look at Our Lady!" We came to Medjugorje. Something started to happen in my soul that

I didn't understand. I began praying, which I never did before. I also meditated a lot. Little by little, the desire to become a priest began to germinate inside of me. Now finally, I am a priest and I am grateful to God for other people."

Information Centre "Mir" Medjugorje, www.medjugorje.hr.

(5/91)
Prisoners Respond To Our Lady's Call

On August 15, 1990, convicts in a prison in New Jersey consecrated their prison to the Immaculate Heart of Mary. As a result of hearing Her call from Medjugorje, they have dedicated their lives to prayer.

One of the inmates, Jim Jennings, was released during Christmas. While at prison, he wrote about Medjugorje:

"We here at the prison (some of us) are very interested in Medjugorje and try to live the messages of Our Lady. Several of us have made the total Consecration to Jesus through Mary according to St. Louis De Montfort's formula.

"Also, as a result of Medjugorje, we have a daily Rosary group in all three phases of this prison. So, as you can see, God's graces being given to the world through Our Lady at Medjugorje are not passing over this place without bearing fruit. When hardened convicts, having been away from the Church for as many as twenty-five years, return to weekly confession, daily receiving the Eucharist, and daily praying the Rosary in groups as well as alone, it can only further prove the reality of Medjugorje, because only a miracle can cause things like this to happen in places like this. I've spent 18 years of my life in various prisons and I've never seen anything like this happen anywhere, especially with the sincerity these men display. We are not saints, nor especially holy men, but we love Our Lord and Our Lady, and because of this tremendous sign of God's love for mankind in these days, we try to at least try... I've been no saint in my life - nowhere near a saint. I've satiated myself in every vice imaginable, yet I've never ever experienced anything that can even begin to compare with what's going on inside of me for almost three years now (since first hearing Our Lady's call from Medjugorje)!"

On September 4, Archbishop Nicolai Rotunno, a former member of the Vatican's diplomatic corps, was at the facility to help the prisoners establish a halfway house based on "Oasi della Pace," a Medjugorje-inspired religious community with houses in Italy, Austria, and Medjugorje. ("Oasis of Peace" was instigated at the request of Our Lady during an apparition in 1985.) The prisoners desire to continue lives centered on responding to Our Lady's call from Medjugorje after their eventual release. (The community's religious habit was designed by Marija Pavlovic, based on how Our Lady is dressed each day when She comes to Medjugorje.) The Plan of Life of the community, having received enthusiastic support from Cardinal Ratzinger and the Holy Father, has been approved by the Magisterium. It also successfully met the first step in the process of gaining official recognition as a new religious order within the church – the approval of the local bishop.

(11/94)
Our Lady and the AIDS Patient
By Sister Emmanuel

In France, a young man told me his story. After 7 years of studying pharmacology, he was not allowed to take the diploma, as he had AIDS. Moreover, he had suffered other kinds of rejection as a homosexual. It was too hard for him to bear, and he decided to commit suicide and jump from a bridge. In order to summon up the courage, he drank a lot of alcohol. He no longer remembers how he jumped, but found himself bleeding in a hospital in a coma. As he was gradually recovering, he saw the image of a woman in front of him, which at first frightened him. But as the days passed by, the image attracted him more and more, and even gave him comfort. In his religious ignorance, he said to himself, "Perhaps it is a saint." On leaving the hospital, he was still very weak, above all because of AIDS, since his lymphatic system was ravaged. By an inexplicable chance, he made a trip to Medjugorje against the advice of the doctor who predicted, " You will die there."

In Medjugorje, shock! He sees in a window the famous image of "the saint," the one in the hospital. He asks who she is and learns that it is the Virgin of Medjugorje (statue of Tihaljina). "Clic-clac" in his head: "It is She then, who came to rescue me from my despair to bring me here." During his pilgrimage, the Gospa takes such good care of his heart that he decides never to leave his Heavenly Mother. Back home, new shock, with the medical check-up: the virus is still present, but all the symptoms have disappeared, his lymphatic system is healthy, and his life is renewed.

Dear Gospa, as Jesus, you come to save what is lost…welcome in our hearts!

Children of Medjugorje, www.childrenofmedjugorje.com

(10/92)
Mary's Rock and Roll Star
By Joan Wieszczyk

Michael O'Brien is a national recording artist. He is a rock and roll star from the Cleveland, Ohio area.

In 1988, Michael made a pilgrimage to Medjugorje. It was there at Vicka's (one of the visionaries) house, that he received a message. The message was written in Croatian by Vicka. In it was a "special inspiration from Our Lady." He was to be a leader with the youth. He was to use that message and his powerful talents and abilities to help turn the youth of today away from the evil one and bring them back to God. Michael has been doing that. He has performed many "gigs" with his band called MOB (the initials of his name).

Michael has become a "welcome guest" at many of the Marian Conferences. He is most popular with his album "Sounds of Medjugorje"…("Hail Mary, Gentle Woman," "Be Not Afraid," "I Believe," …). All who hear him sing at these conferences agree that his talent can be put to good use – for the honor and glory of God.

Michael has been back to Medjugorje a few times. He has found a girlfriend there. She works as a tour guide. Her name is Vesna Misic.

At the Notre Dame Conference in May of 1991, Michael announced to the audience that he was going to propose marriage to her. This was to take place on his birthday, June 25, 1991, which was also the 10th anniversary of the apparitions of Our Lady.

At the Midwest Marian Eucharist Conference in Cleveland, Ohio, on August 22, 1992, Michael announced that he was going to marry her that same evening. It was at this conference that Michael introduced us to his bride-to-be. With joy in our hearts, everyone there stood up and prayed a blessing upon the happy couple.

The marriage was originally to have taken place in Medjugorje. Since the outbreak of the war, plans had to be changed. A priest who was present at the conference just happened to be in the area a week earlier and was asked to perform the ceremony. The "impossible" became "possible."

On August 22 (the feast of the Queenship of Mary) Vesna Misic and Michael O'Brien exchanged vows and became man and wife. Congratulations to the newly married couple, Mr. And Mrs. Michael O'Brien.

Michael O'Brien and Joan Wieszczyk

(7/88)
The Rose
By Joan Wieszczyk

I have made two visits to Medjugorje- one last October, and again this past June, 1988. On my first trip, while others claimed to have seen the sun spin, the Krizevac Cross rotate on the mountain, or have their Rosaries turn to gold, I had none of these things happen to me. Yet the trip was a spiritual one.

Returning home, everyone was filled with the peace of Medjugorje. Our section of the plane was talkative as we shared our days of pilgrimage with each other. It was about two hours before our arrival home when all of the sudden a scent of roses whiffed through the aisle. At first I didn't believe it – maybe someone had perfume on – perhaps the stewardess. No, it was definitely a scent of roses! What a way to come back home! When I arrived at the airport and cleared customs, I met some friends who were leaving for Medjugorje on the very same plane. As we approached each other and began to speak, someone in the crowd again smelled roses. "Could this really come from us?" we asked. Apparently this was our gift from Mary.

On the second trip in June, 1988, I asked Mary to let me witness a phenomenon. However, during the 6½ days I spent there, the same thing happened as before. People around me saw the sun spin, their Rosaries change to gold, and some saw the Krizevac Cross rotate. Nothing for me. I tried to look at the sun, but it was too bright. Nothing unusual happened the whole week. Every time I prayed, I'd ask Our Lady to let me witness something so I could tell my family and friends back home. Still nothing.

On my very last day, I talked to Mary and told Her: "Okay, Mother, if you're going to let me see a miracle, here's your last chance, because I'm leaving Medjugorje right after the 10:00 AM English Mass." I felt very sad that after my second visit there, I still didn't witness anything special.

At this point, Sister Ljudevida, the sacristan, was on her way up to the choir loft in the back of the church with a fresh mixed bouquet of flowers to leave at the site of Mary's appearances. They were beautiful. Before Sister went up with the flowers, I ran and said good-bye and that I was leaving right after Mass. She gave me a hug and as I turned to leave, she called me back, snipped off a flower and gave it to me. It was from the mixed bouquet. It was a rose- from the Blessed Mother's bouquet!

Thank you, Mary. Once again, I received the gift of a rose.

(6/94)
A Psychotherapist Visits Medjugorje
By Sister Emmanuel

Fr. Slavko has reported a very interesting testimony on the part of a psychotherapist who was originally a Protestant, but became Catholic through the Eucharist, and who affirmed after having come to Medjugorje: "I am now convinced that it is truly the holy Virgin who appears in Medjugorje..." "For what reason?" asks Fr. Slavko. "For three reasons: the first, because She appears in a very punctual way; the second, because She says simple things; and the third, because She appears every day."

"But it is just these three things which present difficulties to the theologians!" replied Fr. Slavko. "Why do these points convince you?" "Because as a psychotherapist, I regularly see in people the anguish and profound problems that today are due to the absence of the mother in the families. Society itself is ill because of this absence. There are divorces. And the mothers prefer to go out to work - they have areas of interest other than their children. Now it is precisely these three points – punctuality, simple language and the daily presence of the mother- which are the most necessary for the proper development and for the balance of the child. In Medjugorje, it is truly the Mother who comes, because She remains with us. She gives us precisely these three things which we are lacking. It is the way in which She appears that touches me: She heals us from any of the ill effects of absence."

Children of Medjugorje, www.childrenofmedjugorje.com

(2/96)
Bringing Peace to Bosnia
By Msgr. James Peterson

After I wrote my last article on American troops in Bosnia/ Serbia/Croatia, I read *Return With Honor*, by Scott O'Grady. It is mainly an account of the five and a half days he spent in hiding after his F-16 was shot down over Bosnia by an anti-aircraft missile.

It is a fascinating account of his means of survival and the amazing clear-headedness of his techniques. He knew he had to keep up his spirits and his hopes. He describes his prayer as a constant, his devotion to Mary, his recalling the religious experiences of his early life. Several times, men who were looking for him passed so close to him as he was lying among trees or bushes, that he knew it was only an act of God that kept him undiscovered.

But he also mentions that a friend of his named Anita had told him that she once visited Bosnia, to a "place called Medjugorje, where Mother Mary had reportedly been sighted." Then he goes on to describe his response to Anita. "Never much of a believer in miracles, I filed the story away."

"On the afternoon of my third day in Bosnia, I prayed to the Mother of Medjugorje. Before long I felt a definite presence. It grew more and more vivid, until I could see it shimmering in my mind's eye. It's hard to put this into words, but I saw the vision through feeling it, and the feeling was very warm and good. The international chorus welled up again, praying for my safe return."

"I can't tell you how important that vision was to me. It gave me courage to go on." As I read this myself, it called to mind the times I heard confessions in Medjugorje- the tourists who had come to see, and then became pilgrims, with courage to go on in their own spiritual lives.

For Scott it was part of a continuing realization of a spiritual struggle. He mentions that six years before, he had awakened at two in the morning "and knew I wasn't alone. There was a presence in the room, and incredibly powerful presence – an evil presence. It was a web of hatred and deceit and connivery. It was darker than the night; it was a moral black hole. I wasn't afraid. Somehow I knew

125

that the presence was not out to harm me. It aimed for something more despicable – to entice, to recruit me. It was as if I had to make a choice, then and there, as to what path my life would take."

"It wasn't a hard choice. 'Jesus Christ is my Lord,' I prayed and I denounced evil and all its doing. The presence vanished like a gust of foul wind. I'd never felt it again till the day I landed in Bosnia, when it was amplified everywhere...I felt it each day I was there."

He writes that he realized two wars were going on- the human, political war and the spiritual war – at the center of which was unforgiveness, vindictiveness, even rooted in a fire and brimstone appeal to religion.

But "in Bosnia I caught a glimpse of God's love, and it was the most incredible experience in my life. I'd tapped into the brightest, most joyous feeling; I felt warmed by an everlasting flame. For all my physical complaints, I'd been on a spiritual high since that missile and I intersected."

Needless to say, this has never been on national television. But there is enmity between the devil and the woman. No wonder Mary asks for fasting and the daily Rosary. And faith and trust.

The promise remains that peace will be an answer to prayer.

(1/94)
The Face of Jesus
By Sister Emmanuel

The signs from Heaven are always very present in Medjugorje. I have noticed that the Virgin chooses to manifest Herself above all to the unbelievers and the children. Nevertheless, last month it was a priest (Irish) who was bowled over: he decided to make his Stations of the Cross and climbed the Hill of Krizevac alone. Having reached the 12th Station, he prayed before Christ on the cross, but all of a sudden the face of Jesus began to come to life. Swollen by the blows, losing His blood, Jesus moved His head from left to right, like a wounded person who could bear pain no longer. His eyes, full of love and an unfathomable sadness, met those of the priest. It was a cry of distress, silent but more powerful than a clap of thunder.

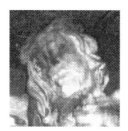

The face of Jesus on the Crucifix on Podbrdo
Photo credit: Jason Smith

The shock was too much, and the priest turned his head away so as not to see this any longer. His heart was at breaking point; he asked himself if he was going mad…he looked once again towards the cross, and Jesus continued to move, to look at him. A long contemplation then began between the crucified High Priest and His priest of our crucified world.

Trembling with all his being, he descended the mountain and rejoined his friends. They no longer recognized their priest, so great was the sweetness in his eyes. They prayed together, and the blessing poured out of him like a peaceful and forceful river.

"The world of today is special," he said. "The wounds of Jesus are intolerable." Only then did he tell his story… he would never be the same: "The face of Jesus is implanted in my heart," he said, "like a seal of wax."

Jesus, in our hearts also, Your blood cries out with Your love!

Children of Medjugorje, www.childrenofmedjugorje.com

(1/96)
Dreams and the Rosary

A reader shares with us her spiritual experiences about praying the Rosary

I say the Rosary daily, but one Sunday, feeling quite tired, I decided I needn't say it this time, as it was Sunday anyway, and having been to Mass already, felt I could take a break. That night, I saw a statue of Our Lady in my dreams. The pupils of Her eyes grew larger and larger, then tears flowed from Her eyes. In my heart, I heard Her say, "You honor me every day of the week. Am I not also your Mother on Sunday?"

I don't miss any days now, tired or not.

Recently, Our Lady visited me again in my dreams. I was kneeling before Her image, praying the Rosary with total devotion and love. She pointed with Her arm, telling me to look. Turning my head, I saw multitudes of people, too many to count. "Who are they?" I said. In my heart Our Lady said, "They are coming to thank you for all your prayers."

At the end of Mass on the Feast of the Visitation, while saying a Rosary in honor of the feast, I wondered how important these prayers really were. I felt a majestic presence, and heard the words, "Your prayers are like gold before the Throne of God." Looking at my beads at that moment, I found the links had turned to gold.

The Medjugorje Sentinel #3

(8/94)
Our Lady and the Unbeliever

By Sister Emmanuel

Last Monday, the Gospa appeared on the mountain and again She prayed for the conversion of sinners. A 14 year-old girl was there, an unbeliever. She only came to Medjugorje to help her handicapped grandmother. At 10 PM, when Our Lady appeared to Ivan, she couldn't believe her eyes – a very beautiful woman was standing close to the Blue Cross. She inclines Her head towards the kneeling group, and Her smile is radiant. The young girl says to herself that maybe it's Our Lady. What an amazing discovery of another world! With a strangled voice, she murmured, "I see Her!" Then, suddenly the meeting of their eyes is brutally interrupted, because the young girl falls from her unstable rock (and her grandmother with her).

While speaking with her the next day, I realized that this young girl is typical of our atheistic society in France: God? I don't know Him. Prayer? I don't know. The reason for life? I don't know.

But her little heart, hungry for love and life, is now turned completely upside down and filled with delight. She naively asks me, "Why was it me who saw Her, when I didn't have faith, rather than one of you who come to pray?"

The response is clear. "It's exactly because you were the one who didn't know Her that She appeared to you. She has searched for you a long time. She loves you infinitely, and She wanted to show you that you are important for Her, and from now on, you are not alone. She will always be with you…!"

Just before the youth Festival, this event was a sign for us: Our Lady cries so much in front of the distress of young people, and is ready to do even miracles in order to reveal Her love and Jesus' love for them, to heal them of emptiness. Before such tenderness, we can only fall to our knees and pray with Her for all those "casualties" of our loveless society which are the majority of the youth in the Western world.

Children of Medjugorje, www.childrenofmedjugorje.com

"Tenting it" at the youth festival
Photo credit: Tom Klins

Statue of St. Leopold near the confessionals in Medjugorje

(8/92)
A Saintly Priest
By Joan Wieszczyk

While in Medjugorje, I met an entirely new priest. When I first saw him, like many others, I wondered who he could be.

There he was- short, chubby, a little old with a Rosary in his hand, standing by a pile of rocks. Most pilgrims thought he was Padre Pio. I knew it was not him. Still I was curious.

Why was his statue in such an odd place, right at the end of the outdoor confessionals? Later, I learned that he was St. Leopold Mandic, the "hidden martyr of the confessional."

He had devoted most of his 40 years as a Capuchin priest hearing confessions. He would hear confessions for 12 to 15 hours daily. Many times he refused to take time out to eat so that he would not miss any penitents.

Many of those who would go to confession to him were priests and religious. Of course, every class of the laity would also come ...the rich, poor, and the educated. He seemed to have the gift of reading people's hearts. He knew their sins before they even confessed.

Once a seminarian came to confession and Father Leopold told him he already knew his sins. But the seminarian insisted on confession. Father let him confess so that he would have peace of mind. When the seminarian finished, Fr. Leopold reminded him of the sins he forgot.

Father Leopold was a prayerful person. He spent many of his childhood days in prayer. He was only a teen-ager of 16 when he left to become a Capuchin. He also was a staunch Croatian. During World War II, he was imprisoned for refusing to give up his Croatian citizenship.

Fr. Leopold spent most of his priestly life in Padua, Italy. This is where he began to hear so many confessions. He himself went to confession every day. He was so close to Jesus and Mary.

While hearing confessions, he would speak only a few words. Fr. Leopold had a speech impediment. Yet many hardened sinners were converted. He had the gift of instilling fear of God in people and also the mercy of God in others.

The pilgrims of Medjugorje were not far off when they thought the statue was Padre Pio. Fr. Leopold was a bit like him. The Holy Sacrament of the Mass meant so much to both of them. Many times during Mass, tears would stream down the cheeks of Fr. Leopold.

Another great love of his was the Blessed Mother. She was his great intercessor. Many miracles were performed through Her. People would come to Fr. Leopold and ask for a cure. He would tell them to go to Our Lady and say, "Blessed Lady, thy servant Fr. Leopold has sent me; grant me the favor I ask."

Fr. Leopold celebrated his Golden Jubilee on September 22, 1940. Soon after, his health began to fail. He no longer could hear confessions. This was a great pain for him. It was worse than his physical pain.

The following summer of 1941, he was well enough to continue. People heard that he was well and began to go to confession to him.

It wasn't until July 30, 1941, at the age of 76, when Fr. Leopold was vesting for Mass, that he suddenly collapsed. As he was dying, his superior began praying the "Hail Holy Queen." Fr. Leopold pronounced the words, "O clement, O loving, O sweet Virgin Mary" and died.

This new Croatian priest that I met in Medjugorje became a newly ordained saint, canonized in 1983, just two years after Our Lady began appearing in Medjugorje.

Now I know why his statue is stationed next to the wooden confessional opposite St. James Church in Medjugorje and near the Adoration Chapel. He is an inspiration to all those in and out of Medjugorje.

Next time you go to confession, remember St. Leopold Mandic. Ask him to help you make a good confession, and maybe he can help you remember the sins you may have forgotten.

Mary asks for monthly confessions. Let St. Leopold be a reminder to fulfill this part of the message.

(7/92)
Medjugorje Relief Flight
Pilgrim's Testimony

I just want to tell you that you've got to keep praying for your loved ones. Never, never give up on them!

It's only because people prayed for me that I got away from the things that were holding me back.

I started taking drugs and alcohol in the 7th grade. I didn't get away from it until I was 22 years old.

I firmly believe to this day, the reason this came about was that I didn't bother going to church since I was 10 years old, and I hadn't gone to confession. But my dear parents never gave up on me. They kept praying.

The experience that I had in Medjugorje was tremendous. I know many others felt the same. I just want to share with you because I consider it a miracle.

I hadn't been saying the Rosary very long, maybe the last month or two. It was then that I was determined to live by the messages that my parents turned me onto-Medjugorje. So I started to go to church every day and began saying the Rosary. It was during this time when I heard about the trip to Medjugorje. So I went, but I wasn't sure why, other than to deliver the medicine. While I was there, I wanted something inside to happen to me, but it didn't. So I thought, "Well, this must be it," and I was satisfied just the same.

But when we went to see Fr. Jozo and he gave us those pictures of Mary…(I've seen that picture a million times) and he said, "Kiss your Mother," it was at that moment when my heart exploded. It's as if I never saw my Mother before and all of the sudden when I said, "Hail Mary," my eyes just cried with love. It was so wonderful!

Picture of Our Lady that Fr. Jozo gives to pilgrims

This place is a miracle in itself. Everyone who goes to Medjugorje should bring a portion of it home. I understand that there have been 15 million people here. That's a whole lot of people in this world. If only each one would go home and touch one life or another.

I encourage you all to encourage others to come back to pray and above all to remember your loved ones in your prayers, especially those people who are into substance abuse.

Yes, I seemed to have had everything in life, but then I had nothing inside. I went into the occult and into the new age. I was into drugs and alcohol and all kinds of garbage, and I got NOTHING! But today I felt it! I felt it!

Here in Medjugorje – I FELT "PEACE !!!"

Editor's note: The pilgrim who gave this testimony remains anonymous.

(4/95)
Speaking in Her Mother Tongue
By Sister Emmanuel

Marija is here (in Medjugorje) for a few days, and yesterday during her apparition, something unusual happened. The Gospa prayed in Croatian, then after a moment of silence, She continued to pray for a long time "in Her mother tongue." As this happens very rarely, I tried to understand Her reasons, and I noticed that Our Lady does this when a Jewish person is present, or someone strongly linked to the Jewish people. Besides, yesterday, there were about ten of us with Marija: a Jewish girl (baptized a Catholic) and my community (the Beatitudes) whose vocation is to pray for the enlightenment of Israel. The Gospa has wished to show that She found Herself at home. But more than that – by praying in Her mother tongue in Medjugorje, She wishes to underline the importance of the role of the Jewish people in the plan of salvation, and how in Her heart, Israel and the Church are one. She gives us here an important sign, a prophetic sign, for the end times. She shows us also that Her messages are coming straight from the Bible, and that we should read their words in the light of their Hebrew roots to understand their depth…

Dear Gospa, Daughter of Israel, "Glory of Jerusalem," you are marvelous!

Children of Medjugorje, www.childrenofmedjugorje.com

(1/92)
The Story of Audrey Santo
By Joan Wieszczyk

August 9, 1987, was a normal, hot, summer day, when little 3 year-old Audrey Santo was playing with her brother Stephen and other neighborhood children. This was also the day that Audrey, who was afraid of the water, drowned.

Audrey recovered, but was rushed to the hospital for observation. The doctor prescribed Phenobarbital for sedation to prevent brain swelling and consequently, brain damage. But, the doctor prescribed too much, 750 mg., and Audrey stayed in a coma.

The first six weeks after the accident, things became worse for Audrey when her fragile body was broken and her arm was dislocated by the hospital's physical therapists. Her doctor required the painful insertion of a tracheotomy tube. Audrey's father left the family due to the stress of the situation.

Audrey remained in ICU with 24 hour nursing care. However, Audrey's mother, Linda, felt that her daughter would receive better care at home from her family. Converting the den area into a sophisticated care unit, the family brought their little girl home, twelve weeks after that hot summer day.

Being a woman of great faith, Linda sought medical permission in 1988 to transport her daughter to Medjugorje, Yugoslavia. There she would ask for a healing for Audrey through the intercession of the Blessed Mother. Millions of pilgrims have journeyed to this tiny remote village, and many people believe that Medjugorje is a special place where Mary appears every day to four young people. It is a present day Lourdes or Fatima. Therefore, with permission slips in hand, and after meticulous planning, Linda made the long trek to Yugoslavia with a nurse and her comatose daughter.

The pilgrimage experience in Medjugorje is difficult to explain. Linda and Audrey got into the balcony where the apparitions take place. There, Linda asked the Blessed Mother to either heal her daughter or take her. Audrey started to show immediate signs of recovery after the apparition, but later that evening she went into cardiac arrest. Linda and the nurse used every means possible and beyond to stabilize Audrey and rush her to the nearest hospital in Mostar. Because Audrey was so critical, no commercial airline would bring her home. The U.S. military medical plane, MedSTAR, had to fly from Germany to Yugoslavia to pick them up and transport them back home to the United States at the cost of $25,000.

Although caring for Audrey was a tremendous burden, Linda could not stand by and do nothing. If Audrey had died, this story would be only another tragic tale, but a miracle happened. Why is Audrey still alive? Is it because a mother fought for her daughter's life and couldn't let her go? Maybe…but with faith there is another explanation.

Audrey is like St. Therese, the "Little Flower," who came into contact with few people, but strongly influenced and changed many lives. St. Therese was a cloistered nun living her life as God wished and shining forth as an example to others. Audrey lives in her family's den, not moving, not speaking, but shining forth.

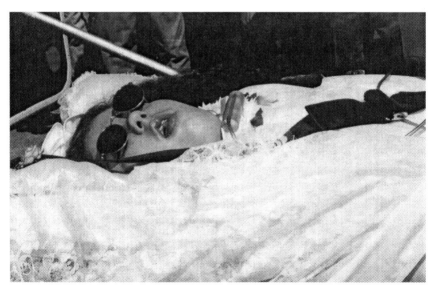

Audrey Santo

After returning home from Medjugorje, Audrey received the "stigmata" in her hands and feet. The wounds of Christ will appear on Good Friday and on different holy days of the Catholic Church. Many conversions and healings are occurring through this child.

During the weekly Friday night Rosary, Linda doesn't know if 2 or 20 people will show up to pray. Rev. Sylvester Cattalo claimed, "This child is truly a victim soul. Many souls are being saved through her suffering." Rev. Charles Babbit of Rhode Island calls her "a living little saint."

Audrey, it seems, was given a choice in Medjugorje – to be well or to offer herself up to God as a "victim soul." Although this is a great mystery in the Catholic Church, and difficult to understand, it appears that Audrey made this decision with her own free will. She chose to offer herself up to God. Rev. E. Charles McCarthy, her spiritual director, has obtained permission for Audrey to receive Holy Communion every day. The Eucharist is the ONLY solid food Audrey can receive by mouth.

As difficult as life for this family sounds, their home is so peaceful and full of love. When you meet Linda, you would not think she has a care in the world. To write about Audrey would easily make up an entire book. This outline is meant to lead you to this child so that you will remember her and her family in your prayers. If possible, please offer up a special prayer, or a Rosary, something for this little "Victim Soul."

Audrey still lives at home, which is just outside of Boston. You can write, care of her mother. Linda will read your letter to Audrey. Also, when writing it is important to please send a self addressed stamped envelope for a reply. Audrey was 8 years old on December 19th. Her address is: Miss Audrey Santo

> 64 South Flagg St.
> Worcester, MA 01602

Editor's update: Joan was the very first one to ever write about "Little Audrey," as she is known. At this writing Audrey is almost 21 years old. Many miracles have been attributed to her intercession. There are 4 Eucharistic miracles (bleeding Hosts) in the chapel in her home.

(12/95)
Fruits
I Received My Vocation after Converting in Medjugorje

At the beginning of October, Friar Christopher Amanzzi visited Medjugorje. This is what he told us on that occasion: "I came to Medjugorje for the first time in 1987. I was 32 years old. This is the 13th time I am visiting the shrine. When I came for the first time to Medjugorje, I planned to stay for just two days and then go to the coast because, as an economist, I was engaged in demanding jobs and felt tired. However, I stayed for two weeks and I profoundly experienced the love of God. I came back to sacramental life which I had given up ten years before. Till that time I was centered on myself, but then God became the center of my life. That year my walk in faith began, and continues still today. All of my friends ask me,'Why don't you decide to become a priest?' I deliberately rejected it then. After later visits in Medjugorje in 1988, something systematically changed in me. I opened myself to the will of God! I started to feel the vocation to which God was directing me. I thought over and searched for my way. Inspired by Our Lady's messages, I came closer to the Gospel which itself began to direct me and invite me to leave everything and dedicate myself to God.

"After my pilgrimage to Medjugorje in 1989, I contacted the Franciscans of the Rome Province and entered the monastery in January 1990. I made my perpetual vows this year on September 17, after which I came to Medjugorje for the 13th time. This time it is my thanksgiving to the Blessed Mother for the grace of conversion and my vocation to the priesthood. I have to admit that my entire family with the exception of my mother, went completely away from God and the sacramental life. After my conversion they have all come back to God, the sacraments, and the Church. In the first place I am grateful to God and Mary for my vocation, but I owe a lot to the perseverance and prayers of my own mother. I want to tell all mothers not to get tired of praying for their children, even when it seems that they have reached bottom. At the end, I want to say that I owe a lot to Medjugorje. Everything in it always reminds me of the person of Jesus Christ. Medjugorje, the messages Our Lady gives us here, by their simplicity, heal all of us who carry the wounds of life in our times. The men of today, wounded and exhausted by the spirit of the civilization in which they live, need Medjugorje."

Information Centre "Mir" Medjugorje, www.medjugorje.hr

(2/95)
The Pope and the Medjugorje Rosaries
By Sister Emmanuel

Mary Jo Chenevert, a 37 year-old nurse from Michigan, USA, spends most of her holidays in Medjugorje. The Gospa stamped Her beauty on her fresh and joyful face. One day, the Lord whispered to her heart that she would personally meet the Holy Father. From a practical point of view, this was totally beyond the realm of possibility. Then a Polish priest, Fr. Mike Dylag, a personal friend of the Pope, invited her on a seven- day pilgrimage to Rome, and this included several private audiences with the Holy Father! Mary Jo then made a secret plan: She will speak to the Holy Father about Medjugorje.

But on her arrival in Rome the Pope broke his collar bone and all the audiences were cancelled.

Mary Jo remained firm in her hope; she knew she would see him. And effectively, the last evening, she was admitted by some miracle in front of his private apartments with a Polish group. Then John Paul II appeared with his arm in a sling, obviously suffering in pain of the fracture. Against all odds, he stopped close to Mary Jo and seized her strongly by the shoulder with his free hand. Then something quite exceptional, he traced on her forehead a big sign of the cross with his nail, as if to engrave a deep furrow.

Surprise, pain, and joy! Mary Jo forgot all about Medjugorje... The Holy Father spoke to her in Polish, but she did not understand a word. He caressed her face for a long time and she could only whisper: "My God! My God!" so strongly did she see the suffering Jesus in him.

Then the Pope moved on about 10 meters, his back turned, he was leaving…She had nevertheless decided to speak to him about Medjugorje! Was this chance to be missed? Then she remembered the Rosaries which she had brought back from Medjugorje for him, they had been blessed by the Gospa during an apparition. She tried to give them to the guard to pass on to the Pope, but he refused. Then she held them out and cried, *"They are from Medjugorje!"*

At the sound of the word "Medjugorje," the Pope turned around and a radiant smile lit up his face. "Medjugorje?" he asked. Then he came slowly towards Mary Jo. Tears filled his eyes as he delicately took the Rosaries in his one free hand, and said in English:

"Do everything you can to protect Medjugorje!"

"But, most Holy Father, "replied Mary Jo, " I am only a person!" "Pray for the protection of Medjugorje!" he insisted. Then he moved away, he kissed the Gospa's Rosaries and pressed them against his heart. It was November 21, 1993, the Feast of the Presentation of the Blessed Virgin Mary.

Children of Medjugorje, www.childrenofmedjugorje.com

(2/95)
Francesca's Miracle
By Barabra Stufano

It was mid February of 1993. My daughter-in-law, Francesca, 26 years old, and mother of two boys only 10 ½ months apart, was suffering from mild virus symptoms. By that evening her breathing became labored and she began experiencing severe chest pains. Her husband Joe rushed her to Mid Island Hospital.

The emergency team went straight to work, taking the usual tests and statistics. Her breathing worsened, her blood pressure dropped lower and lower. Doctors and nurses surrounded her petite body, pondering the cause of this radical decline in her condition. Twenty-four hours later, on a respirator in ICU, Francesca continued to fail.

At the doctor's advice, she was rushed to North Shore Hospital. Diagnosis…unknown. Every doctor with every specialty was called to her side. For the next 72 hours she hung on by a strand. Diagnosis…unknown. Her tiny figure normally only 95 lbs. was blown out of proportion, unrecognizable. Was it her condition? Was it the medication? Diagnosis…unknown.

Her husband and her family never left her side. A twenty-four hour vigil began.

A life sustaining piece of equipment was attached to her. Francesca never closed her eyes through all this. Even morphine injections couldn't lull her to sleep. She was afraid if she closed her eyes they would never open again. Although her eyes were only slits because of the extreme swelling of her body, they never closed. This frail wisp of a girl hung on and wouldn't give into the call of death which hovered over her bed.

On Sunday, a final prognosis from "The" doctor. The hope that we all held on to as she survived one day after another was suddenly lost to the news that Francesca's heart had been destroyed by this illness. Diagnosis…unknown. If she survived another 24 hours, her only treatment or cure would be a heart transplant. Crushed by this news, we just clung together in disbelief. Somehow from the beginning I knew in my heart we would not lose Francesca.

I suddenly remembered about a year earlier a friend of mine visited Medjugorje and brought me back some newspaper articles and a few medals. The story told of the apparitions of the Blessed Mother.

Still in shock, I took a break and left the hospital for home. I was frightened and my confidence in her recovery was shaken. I took one of the medals and returned to the hospital with it.

Francesca's body was covered with tubes and electronic machines. Her nurse suggested we tape the medal to her wrist. By that evening (within 5 hours) her condition for the first time was improving. Her attending physician sat by her side throughout the night in amazement. Twenty-four hours passed, then in total shock, the doctor exited her room for the first time with a twinkle in his eyes and the first word of hope on his lips. The fever broke, the pain lessened, and Francesca continued to improve.

I knew at this point that although the doctors with their vast experience and knowledge couldn't help Francesca, Our Lady of Medjugorje could. Our Lady heard our prayers and answered them. Francesca continued to improve. After 19 days on a respirator in

ICU, the threat of losing her life was over. Francesca's miracle continued, as the possibility of losing her right leg or her foot as a result of the medications threatened her. Even that was healed through the grace of our Beloved Lady.

A few short days later, Francesca was discharged from the hospital. As she walked from her room, the doctors smiled in amazement and applauded her -her heart near perfect, her leg and foot almost normal, and grinning from ear to ear as she left the hospital.

What was it? How did she get it? Will it come back again? Diagnosis…unknown. The only answer we had was the cure. It was truly the intervention of Our Lady of Medjugorje.

We are dedicating our lives to spread the devotion of Our Lady of Medjugorje because of this miracle. Francesca's miracle has led us to others. A few weeks later as I lay in bed, the phone rang; it was my son. He told me of a young boy who needed the blessing of Our Lady. I took another medal from the case where I kept them and placed it next to my bed. My intention was to deliver it to my son the next day so that he could present it to the troubled child. That evening I said the Rosary. I then took the silver medal and placed it on the box where I kept my Rosary. The next morning to my amazement, the silver medal had turned to gold. The miracle continues.

Used with permission from "Mary's Mantle" by Our Lady Queen of Peace Prayer Group

(9/91)
An Answer To A Prayer

Father Ken Roberts asks, "What is the most important thing about Medjugorje? The most important thing is that the world is beginning to pray. It is prayer that Our Lady of Medjugorje is talking about."

Father says when we pray we must pray with all our might. So many of us think that our prayers don't make any difference. Do you really believe that? Do you believe that when you pray in a group that there is power in prayer? Father does.

Last year when Father Ken was in Medjugorje he met a couple, the woman being in her mid-forties. They had their little girl, Bridget, with them. She was 6 years old. They asked him if he was going to be the celebrant at Mass that week. He said he was. Then they asked if their daughter could make her First Holy Communion in Medjugorje. They felt that she was ready. Father thought that she was too young, but he began to question her, asking her about the Faith. He wanted to make sure that she knew what she was doing. As it turned out, she knew all about First Holy Communion, about Jesus in the Eucharist, the sacraments, and her prayers. She knew as much as any 4th or 5th grader, and she was only in the first grade. Father had never seen a child more ready to receive First Holy Communion. He told her parents that it was up to them – he gave them the "go ahead."

Bridget's big day came. She was dressed in a white dress and veil. It was in St. James Church in Medjugorje that she received Jesus, her First Holy Communion.

After Mass, Father Ken was preaching in the pavilion outside behind the church to the pilgrims, many of them youth. Someone took a snapshot of him. In the snapshot you could see a ray of light coming into his hands. It seemed to go right through him and also to that little girl who just made her First Holy Communion.

When Father returned to the United States, he received this photo in the mail from a lady in Cincinnati. He had no idea what it was all about. A week later he traveled to North Jackson, Ohio, site of the Shrine of Our Lady of Lebanon. Father Ken bumped into the little girl's parents. They approached him saying, "Father, you're never going to believe what happened to us in Medjugorje." He said, "Oh yes, I will, but what happened?"

The mother said, "I got pregnant on my daughter's First Holy Communion Day." She was forty-four years old. She explained that she found Bridget crying one day while praying the Rosary. She asked her why and she said, "Mommy, you told me that anything I asked God for on my First Holy Communion Day He would answer." And the mother said, "Well, my dear, what did you pray for?" She said, "I prayed for a little baby brother or sister."

The baby sister was born on the feast of Our Lady of Lourdes and is named Monica Therese.

Father Ken showed them the picture he had received with the ray of light. He thought maybe the message of the spear of light was for Bridget. The little girl said, "Oh, I know all about that." Father was amazed. He asked, "You do?" Bridget said, "Yes. I asked Jesus to bless your hands because you gave me Holy Communion." That ray of light goes through Fr. Ken to Bridget.

Ray of light going through Father's hands to Bridget

That's the power of prayer – visually! Bridget's prayers for a baby sister or brother had been answered. The photo confirmed her childlike faith. The ray of light represented her prayers being answered!

She prayed with all her might. Let us pray the way Our Lady of Medjugorje is teaching us- "with all our heart!" Then and only then will our prayers be answered.

Editor's update: I met Bridget on my first pilgrimage to Medjugorje in 1998. Her sister Monica was making her First Holy Communion! Bridget met her future husband on that pilgrimage and as of this writing, they have a little girl, and another baby on the way!

(8/94)
The Rosary Tape
By Sister Emmanuel

Last June one of my brothers was driving on the highway, praying the Rosary. They were listening to a tape made here (in Medjugorje), where each decade is followed by a message of the Gospa. One of the tires blew out, and the car rolled over several times, hit the barrier and came to a halt on its roof. Everything stopped in an anguished silence... except the tape, which continued... "4ᵗʰ Sorrowful Mystery... Hail Mary, full of grace..." Everybody was safe, and got out through the windows, except Yves, who was trapped, feet in the air. Fire was a threat, because petrol was leaking. The voice on the tape reassures, "My children, do not be afraid. Satan can do nothing against you. Be at peace!" Yves receives great peace; Mary is with him. He continues his Rosary. A fireman wants to stop the Rosary tape, but Yves shouts, "No!" The voice continues, "First Glorious Mystery, the Resurrection... Dear children be enthusiastic for the Resurrection!" Yves understands that he will be saved at the end of the Glorious Mysteries, and when a priest approaches to offer his services, he responds, " I'm all right, thank you. I will finish my Rosary." Effectively, during the last hymn in Croatian, the fireman manages to release him. He only has 4 broken ribs. The car is in pieces, but Yves' heart will never be the same: "Yes, I just love the Resurrection. My life is only just starting, and it will last for all eternity."

Vicka repeats it unceasingly: "Satan wants to destroy your families. The weapon against him is to pray the Rosary as a family, as when you are united in prayer, Satan can do nothing against you."

Children of Medjugorje, www.childrenofmedjugorje.com

(7/90)
"Queen of Peace" Portrait

While on a pilgrimage on the miraculous Feast of the Assumption on August 15, 1988, at St. John Church in Lubbock, Texas, ecclesiastical artist Eduardo Nandin Esparza from Austin was confronted by a lady from Corpus Christi who had just returned from Medjugorje, Yugoslavia. She had in her possession two photographs of Our Lady which had been taken by a Vatican nun in the apparition room of St. James Church in Medjugorje. She claimed that Our Lady would show her who one of them would belong to. Among tens of thousands of people that were in Lubbock for the pilgrimage, she called Eduardo aside and said, "The Blessed Mother wants you to have this photograph."

Eduardo cannot explain the spiritual feelings and blessings he has received since he has had this picture. He has cherished it with all his love.

A year later, Eduardo's wife, Felicitas, received a book from a Christian friend entitled, "Medjugorje, the Message," written by Wayne Weible. The cover of the book has the same picture of the Blessed Mother that Eduardo received in Lubbock. After his wife read the entire book, which was so touching and revealing to her, Felicitas received an inner message, which she felt came from the Blessed Mother, that Eduardo was to paint a portrait using the face as his model. As she shared these feelings with Eduardo and they began to pray together, a very spiritual, warm and loving feeling filled his studio. Eduardo realized why the Blessed Mother wanted him to have Her picture. He has always felt a deep affinity with Mary and She is frequently the subject of his paintings. Eduardo has since done the "Queen of Peace" by pencil, blessed olive oil, holy water, and finally completely in oil on canvas.

Throughout this painting, Eduardo took photographs as the different stages of his work progressed, as he usually does for documentation purposes. Three months after the completion of this oil painting, the film was processed, and a most remarkable picture taken during the early stages of the portrait done in pencil was developed. This portrait was so inspiring that Eduardo decided to share this picture with all the world.

"Queen of Peace" portrait

However, in reproducing the prints, something miraculous took place. A light appeared on the left side of Our Lady's portrait, which seems to glow from behind Her and reflects through Her veil and onto Her cheek and forehead. A broken heart is apparent on Her chest, and a smaller heart below Her left eye. Production of the prints are in gold tones since the initial photography taken of this work in his studio appeared in gold. Two prints among them all have a tear on the left cheek.

While Eduardo is a devoted Catholic and apostle of the Blessed Virgin Mary, the photographic and printing companies that assisted in this production are Baptist and Jehovah Witness. They find themselves at a complete loss for words, knowing that this picture is truly a miraculous one and could not have been the work of man alone. As Eduardo says, "She wanted it that way." There is a message in this picture for the world to see.

Our Lady has chosen Eduardo to be Her artist, as She has chosen numerous others throughout the ages. Eduardo discerned the message in Her portrait as follows: "Our Lady is saying She is the Queen of Peace, Mother of Light and Hearts, as Jesus is the Light of the World, and stands beside Her as well. Her broken heart is visible on Her chest because of our sins. She also shows us that She is yearning for our hearts as She displays our hearts on Her face below Her left eye. In two of the prints, She miraculously shows tears that wash away our hurt and problems. With Her mercy, She softens cares and prepares them for Her Son Jesus Christ who heals and delivers us."

(6/90)
Do You Know That Nun?
By Kay Mule

"In 1968 I was stationed at a parish in Gulfport, Mississippi," began Fr. John Izral at a Peace Mass at St. Matthew the Apostle Church in River Ridge, LA. "One day I received a call from a Baptist woman. 'Father, I must see you,' she said. 'I met a nun and I want you to tell me who she is.'"

Since Fr. Izral knew the nuns of the area, he agreed to come to her house. When he arrived, the woman began to tell him of her life. Her husband was a drinker and had physically abused her. If she went to church, he would beat her. If he found her reading the Bible, he would tear it up. When he was very drunk he would bring other women home. If his wife complained about his habits, he would beat her. She had a nine year-old son who was following in his father's footsteps. He had been in trouble with the law on several occasions.

One day when her husband came home drunk, the woman could take it no longer. When he went into the bedroom she fell on her knees near the kitchen table. "God," she prayed, "please help me."

A few minutes later the door bell rang. Standing there was a beautiful woman with street length clothes, blonde hair and blue eyes. She had never seen her before. "Father," she questioned, "Do you know this nun? I want to talk to her again." She continued, "The 'nun' sat at the table with me and described my life – how my husband has acted and the abuses I have had to endure."

The "nun" gave her some advice – not to worry about getting to church if her husband would not let her, and for her to read the Bible when he was not at home. She also taught her to say the prayer to St. Michael the Archangel, which she was to pray daily. "I was amazed," said Fr. Izral, "that she could recite it after hearing it only one time."

Inspired by this visit, the woman called her husband to meet the guest. He came to the bedroom door and was knocked back, as a strong invisible hand slapped him across the face so vigorously that he fell to the floor. He didn't dare to come out of the bedroom until long after the visitor left.

Then the son came into the kitchen. His eyes riveted on this beautiful visitor. She then hugged the wife and walked out the door. Immediately her son asked, "Mother, who is that lady?"

The woman, realizing she had forgotten to ask the name of the visitor, immediately opened the door; no one was there. Earlier, when the visitor arrived, the wife had noticed there was no car parked nearby. As she looked up and down the street, there was no car and no one on the street.

Fr. Izral told the woman, "That was not a nun. You were visited by the Blessed Virgin Mary." He continued, "Though it went against everything I learned in the seminary, I seem to have the absolute certainty that this was Mary."

Fr. Izral spoke to the woman six weeks later. She had followed the advice given by the visitor. Her husband no longer was drinking.

Her son had changed too, and their family life had improved greatly. She was still praying the daily prayer to St. Michael.

When Fr. Izral heard about the apparitions in Medjugorje he remembered the Baptist woman's story. Why could She not appear to six children with messages for a troubled world? If She appeared to a troubled, abused Baptist housewife, would She not also appear when we Catholics were also in desperate spiritual need?

"To me," said Fr. Izral, "the real message of Medjugorje is that Mary loves us as totally, as unconditionally as Her Son Jesus does, and She is calling us to a total surrender and service to Him."

The Medjugorje Star

(6/94)
Healing of Hearts
By Sister Emmanuel

Medjugorje continues to be the place for physical healing and for the healing of hearts. For example, two young AIDS victims came here two days ago. The illness has been transmitted through homosexual practices. The Gospa totally overwhelmed them, and one of them saw Her. She spoke to him and explained some of the messages, as he had never heard of them. We do not yet know if a physical healing has taken place since this can only be revealed by a blood analysis, but for these two it is really Heaven which has come into their hearts to embrace them in their distress.

A woman afflicted with sclerosis and in braces was carried up Podbrdo on a stretcher; she walked down, having regained the suppleness of her body. A 23 year-old person, who smoked almost 3 packages of cigarettes a day, felt a great disgust for cigarettes, and no longer smokes. The same thing for a man, a smoker and an alcoholic; he no longer smokes and now has no more than three glasses a day. Two couples with children, who married in a civil ceremony (previous divorces did not allow them to be married in church), made a decision to live as brother and sister in chastity. A little example of the graces granted here…

A pilgrim saw a grandmother who was making hay, and noticed her shining expression, saying to her: "How lucky you are to have been born in Medjugorje, in this village chosen amongst all others!" "To be from Medjugorje," she replied, "is not to be born in the village, but to do everything the Gospa asks!"

How beautiful! Each one of our hearts would become a little Medjugorje if the Gospa filled them.

Children of Medjugorje, www.childrenofmedjugorje.com

(4/93)
Siroki Brijeg – 1992

A pilgrimage to Medjugorje would not be complete to any of us if we didn't get to see at least one visionary before we left. Traveling all that way and not getting to see Fr. Jozo Zovko, OFM, would also seem unfair. As we got to know the visionaries, we got to know Fr. Jozo. Even if it meant an extra trip to Tihaljina, it was something special. He has that certain look. He has the gifts of the Holy Spirit. This is very evident.

So time was set aside for our group to meet Fr. Jozo. We didn't have to travel to Tihaljina. Fr. Jozo is no longer stationed there. He has been transferred to the monastery of Siroki Brijeg. It's about a 45-minute drive from Medjugorje. As we traveled along, I wondered why he had to leave Tihaljina. It was through Fr. Jozo that the statue of Mary in his church in Tihaljina became so popular. To me, she was known as "Our Lady of Peace." Isn't that what Our Lady of Medjugorje is? The Queen of Peace.

When we arrived at Siroki Brijeg and our guide Anka began to describe the history of that area, I realized why Our Lady sent Fr. Jozo there. She is using him to inform the faithful (from all over the world) of the martyrs that are buried there. I'm sure he will be very instrumental in having them canonized saints some day. In February 1992, a commemorative service was held in their honor.

A little background – in 1945, thirty of the monks living there at the time were killed by the Communists (three of them were from Medjugorje). Twelve were killed and burnt in the air-raid shelter in the monastery garden. Among these were eight young deacons. Five were shot with their chaplain in the neighboring parish. Eight

Entrance to the Cave of the Martyrs in Siroki Brijeg

monks were tortured and killed after being taken in the direction of Split from the Hydroelectric Power Plant. Two were killed in the environs. One from Izbicna was tortured and killed. Another was killed in Mostar and thrown into the Neretva River. One was killed in Slovenia.

The bodies of the twelve killed and burnt in the air-raid shelter along with the six killed in Mostarski, Gradae, were recovered only after a long silence concerning their deaths was revealed. They were transferred into the church in Siroki Brijeg called "Our Lady Assumed into Heaven." Above their tombs on the wall of the sanctuary is a huge poster, encased in glass, with the names of the thirty Franciscan martyrs.

The building next to the church used to be a seminary. At one time there were 120 students studying to become religious. Then the Communists came and confiscated the building. Out of the 120 students, only 12 were allowed to remain and finish their seminary schooling. They later were ordained. One of them was Fr. Jozo.

It is no wonder why Our Lady has chosen Yugoslavia for Her apparitions. Her Franciscan priests and brothers have defended their faith even unto death for many centuries.

This historic lesson left many of us in tears, as we were privileged to enter the air-raid shelter where those monks had given their lives.

We then gathered to hear a spiritually uplifting talk by Fr. Jozo. Having the Holy Mass in his chapel was a blessing in itself. As a token of appreciation, he gave each one of us a picture of Our Lady. He told us to "look at your Mother, kiss Her." Then he gave us a Rosary to be used as a powerful weapon against Satan. And finally as a remembrance of this visit, each one of us was blessed by Fr. Jozo Zovko individually.

This was surely a rewarding pilgrimage.

Chapter 4:

Living the Messages

Stones on path leading up to Mt. Krizevac

(11/93)
Five Stones of Medjugorje

Stones picked up from Apparition Hill and Mt. Krizevac are very holy because the Mother of God has appeared many times on that holy ground. Numerous miracles have happened to those who pray and trust in Her and use these holy stones.

Take five of these holy rocks or stones, along with a picture of Mary (the one given by Fr. Jozo) and place them on your altar or table. They will be an everlasting remembrance of your pilgrimage to Medjugorje. It will help you live the messages day by day.

Tell your family, children and friends where you were and what these 5 stones or rocks mean to you. Each one of them symbolizes the 5-part message of Medjugorje.

The first and most important of all is PEACE! This is the reason for Mary's coming. She has appeared for over 12 years now, pleading with each and every one of us to take Her messages seriously. She knows that we have hearts of rock and stone. It is up to us to transform them into a soft warm loving heart, striving for peace with our families, friends, and even our enemies.

We need spiritual ingredients to help us achieve the goal of peace. Mary knows which ones they are. Prayer with the heart is a powerful ingredient. It is the fore-runner of them all. It is prayer that is needed to change the heart. That is because it is the lifeline to God. He is the one reading our hearts when we pray.

Mary hasn't given up on us yet. She asks us also to fast. The second stone represents fasting. We've got to get in the habit of fasting on Wednesdays and Fridays. By fasting we can make Satan depart. Fasting is also a form of penance. When we fast, we are releasing love in the heart and cleansing our soul at the same time.

The third stone is the Holy Eucharist. Jesus becomes Life in you! Your life then becomes Eucharist to others. It is your life and your example that must become bread for others.

The fourth rock or stone reminds us of Confession. We must not only confess our sins and destroy all idols, but we have to realize that in sin, we have lost peace, love and joy. We must be transformed again. God gives us freedom when we are transformed. We are transformed in Confession. Confession means Resurrection, a new life.

The fifth rock is the Bible. The Bible is God's word alive. Fr. Jozo tells us to dust off the Bible. Pick it up and keep it in your arms until you feel your heart pulsating with it. Make this book number one. Do not exchange it with any other book, for He is your Teacher. This is the candle if you are looking for the Light. God's word is your strength.

These five stones are your daily reminder of the main purpose of Our Heavenly Mother's appearances in Medjugorje.

(10/97)
Pray With the Heart
By Joan Wieszczyk

Mary of Medjugorje continually asks us to pray. We have to pray in order to understand what God wishes to say through Her presence and through all the messages She gives us. She wants us to pray with our hearts, not just mumble words. We've got to take Her words seriously.

I began to think just when and how I learned to pray. Perhaps you could ask yourself the same question. Was it in the home when I was a tiny child? Did I learn from the nuns at school? To pinpoint the exact age, I don't know. I do know that I was taught well in knowing and loving God by the time I was prepared to receive Jesus in my First Holy Communion. The Sisters (teachers) did a splendid job in instructing each of us in my class. I also remember the time when I was to receive the Holy Spirit in the Sacrament of Confirmation. It was another joyous occasion in my lifetime. So you see, I was well versed in the love of God. I don't remember being told to pray "with the heart." I guess when you're young, it comes naturally. It's when we get older and the distractions take hold of our minds that we have to be reminded once again of the power of prayer. Prayer is not to escape our lives, but to be a part of it. I know so many Catholics who knew their prayers when they were young, but today don't know how to pray the Rosary. It is no wonder God sent His Mother here on earth to help us get back to Jesus. We can't do it without prayer.

And now that we forgot how to pray, Mary comes as our teacher and instructor. We learn through Her as we listen to the messages over and over. It is only then that we will be able to learn how to pray and how to pray with the heart. She is repeating and repeating until we get the message right. That is why Mary tells us to pray constantly. One member of my prayer group asked, "How can I pray constantly when I'm so busy with my housework, etc.?" Just being aware of His Presence is a prayer in itself. When we pray our morning offering, we offer everything we do or say that day to Jesus and Mary. If doing our housework, etc. is part of the offering, They are in our presence. We could remind ourselves of Their Presence by simply saying little ejaculations...i.e. "Jesus, Mary, I love You," or just "Jesus."

For me, praying with the heart means falling in love with prayer. There are many forms of prayer. They are private prayer, vocal prayer, group prayer, and also meditative prayer, etc. Some vocal prayer can be litanies, Rosaries, novenas and many, many more. Then there is a deeper prayer, the prayer of contemplation. It all depends on the individual and how to enter into prayer.

In the earlier days of the apparitions, when the visionaries were asked how they prayed, their response was...

Jakov: the youngest of them said, to him *each prayer was very precious in his life. It was a heart to heart conversation with God.*

Vicka: *I can say even ten Rosaries, but I'm not made for meditation. God hasn't given me that gift.*

Marija: *I gladly say a Rosary, but I would rather meditate. I simply must retire into solitude. I remain in silence.*

Ivan: *The Bible is the biggest thing in my prayer.*

Ivanka: *Sometimes I use the Bible but seldom. I talk to Jesus in my own words. I pray with the heart.*

This is how they used to pray. That was over ten years ago. I'm sure, by now, their prayer life has grown. Our Lady has been teaching them and us how to pray, pray, pray with the heart.

I myself love praying and meditating alone in silence and in the dark so as not to be distracted. That is when I am in private prayer. I also like to pray aloud the Rosary and the Divine Mercy Chaplet with my family. Then come the prayer groups when the prayers can multiply themselves as we pray together. For Jesus said, "Where two or more are gathered in My Name, I am there in their midst."

Of course, the greatest and most powerful prayer is the Holy Sacrifice of the Mass. Our Lady of Medjugorje tells us to go to Mass as often as we can, daily if possible. When we go, we should go with an open heart, the prayer of the heart. The Mass is the most outstanding miracle happening here on earth. There we partake into the Life, Death and Resurrection of Our Lord, Jesus Christ. We are joined together as one big family with the Trinity and Mary, angels and saints. That for me is Heaven on Earth!

If we were to tell someone how to pray with the heart, I would have to tell them how I try to pray with my heart. First of all, whether I am kneeling or not, I begin with the Sign of the Cross. Then I invite Jesus and Mary along with my guardian angel and all the other angels and saints to be with me at that moment. I invoke the Holy Spirit to fill me with His love. Closing my eyes and depending on what I am meditating on, I can visualize Jesus, as a baby in the crib, as the Resurrected Lord, as a member of the Holy Family, on the cross and in so many different ways. I try to picture Mary as being my Mother also. I see Her as Our Lady of Medjugorje and under so many other titles. In Their presence, I begin to pray with my heart, asking forgiveness of my sins. I thank Them all for what They have done for me. Then I begin to pray for Mary's intentions, the unbelievers, conversions, peace in my heart, in my home and in the world. I pray for my loved ones, family members, relatives and friends, the Pope, bishops, my pastor and priests, and all the religious nuns and brothers. I can't forget the sick and the poor souls in Purgatory, and also for the other intentions that I did not include.

I also ask for the Lord's help, and most of all, I pray for a happy death and to be with all of Them in Eternity. During all this time, I am holding my Benedictine Crucifix in my hands, bringing it close to my heart, and at times kissing Jesus.

This is just some of the ways that I try praying with the heart. It is the perfect way to be in constant touch with Jesus and Mary.

But what about the times that we can't pray? I am speaking about the "dry times, the dark night of the soul" - when it is really hard to pray with the heart, especially when we are ill or when some kind of catastrophe strikes us. If it is any consolation to you, we know that God sees our heart. He knows how much we want to pray and how hard it is for us. This silence, this suffering, too, can be a prayer of the heart. All we have to do is lift it up to Him.

It is only through prayer that we can realize just how much Our Lady, with the love of Jesus, loves us. That love is boundless!

Fr. Jozo emphasizes Our Lady's request to read the Bible daily.
Photo credit: Bernard Gallagher

(2/96)
The Bible
By Joan Wieszczyk

I recently read of Father Joseph A. Fitzmeyer, a Jesuit, who had said in an address in Ireland, that there has been a remarkable return to the Bible in Catholic life. Father is a Professor Emeritus of Biblical Studies at the Catholic University of America in Washington, D.C. He said an encyclical by Pope Pius XII on biblical studies encouraged the emergence of the Catholic Biblical Movement in the mid-1950's.

I would hope we could credit a great deal of this return to the Bible to those who have been following the messages of Medjugorje. Mary has been asking us to read the Bible every day. I myself never read the Bible often. It was only after I got to know the messages that I realized how inspirational it was and how pleasing it was answering the request of Our Heavenly Mother.

There is no other book that compares to the Holy Bible. It is holy because it contains the Word of the Lord. We are asked to place it in a special visible spot in our home. In other words, don't hide it in a drawer or on the back shelf. Have it in an area where it is easily obtainable. We are encouraged to pick it up, read it, and pray. It should be read together with the family, and at times be read by oneself at quiet times for personal spiritual reading.

The Bible is the greatest book in the world! The word "Bible" means "The Book." God is the author, and therefore it contains no errors (in faith).

The Bible is a source of divine revelation. God has spoken to men in two ways – through Scripture and through Tradition. The Council of Trent stated that both founts of revelation, Scripture and Tradition, are to be esteemed equally.

It was during a period of 1400 years that God inspired chosen men to write the books of the Bible. It is composed of 73 books, 46 in the Old Testament, and 27 in the New Testament. The Old Testament was written before Jesus was born. The New Testament was written after His birth.

The New Testament contains 4 Gospels, the Acts of the Apostles, 21 Epistles (sometimes known as Letters), and also the Book of the Apocalypse.

The Gospels are 4 short records of the life and teachings of Our Lord Jesus Christ. The Acts of the Apostles record the work of the Apostles, especially St. Peter and St. Paul during the 30 years after Jesus' Ascension. During their travels, they wrote many letters to their Christian communities. These are filled with the inspiration of their zeal to do what Christ asked of them, which was to preach His Gospel throughout the world.

The book called the Apocalypse was written about 96 A.D. Christ entrusted this task to St. John to let us know something about the end of the world, of His return to it, and also of Heaven.

Reading of the Bible is a part of the message of Medjugorje. It's filled with inspiration. It is God speaking to us. We are to read it daily and listen. Listen to the Word of God. In this way, we will be growing in holiness, the path that Mary is calling us to.

Make sure your children have their own Bible early in life. It makes a beautiful spiritual gift for any occasion – be it Baptism, First Holy Communion, Confirmation, birthdays, Christmas, Easter, and many other occasions in their lifetime. It is a religious book to be used also for one's personal spiritual life. No better book of personal spiritual reading could be found!

Keep the word of God alive in your home. Read the Bible!

Mass at St. James Church in Medjugorje

(10/97)
Unite the Rosary with the Mass
By Fr. Luke Zimmer, SS.CC

We need to pray the Rosary, and it is not just for simpletons, for those who are unlearned, those who cannot read – it is for everyone, and I say especially for those who are intelligent, because when you meditate upon the mysteries of the Rosary, you are never, ever going to exhaust the treasure it holds.

It teaches you your faith. So we should get in the habit of praying the Rosary, and for those of you who have the time, I ask you to pray the fifteen decade Rosary. Those of you who are elderly, you have time. Those who are lonely, do not waste your time on those stupid soap operas. But if you would try one Rosary after another, you would be contributing to the welfare of the whole world. We need your prayers.

We should learn to pray the Rosary in union with the Mass, praying it outside the Mass, before the Mass, after the Mass, but always uniting our prayers with the Mass.

When we are praying the fourth Joyful Mystery, the Presentation unites itself with the Offertory of the Mass. Offer this with each Mass and your prayers will be united with 400,000 Masses being offered each day to the Heavenly Father.

At the Consecration, offer everything to the Father - your suffering, your intentions, everything.

Then in the third Glorious Mystery, the Descent of the Holy Spirit unites itself with the Communion of the Mass because when we receive Jesus as the Eucharist, the Holy Spirit takes over and transforms us, making us like Jesus.

So you can see how you can live the Mass, how everything can be united with the Mass – your prayers, your works of charity, your work of service to others. Unite everything to the Mass, and you will be praying always. We need to be a living prayer, not just a Novena, not just for a few days for this or that, but praying always.

Here is the Mystical Mass Prayer:

Eternal Father, we offer to You, through the Immaculate and Sorrowful Heart of Mary, in the Holy Spirit, the Body, Blood, Soul and Divinity of Our Lord Jesus Christ, in union with each Mass celebrated today and every day until the end of time.

With Mother Mary, St. Joseph, each angel and saint in Heaven, each soul in Purgatory, each person in the Body of Christ and the family of God, we offer each act of love, adoration, praise and worship. We offer each act of thanksgiving for blessings, graces and gifts received. We offer each act of reparation for sins that have been, are being, and will be committed until the end of time. And we offer each act of intercessory prayer. We offer all these prayers in union with Jesus in each Mass celebrated throughout the world until the end of time.

We stand before You, Triune God, like the Prodigal Son, asking to be accepted, like the Publican, asking for mercy and forgiveness, like the Paralytic asking for healing and strength, and like the Good Thief asking for salvation.

We consecrate ourselves and all of creation to You.

Eternal Father, we ask You, in the name of Jesus, through the power of His Precious Blood, through His death on the cross, through His resurrection and ascension, to send forth the Holy Spirit upon all mankind.

Holy Spirit, we ask for an outpouring of Your graces, blessings and gifts upon those who do not believe, that they may believe; upon those who are doubtful or confused, that they may understand; upon those who are lukewarm or indifferent, that they may be transformed; upon those who are constantly living in the state of sin, that they may be converted; upon those who are weak, that they may be strengthened; upon those who are holy, that they may persevere.

We ask You to bless our Holy Father, the Pope. Give strength and health in mind, body, soul, and spirit. Bless his ministry and make it fruitful. Protect him from enemies.

Bless each cardinal, bishop, priest, brother, sister and all aspiring to the religious life, especially…, and grant many the gift of a vocation to the priesthood and religious life.

Bless each member of our families, relatives and friends, especially…

Bless the poor, the sick, the underprivileged, the dying and all those in need…

Bless those who have died and are in the state of purification, that they may be taken to Heaven.

We offer and consecrate ourselves and all creation to You, Heart of Jesus, Mary and Joseph. We ask you, Mary and Joseph, to take us with all our hopes and desires. Please offer them with Jesus in the Holy Spirit to our Heavenly Father, in union with each Mass offered throughout all time.

We consecrate ourselves to Archangel Michael, Gabriel and Raphael, and each angel, especially our Guardian Angel. We ask, in the name of Jesus, through our Mother Mary, Queen of all Angels, that You, O Heavenly Father, send forth legions of angels to minister to us: Archangel Michael with his legions to ward off the attacks of the world, the flesh and the devil; Archangel Gabriel with his legion to teach us that we may know and do Your will, and that they may help us to catechize and evangelize; Archangel Raphael with his legions to heal our woundedness, supply for our limitation, and strengthen us in our weakness to overcome demonic depression, to give us joy in the spirit, to protect us in our travels, and supply all our needs.

Finally, we ask for the gift of unconditional love, that we can live the love-life which was reflected in the Holy Family at Nazareth, thus bring about justice and peace throughout the world. Amen.
Nihil Obstat: The Very Rev. Richard Danyluk, SS.CC, Provincial
Children of Medjugorje,www.childrenofmedjugorje.com

Priests hearing confessions on the lawn, during a busy time in Medjugorje

(8/92)
Confession:
Sacrament of Penance
Sacrament of Reconciliation
By Fr. Dennis, C.S.S.R.

Whatever you call this sacrament, it is the "Sacrament of Peace." You know it as "Confession" if you have been away from it for a long time; it's the sacrament of "Penance" if you last received it in the late seventies or early eighties; you know it as "Reconciliation" if you receive this sacrament now.

I call it the "Sacrament of Peace." I liked it when we called it Penance because our word "peace" is included in the word "Penance." But whatever you call it, it is time to rethink this wonderful sacrament... maybe I'm targeting this article to those who have not been to Confession for 15 or 20 years...or to those who have not received the sacrament of Penance for 10 years. If you are in either category, read on.

Remember when you sinned seriously... how worried you were that you might die without going to Confession. We never looked forward to Confession, but after we made a good one, we knew peace. We knew that our sins were forgiven. Now we could die.

Though we Catholics often carried a lot of guilt, we left most of it in the confessional. Most of us knew that our sins had been forgiven.

The vast majority of Catholics are not going to church now, and I believe that many would return to the Church if they understood more about this sacrament. I believe the fear of Confession is keeping many away.

Memories of past difficult confessions, fears about how to confess serious sins stretching back many years, fears about face to face Confession... these all keep many away from Confession and away from Church.

Then a friend of yours – forty-five years old – drops dead suddenly. More fear... could that have been you? Was he ready? Are you ready? More fear.

Where there is fear, there is no peace. Jesus wants all to have His peace. We have the "Sacrament of Peace" and we are afraid of it. How sad! Some ideas about our fears about this Sacrament of Peace:

Every sacrament has a human side and a spiritual side. With this sacrament it is the human side that scares us. Nobody doubts God's forgiveness (the spiritual). Many doubt the human problems related to making that confession.

We were taught that we must confess all our serious sins…that has not changed. **We must confess all our serious sins.** What has changed is that we can now confess our sins differently.

The priest needs a **confused** knowledge of the state of a person's soul. He does not need a **clear** knowledge. This distinction changes the actual confession of our sins. For example:

Clear knowledge: a married man confesses to the priest that he had an affair. He would mention what he did with this other lady, how many times he did it, how long the affair lasted, etc.

Confused knowledge: a married man simply states to the priest that he was unfaithful to his wife.

In the first instance, the man would go into much detail. In the second instance, he would simply state the sin. The statement of sin (in most cases) is sufficient. No great detail is necessary. Most sin can be put into a word or phrase and said briefly: I had an abortion; I over-reacted with my children; there is a personal sexual sin; I compromised with my husband.

These are examples of how one might confess some difficult sins that keep many away from this sacrament. Most priests do not ask a lot of questions… some do… but most do not. We priests know how difficult some sins are to confess. If a penitent were to go to a counselor, it might take many sessions before the patient could even mention some embarrassing problem. We cannot expect someone to come into the sacrament of Penance and just speak it. We know these sins are difficult to speak.

Hallmark cards makes millions of dollars saying "I love you" because a woman cannot say that to her husband. How can we expect someone to come into the sacrament of Penance and confess difficult sins.

We presume the person is confessing as well as possible. That is all the Lord asks. Simply confess your sins as well as you can. We priests, sinners all, know well from our own lives that this is not easy. But, we also know from our own lives how peace-filled this sacrament is. When we free ourselves of these sins, we do indeed understand this sacrament of peace.

If you have been away a long time or know someone who has been away from the Church a long time, do something about it. Go to Confession. Encourage others to return to experience the peace so many long for.

Don't be afraid to start your confession. "Bless me, Father, for I have sinned – it has been a long time. Please help me." The priest will then walk you through your confession **gently**.

(11/88)
To Pray Well, Fast
By Rev. Albert Shamon

Prayer is the breath of the soul.

Fasting is the prayer of the body.

Prayer and fasting are as necessary to our spiritual life as breathing and eating are to our physical life.

As breathing and eating are interrelated, so are prayer and fasting. When you fast, you can pray better. Try it and see if that isn't true.

But we have virtually forgotten about fasting. Our Lady of Medjugorje asks: "Fast strictly on Wednesday and Friday..." (8/14/84)

Fasting opens you up to others and to God. Fasting helps you experience how it is to be poor. The poor hunger by necessity. They know what it is to need; and so they are open to help. The poor person is open to trusting God, for he has no one else in whom to trust. That is why Mary said God gives good things to the hungry (Lk. 1:53). Her Son echoed Her sentiments when He said, "How blest are the poor in spirit; the reign of God is theirs." (Mt. 5:3).

Self-sufficiency can shut out God. If we have no sense of need, then we see no need for turning to God. Our Lord Himself said that it is hard for a rich man to enter the kingdom of Heaven. One reason is because a rich person tends to be self-sufficient, to trust in his own resources, and not in God. Only when the well is dry will you know the value of water.

Fasting does not mean not eating. When you fast, you eat, but you do not eat what your palate craves. How often we eat because something tastes so good! Fasting denies those tastes, jaded by our abundance.

To drink sugarless coffee and one slice of toast on a Friday morning and the same with a couple of slices of toast for lunch is not too appetizing – but it is sufficient. You eat, you see, but not what you would like to eat. You are, in reality, denying yourself. And that is good!

Such fasting is so good because it also helps toward self-mastery. We all experience the rebellion of the flesh against the spirit. St. Paul cried out that because of the sting of the flesh, he did not do what he wanted to do, but what he hated. "I do, not the good I will to do, but the evil I do not intend." (Rom. 7:19)

If you starve a lion, you so weaken it that you can master the beast. Fasting starves the passions and so weakens their power that it becomes possible for your reason and will to gain the upper hand in your life.

Lastly, you can almost say that fasting is a physical necessity. More graves are dug by knives and forks than by accidents. So, thousands of people diet or go to health clubs. Fasting is not so strenuous and difficult as dieting and exercising, yet it is more rewarding; for it not only slims the body, but it also shapes the soul.

Mark's gospel tells of five conflicts between Jesus and the Scribes and Pharisees. The third clash was over fasting (Mk. 2:18-22). Our Lord did not attack fasting – but only the way the Scribes and Pharisees fasted.

You must fast, but never to lord it over others who do not fast (Lk. 18:9-14).

You must fast, but not to be seen by men, to show off (Mt. 6:16-18).

You fast to atone for past sins. When you do, fasting is called "penance."

You fast to make up for the sins of others. When you do, fasting is called "reparation."

You fast to gain future strength in the struggle against the world, the flesh and the devil. When you do, fasting is called "mortification." Mortification opens up the heart to God and to others and disposes you to follow the dictates of your reason illumined by faith.

So important is fasting that Jesus began His public life with it. It empowered Him to conquer the temptations of the devil. He is the Way.

There is another kind of fasting we can do. It is this: pick out two days each week for no television. Replace the time with family games, family prayer, family Bible reading, visits to friends and shut-ins, letter writing.

One day, Our Lady, in asking the seers to prepare for Christmas, said, "I tell you, turn off your television sets, your radios, and follow the program set by God of meditation, prayer and reading the Gospel; foster the development of faith" (1984). She promised such a preparation would bring them the merriest Merry Christmas.

From "Our Lady Teaches About Prayer at Medjugorje"

(4/91)
The Rosary
By Fr. James Peterson

Recently, I was talking to a woman who came to pray to Mary when she was a Protestant. She said as a child she had one relative – a Catholic – who was most gentle and loving, and who taught her to say the "Hail Mary." She found it very comforting.

She also found that she came to a sense of mystery, of awe, of reverence for the Holy Eucharist. Her desire to worship included a desire for sacramental life.

Eventually, she came to learn the Rosary. And more eventually, she knew she should be a Roman Catholic, and was received into the Catholic Church.

Some of her Protestant friends were bewildered. They had many problems with what she was doing. A number of their questions were about Mary and the Rosary.

She explained that "praying" to Mary was not apart from God. Mary's role is to intercede. As she could ask friends on earth to pray for her, she could ask friends in Heaven to pray for her. It is comforting to have part of our prayer group in Heaven.

But then one of them asked, "How can you keep repeating all those words in the Rosary?" And she said, "That's background music." You don't think of every word, but you have a quiet peace-of-mind in which you are able to focus on God, His love for us, His dealing with us.

Certainly, I have known people who learned inner-quiet through the Rosary. And I have known people who learned mental prayer through the Rosary.

And I see the Rosary not simply as a duty, nor as a technique of learning prayer – but as a powerful instrument to open up the kingdom of Heaven to our present understanding, and as a means of showing how the events (the "mysteries") of our lives prepare us to love externally.

Beyond that, it is a means of holding hands with Our Lady, of sharing Her power and intentions in regard to peace in the world, and in our hearts and homes and our parishes and our neighborhoods.

(2/95)
Consecrate Yourself Daily

In the monthly October 25, 1988 message, Our Lady invited us to consecrate ourselves to the Heart of Jesus and to Her Immaculate Heart. Why not begin today to fulfill Her wish by praying the prayer of Consecration to the Sacred Heart of Jesus and the Immaculate Heart of Mary.

"Therefore, little children, I am inviting you today to the prayer of consecration to Jesus, my dear Son, so that each of you may be His. And then I am inviting you to the consecration of my Immaculate Heart. I want you to consecrate yourselves as parents, as families and as parishioners so that all belong to God through my heart."

**Statue of the Sacred Heart of Jesus in Fr. Jozo's former
church in Tihaljina
Photo credit: Diana Stillwell**

Prayer of Consecration to the Sacred Heart of Jesus

Jesus, we know that You are merciful and that You have offered Your Heart for us. It is crowned with thorns and with our sins. We know that You implore us constantly so that we do not go astray. Jesus, remember us when we are in sin. By means of Your Heart make all men love one another. Make hate disappear from amongst men. Show us Your love. We all love You and want You to protect us with Your Shepherd's Heart and free us from every sin. Jesus, enter into every heart! Be patient and never desist. We are still closed because we have not understood Your Love. Knock continuously, O Good Jesus, make us open our hearts to You at least in the moment we remember Your Passion suffered for us. Amen. (Imparted by Our Lady to Jelena Vasilj on November 18, 1983)

Prayer of Consecration to the Immaculate Heart of Mary

O Immaculate Heart of Mary, ardent with goodness, show Your Love towards us. May the flame of Your Heart, O Mary, descend on all mankind. We love You so. Impress true love in our hearts so that we have a continuous desire for You. O Mary, humble and meek of heart, remember us when we are in sin. You know that all men sin. Give us, by means of Your Immaculate Heart, spiritual health. Let us always see the goodness of Your maternal Heart and may we all be converted by means of the flame of Your Heart. Amen.
(Imparted by Our Lady to Jelena Vasilj on November 28, 1983)

(10/92)
Discipline
By Joan Wieszczyk

Discipline is a very important fact in the messages of Medjugorje. Without disciplining oneself, you resist the true meaning of it. Discipline in itself requires much training. "Giving up" is discipline. At first it seems hard. At times we fail and begin to look for excuses. It takes a lot of guts and determination to continue. The more often we practice discipline, the stronger we become.

Prayer and fasting are two important parts of the message from Our Lady of Medjugorje. Fasting, like prayer, takes a lot of discipline.

When wanting to pray from the heart, either with a group or by oneself, you must find time. You must "give up" time you would use otherwise.

The same goes for fasting. We must "give up." We have to learn to discipline ourselves. Once we accomplish this task, we will be able to help others to do likewise. How? Simply by our example. Someone needs to be the example. Why not us?

We should discipline ourselves first by "giving up" mortal sin. Then we must become stronger by working on our venial sins. Go to confession often to rid ourselves of these sins.

Just as prayer is a daily requirement, we can make fasting from sin a daily requirement.

Mary is asking us to become Her disciples, Her followers. She wants us to spread the messages of Medjugorje. These messages are simply the Gospel. If we want to be Mary's disciples, we must discipline ourselves. Notice how closely these two words are related-discipline and disciples.

It seems like She wants us to give of our whole selves so that we can give ourselves wholeheartedly to Jesus.

For almost 12 years, Mary has been coming down from Heaven to teach us how to discipline ourselves. She wants us to become like little children again - Her "dear children." She is a loving mother, teaching us about discipline. She herself does not discipline. Instead She wants us to discipline ourselves. By this, She is asking us to "give up" something on Wednesdays and Fridays, preferably food. In other words, to live on bread and water. On those days, let your hunger and thirst be for the Lord. In this hunger, you may find yourself wanting to participate more often at daily Mass. "Happy are those who come to His supper."

All in all, when one learns to discipline oneself, then and only then, can the message of Medjugorje become alive in your life.

In the Gospel we learn that "Jesus must increase and we must decrease." This can come about when we practice the virtue of discipline which is an important part of the message of Medjugorje.

(6/96)
Family Altars
By Joan Wieszczyk

The messages of Medjugorje have to hit home. Why don't we begin now in this 15th year of the apparitions. Let's take them seriously and place them in our hearts. Is it not true, that the home is where the heart is? Then, let's make our homes a home where the King and Queen of Peace reign.

Fr. Jozo reminds us all to set up family altars. In this way, your family and friends can be at ease when they can feel the Holy Spirit's presence as they enter into your home.

Please tell all families to set up family altars. On this altar in your home do the following:

1. Place a family cross.
2. Below the cross, place a picture of Mary who stood beneath the cross, and was given to us there by Our Precious Savior.
3. Place your weapon – the Rosary on the altar.
4. Place God's Divine Word – the Bible
5. Place holy water to remind you of your Baptism.
6. Bless yourselves and your homes often with holy water, for this is our clothing of protection.
7. Families, please use your altars!

A family altar
Photo credit: Carolanne Kilichowski

(1/89)
You Need To Pray
By Rev. Albert Shamon

Because we do not see the value of prayer, we say we have no time for prayer.

First, *we need to pray, because our salvation depends on it.* St. Alphonsus Ligouri said, " If I had only one sermon to preach. I'd preach it on prayer." "For," he said, "if you pray, you will be saved; if you do not pray, you will be lost."

Someone put it this way in rhyme:

If you pray well, you'll live well.

If you live well, you'll die well.

If you die well, you won't go to hell.

And if you don't go to hell, then all is well.

The plight of the world today and the victories of Satan in the world can be attributed to the single fact that we are relying too much on our own resources – ourselves, our sciences, our technologies – and not at all on prayer.

Yet, St. Paul warned us, "Our battle is not against human forces, but against principalities and powers and the evil spirits in regions above. You must put on the armor of God…at every opportunity, pray…" (Eph. 6:12-13,18)

When we do not pray as Our Lady asked, we are fighting without the armor of God. We are defenseless and vulnerable, sitting ducks for Satan. And he, with his angelic powers, is making fools out of us. Believe it or not, he even has Satan worshippers in this supposedly so enlightened nation of ours.

Prayless, one becomes Godless, one can turn to demons. This is actually happening here in America.

"In America," wrote *Mike Warnke, "about eighty different occults are practiced… tarot cards, astrology, witchcraft, reincarnation, astral projection, ESP, thought transfer,… an estimated 40 million Americans consult the horoscope, aided by 10,000 professional and 175,000 part-time astrologers who make astrology a $200 million-a-year business. Also, about five million people plan their entire lives by their daily horoscope and won't even get out of bed before consulting it."* (**The Satan-Seller**, p.84)

Hence, the urgency of Our Lady's call to prayer. Prayer has no sword nor saber/No mighty bayonet/Threats not to crush its neighbor 'neath its heal'/And yet, when all else fails, prayer prevails.

It is significant that Mike Warnke, a former Satanist high priest, was able to break his ties to Satan, only through prayer – his own prayers, and especially those of his devout wife Sue.

Mike advised:

"Fight fire with fire. Go directly to the greatest source of supernatural power of all. Pray, pray for all of us… and also pray for specific people involved in the occult…" (Idem, p.213)

"Pray - pray - pray – Jesus is the only effective answer to those who want deliverance from the occult...Don the full gospel armor, pray, and ask others to pray that He will guide you. He will!" (Idem, p.213)

Secondly, *we pray to meet God.*

Why did the Wise Men follow a star? Was it not to find God? Why does Our Lady appear at Medjugorje? To lead us to Christ.

That is why prayer requires time. We pray to meet God, but we must pray long and often in order to become friends with God. Aristotle said, "To become friends, you must eat a bushel of salt together." At every meal, you eat at most only a pinch of salt. To eat a bushel of salt would require countless meals together. What Aristotle meant, then, was that forming a friendship demands countless encounters together. Likewise, intimacy with God demands continuous prayer.

Thirdly, *we pray to be changed.*

St. Thomas wrote, "You pray not to make your needs known to God, but to make known to yourself your need for God."

"You pray not to change God's mind, but to change your mind to His."

"You pray not to move God to do your will, but to be moved to do God's will."

If prayer is not changing you, then you are not praying well. Our Lady asked, "Why are you praying? To be with God, to experience, God within. After five minutes of prayer something ought to happen within you, if you do it properly."

Lastly, *we pray to open up the hearts of sinners.*

In our prayers, we should pray for the opening of hearts gripped by sin. On April 18, 1985, Our Lady said, "Dear children...pray so that the hearts which are under the burden of sin may open up. I so desire it." Our Lady requested such prayer from Mirjana, perhaps because at the University of Sarajevo, she no doubt was having firsthand experience of atheism.

Our Lady begged for prayers for unbelievers and atheists, because as She said to Mirjana, "They are my children too, and I suffer much because of them." She suffers especially for them, for She knows the hell to which their atheism can lead them. Thus, Our Lady went on, "If they only knew what would happen to them, if they are not converted. Mirjana, pray for them." (3/18/85)

Our Lady is asking us to have both Jesus' and Her scope of vision in prayer: to pray for everybody, especially sinners. She made the same request at Fatima when She asked us to pray after each decade of the Rosary: "O my Jesus, forgive us our sins. Save us from the fires of hell. Draw all souls to Heaven, especially those most in need of Your mercy" – namely, poor sinners.

From "Our Lady Teaches About Prayer at Medjugorje"

(11/96)
The Holy Souls
By Brother Craig Driscoll

Dear Children,

During the month of November people pray especially for their relatives and friends who have died. We call these people the "Holy Souls." They are in Purgatory "getting ready" to go to Heaven. In Purgatory they are being made perfect. It's kind of like getting all cleaned up after working in the garden before going to a very special party. The only thing is, the Holy Souls are really in a hurry to go to Heaven, but they have to wait. So we pray for them so they won't mind waiting so much. It's kind of like that. So this November let's pray for the Holy Souls.

Until next time, may Our Blessed Mother bless you.

Editor's note: We include this article as it has such a simple explanation of Purgatory for those who may not be familiar with it. To expand on what Br. Craig wrote, we would like to add that Our Lady has asked us to pray DAILY for the Holy Souls though, not just in November.

(8/91)
Make My Heart Like Unto Thine
By Joan Wieszczyk

Jesus and Mary want to change your heart. They want to create a new one in each and every one of us – a heart full of peace, love and joy.

Mary wants to take your heart and change it into the heart of Jesus. Jesus wants to take your heart and change it into the heart of Mary.

Do you know of anyone who has had a transplant? How about someone with a pace maker or a heart by-pass? Perhaps you yourself have survived a heart attack. Traumatic experiences such as these require the person to change his or her lifestyle in order to survive. Most are happy and thankful for having been given another chance. It's time to appreciate the gift that God gave each and every one of us. It's the gift of life!

Sr. Claire Marie of the Oasis of Peace was right when she said that "Medjugorje is a hospital and Mary has the prescription." Better still, Mary is the prescription, for it is "through Mary to Jesus."

Ask anyone who has been to Medjugorje if they found peace in that holy place. People don't go there just to have their Rosaries change to gold or witness the miracle of the sun. These are only a tranquilizer compared to the real thing. For many, Medjugorje is a bit of Heaven on earth. It is there where a person experiences a "change of heart." It is there where one gets a spiritual heart transplant, a spiritual pacemaker, or a spiritual by-pass and a time of grace. In other words, another chance. For this to happen, your whole lifestyle must change.

Anyone who has been to Medjugorje and hasn't had a change of heart is risking his or her spiritual life. They may even lose their souls.

As mentioned before, the prescription for a change of heart comes from Mary. If followed, it is a guarantee to a new life (Heaven).

Some people need a refill. They go back to Medjugorje for it. Those of us who have been there are required to be witnesses to this miraculous cure. Not only that, but we are told to pass it on to others. Let them have the cure.

The good news is that you don't have to travel to Medjugorje. You can get the same prescription here. It never changes. All you have to do is follow it. Following it means living it – living the five-part message of Medjugorje. So put your whole heart in it. Make your heart a heart like Jesus and Mary. Make it a faithful heart.

1st – PUT GOD #1 IN YOUR LIFE. Be Christian in everything you do. If you're Catholic, be a good Catholic. Remember to follow the Vicar of Christ on earth, the Pope. If you're of another faith, do the best you can.

2nd – HAVE A FORGIVING HEART. Go to confession at least once a month. Dump the trash in your life. Get rid of the grouchiness, impatience and ill temper. Forgive those who have hurt you. Remember to ask forgiveness. If you don't forgive, how can God forgive you?

3rd – HAVE A PRAYING HEART – Pray, pray, pray from your heart, not just rattling off some words. Know and truly mean what you are praying. Take time for yourself and absorb the Word of God as you read the Bible. Carry your Rosary, the spiritual weapon, so you can pray and meditate on the mysteries. The greatest prayer one can have is going to daily Mass.

4th – HAVE A LOVING HEART – Self-discipline yourself for the love and glory of God. Begin fasting on bread and water on Wednesday and Friday. Fasting is a sacrifice and a proof of true love. Christ sacrificed His life for us. Can't we sacrifice a little for Him? We can – by our fasting.

5th –HAVE A PEACEFUL HEART – Each day, offer everything you do or say. Give your heart to Jesus and Mary. Remember to live the message of Medjugorje, for then only can come true "peace." Share with others the peace that comes from above.

Just a reminder that the clock is ticking. The "time of grace" is NOW!! Take this grace which is given to us by the Mother of God who is "full of grace" and use it for what it is worth…

A CHANGE OF HEART !!!

(8/91)
Intercession
By Fr. James Peterson

Among the most basic of Mary's instructions to the modern world is the need of intercession – for souls, for conversion of sinners, for the conversion of all the sinners of the world. And we who are asked to pray are included among those prayed for. We have sinned – in thought, word, deed, and omission.

We need, then, to look again at what it means to intercede.

In a human relationship, if someone is in legal trouble and wants to find a person to intercede for him, what does he look for in an intercessor? A person who is somehow approachable, who will have enough concern to find time for the person in trouble, to investigate his or her needs, to listen to the reasons for hope or understanding, to hear the promises of the future. Then the one who is interceding must be able to approach the judge or the council or whoever has the problem. The more status he has with the judge, the more effective is the intercessor.

Therefore, when someone asks you to pray for him, he must think you have stature with God - and are concerned enough about the needy person to take time and use effort in his behalf.

And if Mary asks you to pray for others, She must think you have stature with God. For you to intercede effectively you must believe you have stature with God. Otherwise, you pray without confidence, and your prayer is not heard – does not even pierce the clouds.

Jesus says where we are gathered in prayer He is in the midst of us. To be in the same room or the same pew or the same hymn does not mean we are together. We need to accept one another, to be open to one another, to share entrance into the consciousness of God.

But then what stature we have! Jesus says, "He who hears you, hears Me." That's people. That's God.

When we say the Rosary, we are joined with Mary. When we say it together, Christ is in the midst of us. What stature! With what daily responsibility and with what confidence, we ought to pray, "Lead all souls to Heaven."

Sinners, praying for all sinners, now in Christ, in union with the saints and angels. With great confidence as we approach. God has loved us in Christ, before the foundation of the world.

Let us pray.

Couple getting blessed by Fr. Jozo with the cross

(1/89)
Marriage and the Cross in Croatia

Below are excerpts from a conference given by Father Jozo, pastor of St. James Church in 1981 when the apparitions of the Blessed Mother started in Medjugorje. He is now pastor of St. Elias Church, a short distance away, and frequently addresses pilgrims who make the "side trip" to his parish.

"...You are currently in a country where people get married according to a particular custom. When a couple decides to get married, they buy a cross. At the wedding ceremony, the priest blesses the cross. While the priest still holds the cross, the couple join their hands and hold the other part of the cross and pronounce their vows for the sacrament of marriage. They kiss the cross, take it home, and place it in a designated spot. This spot becomes where they pray. Everybody looks at the cross when leaving or entering the house. Children, too, learn to look at the cross. And the cross gives strength. Daily life is organized in such a way that prayers are always said in front of this cross of the marriage. And this is the place, in front of the cross of marriage, where husband and wife come for a reconciliation and ask forgiveness from one another after a fight.

"...The wedding vows get strengthened in front of the cross of the marriage. When children and/or hard times come, one can talk or cry in front of the cross. Husband or wife would not think of abandoning their spouse, for they would also be abandoning Jesus. For it is from the cross that comes the sacrament of marriage. And it is in front of the cross that one keeps the vows.

"We do not know divorce in this country. I can't even imagine how it can happen. Since marital love is based on Jesus, how could it disappear since Jesus and the love of Jesus are the basis of the sacrament of marriage? There are unfortunately few Christian families in this world. There can't be a Christian family unless that family prays together. And when they don't, they don't grow spiritually.

"...Everyone receives many spiritual gifts from God, and two-thirds of these gifts are grown in the families. Why is there such a lack of charity in people's hearts? Because families don't pray together. That's why the Virgin Mary wants to create a new family on the same principle as in Medjugorje. She wants to create it all over the world. For that which exists any more in the families, the Virgin Mary wants to happen in Medjugorje when people of different cultures, races, from all over the world pray together and tell everybody, 'I learned to pray at Medjugorje...I felt love...I saved my marriage'."

(2/90)
From the Heart
By Hubie Mule

We need to take time in our lives to pray. Our heavenly Mother is pleading for our help in the battle against evil. Mary has been in God's plan from the very beginning. "I will put enmity between thee and the Woman, and between thy seed and Her seed; She shall crush thy head, and thou shall lie in wait for Her heel." (Genesis 3:15) Mary's role is great in the salvation of souls. Mary's message of Feb. 13, 1986, Medjugorje: "Turn off the television and renounce other things which are useless."

I was a "TV hound" until I read this message of Our Lady in Medjugorje. When I realized that it would be impossible to live the messages while spending 3-4 hours in front of the TV every day, I turned it off. It has been three years since I've wasted time with the TV.

Jelena, who receives inner locutions from Our Lady, once saw Satan, in a thoughtful mood, think, "I will entice others with several films, so that after Mass, they will rush home to watch TV."

In the meditations for spiritual growth in the Vatican II Weekday Missal we find when Seattle had no newspaper or TV, suicides there dropped 43 per cent... *The whisper of the Holy Spirit cannot be heard above the radio and TV."*

I feel that Jesus is telling us that TV leads to lewd and sensuous living. The permissiveness suggested on TV may lead one to separation or divorce, pre-marital sex, incest, drugs, filthy language, alcohol, laziness and most importantly, away from God and the salvation of the soul.

Children are our treasures. Each is like an unpolished gem. Parents have the responsibility to polish their gems and make them shine. Don't let TV be the polishing stone.

In Medjugorje on July 29, 1986, Fr. Tomislav Vlasic said, "We are all aware of the fact that if the world carries on as it is doing, it will end up in total ruin, and for this no message from Heaven is needed."

Mirjana, who received the tenth secret on December 25, 1982, said, " If God did not give me His particular help, I would go mad." Why? She replied, " because I know what will happen in the world and men are behaving as if God did not exist. They offend Him."

When we turn on the TV indiscriminately, we are inviting Satan into the front door of our homes. Don't let TV ruin you. If you are serious about your conversion, prayer, fasting and the eternal salvation of your children, put God first in their lives. Turn off offensive TV programming and turn on Jesus Christ.

The Medjugorje Star, July, 1989

Pilgrims praying on Apparition Hill

(7/97)
Be Still
By Msgr. James Peterson

One of the most recurrent requests of Our Lady at Medjugorje is for prayer of the heart. That's not simply of the lips nor simply of the mind – though it can involve both of them.

But prayer of the heart means getting inside oneself and letting one's response to God come from deep within.

And that requires some interior quiet. Confusion, rushing, "to get prayer in," pressuring to get on to something else – these things all arrive at superficiality.

When Habakkuk, a prophet, speaks for Yahweh, he says, "Be still and know that I am God." That applies certainly to interior quiet. But it applies also to exterior quiet. Everyone devoted to Jesus and Mary comes to know the need of quiet. Sometimes, some places, it is essential.

I work much in prisons and have long known that one of the most difficult aspects of imprisonment is the lack of peace, the lack of quiet. For me, I think it would be the difficult part of the punishment of being incarcerated.

If you are not in prison, when you put your mind to it, you can find time and place for quiet. Every day you need it; you can find it.

Without it, it's not likely that you will have prayers of the heart. Without that, it is unlikely that you will be sharing in bringing to the world the peace that we all long for.

(10/91)
Who Says the Rosary is Boring?

Too often people say they find the Rosary boring. Sometimes a simple change in approach can do wonders to add zest to something we consider a chore. If you're in a "Rosary Rut" and don't think you're getting much out of it, think about what you're putting into it instead. When you put yourself into the Rosary, you'll receive profound revelations and a deeper understanding of the Mysteries, of God, and of the greatest mystery of all – yourself. You'll discover answers to your problems. Here are some suggestions that just might awaken your interest and stimulate your zeal in praying Our Lady's perfect prayer for peace:

1. Find a book with beautiful pictures of the Meditations. Look at the pictures. Don't try to direct your thoughts as you say the prayers. Soon you'll find yourself falling in love with Jesus, Mary, Joseph, and all the "characters" in the unfolding drama of their lives here on earth. Perhaps later you'll be

able to identify with them. Who knows where this may lead you. Be open.

2. Make up your own mental images (without a book) and move the "characters" around in your mind's eye in their different roles as though you are the producer of a play.

3. Pour out your love in the individual prayers. Say each prayer sweetly and lovingly, like a caress. Make each "Hail Mary" say "I love you." Make it beautiful to Our Lady's ears. Imagine making Her smile, loving you in return.

4. Reverse #3 and feel Her tender motherly love being poured into your very being. Let it penetrate and warm your heart. Now it's your turn to smile!

5. Do the same as #3 and #4 while saying the prayers to Jesus, to Our Father, and/or to the Holy Spirit.

6. Picture yourself in the role of Jesus – how He must have felt in the security of His Mother's arms on the day He was born, how He felt when He was with His daddy Joseph, when He was condemned, when Veronica wiped His face, etc.

7. Do the same as #6 by picturing yourself as Mary, Joseph, Simon of Cyrene or any of the other people involved in Our Savior's life, death and resurrection.

8. Relate the events in the mysteries to events in your own life, in the life of the Church, or in the life of the world.

9. Make comparisons. For instance, using Mary as the perfect model of wife and mother, ask yourself how well you emulate Her, where you fall short, what you can do to improve. How does your family stack up to the Holy Family? Is there something you can do to improve your family situation? Think about Joseph as husband and father. What can you learn from him?

10. Read Rosary meditations from the many books available and use these meditations as a starting point.

11. Use the prayers as "background music" while meditating on the mysteries and allowing your mind to wander in and out of the unfolding dramas.

12. Use any combination of these suggestions. Try different methods at different times depending on your mood and time-frame.

13. Think about why you're saying these prayers and to whom. Think about all Our Lady and Jesus do for you and acknowledge how little a token of your love, the Rosary is, compared to what they offer you.

14. Think about the Rosary as being your share in God's plans for peace, salvation.

15. Pray the meditations and prayers quietly, listening for whatever the Lord or Our Lady may be saying to your heart through the "listening" Rosary.

16. In the Joyful Mysteries think about the joy, beauty and purity of Jesus, Mary and Joseph; in the Sorrowful Mysteries what we did to destroy that; in the Glorious how our God goes on forgiving and loving us despite ourselves, how He restores to us the joy, beauty and purity we lost through sinfulness. Are we prepared to do the same for those who offend us?

17. Think of the mysteries in light of the Gospel.

18. Think of the mysteries in light of Our Lady's messages from Medjugorje.

19. Think of the grace you'll receive. Watch your life and the lives of those around you grow as a result of your perseverance in praying the Rosary.

20. Think of the Rosary as a powerful tool to ward off evil.

21. Make up your own ideas. This list is just the beginning. The sky's the limit!

22. If you can't do any of the above, do it as an act of discipline and offer it up as penance for the salvation of sinners and for peace in our hearts, homes, Church and world. Do this anyway in addition to any of the above.

BORING? WHO SAYS THE ROSARY'S BORING? IT'S ONLY AS BORING AS YOU MAKE IT.

Center for Peace, Concord, MA (closed as of 1/89)

(8/90)
Distraction in Prayer

Before beginning your private prayer, you might want to invite Our Lady, your patron saint, your guardian angel, the patron saints of those you pray for, etc., to join you. In this way, you are forming your own spiritual prayer group. You can also ask Our Lady to help you pray devoutly. If you are distracted, you can offer your unintentional distractions in love, and ask Our Lord to accept them as devout prayers. If you're distracted when praying the Rosary, just continue, and offer your Rosary to Mary with your distractions as a child would offer a bouquet to its mother. Even if imperfect, it is offered with LOVE.

Queen of Peace Center Update, Dallas, Texas

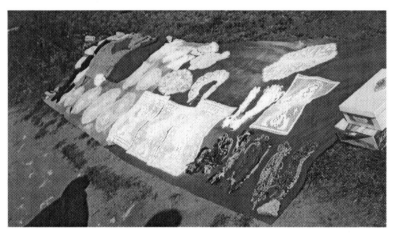

Hand-made Rosaries for sale on the path to Apparition Hill

(10/97)
Sharing the Rosary
By Msgr. James Peterson

Recently I spent a morning with inmates in a State Prison, discussing with them the means of sustaining a spiritual life while incarcerated. They wanted especially to discuss the Rosary. We broke into groups of five for discussion. I wondered how long a time to allow- fearing they might have too little to say. At the end of a half hour, all the groups were still vigorous and intent.

The report-backs were impressive. All of them were aware that the Rosary lifted them – from the edges of discouragement, from being immersed in the exterior dullness of a given day. It helped them to see how Joseph and Mary and Jesus entered into the events of their own lives, the mysteries God had prepared for them.

After the main report-back, I was talking to an elderly inmate. He was peaceful, but very thoughtful. The Gospel at the Mass we had shared was the parable of the master who had entrusted his servants with 5,000 silver pieces, and 2,000, and 1,000. The one who had received the 1,000 buried them because of fear. The master on his return punished him severely. With this on his mind, the man said to me, "You know someday us Catholics are going to have to answer for burying the Rosary. God has entrusted it to us. It is powerful and does so much for anyone who uses it. It doesn't belong only to Catholics. We deserve to be punished if we hide it."

That's part of the message.

Mary calls us to know the power of the Rosary, to use it, to share it.

Peace will come as an answer to prayer. That's the message.

(9/88)
Forgiveness Prayer
By Fr. Robert De Grandis, S.S.J.

Forgiveness is central to Christian faith. Remember what Jesus said as He was dying on the cross. "Father, forgive them..." Often, a prayer such as this one will bring to mind other areas that need forgiveness. Let the Holy Spirit move freely and guide your mind to persons or groups that you need to forgive.

Lord Jesus Christ, I ask today to forgive EVERYONE in my life. I know that You will give me the strength to forgive and I thank You that You love me more than I love myself and want my happiness more than I desire it for myself.

Father, I forgive YOU for the times death has come into my family, hard times, financial difficulties, or what I thought were punishments sent by You and people said "It's God's will," and I became bitter and resentful towards You. Purify my heart and mind today.

Lord, I forgive MYSELF for my sins, faults and failings, for all that is bad in myself or that I think is bad, I forgive myself; and I accept Your forgiveness.

I further forgive MYSELF for taking Your name in vain, not worshipping You by attending church, for hurting my parents, getting drunk, for sins against purity, bad books, bad movies, fornication, adultery, homosexuality. Also, for abortion, stealing, lying, defrauding, hurting people's reputation. You have forgiven me today, and I forgive myself. Thank You, Lord, for your grace at this moment.

I also forgive MYSELF for any delvings in superstition, using ouija boards, horoscopes, going to séances, using fortune telling or wearing lucky charms, I reject all that superstition and choose You alone as my Lord and Savior. Fill me with Your Holy Spirit.

I truly forgive my MOTHER. I forgive her for all the times she hurt me, she resented me, she was angry with me and for all the times she punished me. I forgive her for the times she preferred my brothers and sisters to me. I forgive her for the times she told me I was dumb, ugly, stupid, the worst of the children or that I cost the family a lot of money. For the times she told me I was unwanted, an accident, a mistake or not what she expected, I forgive her.

I forgive my FATHER. I forgive him for any non-support, any lack of love, affection, or attention. I forgive him for any lack of time, for not giving me his companionship, for his drinking, arguing and fighting with my mother or the other children. For his severe punishments, for desertion, for being away from home, for divorcing my mother or for any running around, I do forgive him.

Lord, I extend forgiveness to my SISTERS AND BROTHERS. I forgive those who rejected me, lied about me, hated me, resented me, competed for my parents' love, those who hurt me, who physically harmed me. For those who were too severe on me, punished me or made my life unpleasant in any way, I do forgive them.

Lord, I forgive my SPOUSE for lack of love, affection, consideration, support, attention, communication, for faults, failings, weaknesses and those other acts or words that hurt or disturb me.

Jesus, I forgive my CHILDREN for their lack of respect, obedience, love, attention, support, warmth, understanding; for their bad habits, falling away from the church, any bad actions which disturb me.

My God, I forgive my IN-LAWS, MY MOTHER-IN-LAW, FATHER-IN-LAW, SON/DAUGHTER-IN-LAW AND OTHER RELATIVES by marriage, who treat my family with a lack of love. For all their words, thoughts, actions or omissions which injure and cause pain, I forgive them.

Please help me to forgive my RELATIVES, my grandmother and grandfather, aunts, uncles, cousins who may have interfered in our family, been possessive of my parents, who may have caused confusion or turned one parent against another.

Jesus, help me to forgive my CO-WORKERS who are disagreeable or make life miserable for me. For those who push their work off on me, gossip about me, won't cooperate with me, try to take my job, I do forgive them.

My NEIGHBORS need to be forgiven, Lord. For all their noise, letting their property run down, not tying up their dogs who run through my yard, not taking in their trash barrels, being prejudiced and running down the neighborhood, I do forgive them.

I now forgive all CLERGYMAN, my CONGREGATION and my CHURCH for their lack of support, affirmation, bad sermons, pettiness, lack of friendliness, not providing my family with the inspiration we needed, for any hurts they have inflicted on me or my family, even in the distant past, I forgive them today.

Lord, I forgive all those who are of different PERSUASIONS, those of opposite political views who have attacked me, ridiculed me, discriminated against me, made fun of me, economically hurt me.

I forgive those of different religious DENOMINATIONS AND BELIEFS who have harassed me, attacked me, argued with me, forced their views on me or my family.

Those who have harmed me ETHNICALLY, have discriminated against me, mocked me, made jokes about my race or nationality, hurt my family physically, emotionally or economically, I do forgive them today.

Lord, I forgive all PROFESSIONAL PEOPLE who have hurt me in any way: doctors, nurses, lawyers, judges, politicians and civil servants. I forgive all service people: policemen, firemen, bus drivers, hospital workers and especially repairmen who have taken advantage of me in their work.

Lord, I forgive my EMPLOYER for not paying me enough money, for not appreciating my work, for being unkind and unreasonable with me, for being angry or unfriendly, for not promoting me, and for not complimenting me on my work.

Lord, I forgive my SCHOOLTEACHERS AND INSTRUCTORS of the past as well as the present. For those who punished me, humiliated me, insulted me, treated me unjustly, made fun of me, called me dumb or stupid, made me stay after school, I truly forgive them.

Lord, I forgive my FRIENDS who have let me down, lost contact with me, do not support me, were not available when I needed help, borrowed money and did not return it, gossiped about me.

Lord Jesus, I especially pray for the grace of forgiveness for that ONE PERSON in life who has HURT ME THE MOST. I ask to forgive anyone who I consider my greatest enemy, the one who is the hardest to forgive, the one I said I will never forgive.

Lord, I beg pardon of all these people for the hurt I have inflicted on them, especially my mother and father, and my marriage partner. I am especially sorry for the three greatest hurts I have inflicted on them.

Thank you, Jesus, that I am being freed of the evil of unforgiveness. Let your Holy Spirit fill me with light and let every dark area of my mind be enlightened. AMEN.

The Medjugorje Star May, 1988

(7/90)
Television
By Fr. James Peterson

While I was waiting in a doctor's office the other day, I saw a segment of "Oprah," and was dismayed. She was asking young women about what tricks they use to win men back to them. Their answers were unadulterated trash. The audience, many of them older women, joined in with a kind of acceptance of living together, and moving in and out, and getting even.

What further distressed me was the way the young women and a few young men paraded their escapades for all the public, so that if there had been any real possibility of reconciliation, the television program itself would make reunion almost impossible.

Beyond that, there is sadness in realizing that the hostess or host of the talk show chooses subjects that will get the attention of an audience and hold them. If this is what interests the American public, and if people watch hours and hours of television every week with a kind of uncensored idleness, it is easy to understand why Our Lady came to Medjugorje and not to New York, or New Orleans or San Francisco.

And if Her coming to Medjugorje was intended for the whole world, then one of the great works of any people in America who want to spread Mary's message, is to wage war against television.

How?

For one thing, by self-discipline. One very simple fast for Wednesdays and Fridays is to give up television watching entirely on those days. Another would be to restrict programs - just a few a week, chosen thoughtfully and frugally -some news programs, some with real value of content (though they are rare). With that, there could be a program of reading: Scripture, lives of the saints, and some wholesome classics.

Another way is to talk to others about television-as-a-problem. Children and young people who hold on to television are deprived of many forms of exercise, of creative activity, of responsible interaction with other human beings. Adults forget the presence of others, and lose the joy of sharing little things.

Positively, a home without television has more time for communication, for sharing, for peace of heart, and for a family Rosary. More time for real people. More time for God.

(11/94)
So, What About the Souls in Purgatory?
By Susan Tassone

It all started last October. I was reading a book on Purgatory called *Read Me or Rue It*. I was fascinated with the stories about the Holy Souls and how they help and intercede for those who relieve their sufferings. It said the most powerful thing you can do for Holy Souls to release them from Purgatory is to have a Mass said for them. The Holy Souls need the Precious Blood of Jesus. When the priest raises up the chalice in consecration, we should offer it up for the Holy Souls. The book also said that the souls will repay you 10,000 times over for what you do for them. In other words, they become your intercessors in Heaven.

Our Lady has said many times in Her messages to pray for the Holy Souls. Coming from Our Lady it is good enough for me.

I then decided to have Masses said for the Holy Souls. I proceeded to take up a collection from my colleagues at the office for the Holy Souls. The dollars grew and grew - $200 to $400- then $600, and all the way to $765. Over 100 people of every faith contributed. I was thrilled.

Excitedly, I called my parish priest and told him I wanted Masses, Masses, Masses for the Holy Souls. He told me he could not accept the money. He explained that because of the shortage of priests in the parish it was impossible to have the Masses said since the Mass intentions for the year were booked. I learned this is true in many parishes. However, the priest told me he had recently received a letter from the Missions Office at the Chancery appealing for Mass stipends to be sent to the Missions.

I reluctantly made an appointment with the Director of the Missions Office. To my great surprise, she said Bishops from all over the world send her letters BEGGING for Mass stipends. The Masses would be said quickly for a donation of $5 each. The Director said the Masses are offered by missionary and native priests in Asia, Africa, Central and South America, and the stipend is often the only salary they receive. It also buys the bread for the Holy Eucharist. She also informed me that stipends for Masses had diminished greatly over the past few years, so these Masses were especially welcome. I was ecstatic! I knew this is where Our Lady wanted our donation to go. Over 150 Masses were said for the Holy Souls AND we were supporting the Missionary priests as well! I later received confirmation when I read that God is very pleased when we help the Missionaries. *"And the king (God) answering, shall say to them: Amen I say to you, as long as you did it to one of these my least brethren, you did it to Me."* Did the Holy Souls repay me for my efforts on their behalf? More than I ever could have imagined! The day after the Feast of the Holy Souls (November 3) I was offered a free trip to the Holy Land, then a free trip to Medjugorje, and THEN a new consulting contract which would give me spending money! On December 12, at noon my Rosary links turned to gold as I was praying. I was floored to say the least! The best part of it all is that

I now truly feel the presence of Jesus, Mary and the Holy Souls in my life.

I urge you, as Our Lady has been doing for the past 13 years, to pray, pray, pray for the Holy Souls. When your prayers and Masses release them and they reach Heaven, they, in turn, pray unceasingly for you before the throne of God. They become your most loyal friends in Heaven and will help you on earth and see you safely home to Heaven. Can one ask for more than that?

All of us cannot afford Mass stipends, but we can afford to offer our prayers, the Rosary, Stations of the Cross, the St. Gertrude prayer, lighted candles, ejaculations, and acts of charity for them.

For Masses, write to:

Catholic Mission Office

721 N. LaSalle

Chicago, IL 60610

Website: www.spiritualtreasury.org

Include Mass intention with stipend. Intentions can also be for your own deceased family members, and don't forget yourself.

*Editor's Update: Over $350, 000 has been raised for Mass stipends. Susan likes to think of it as 350,000 souls released from Purgatory. Susan Tassone has brought the Holy Souls to the Vatican and has had the privilege of two private audiences with His Holiness Pope John Paul II. Susan is best selling author of **The Way of the Cross for the Holy Souls in Purgatory, Praying in the Presence of Our Lord for the Holy Souls, The Rosary for the Souls in Purgatory, 30 Day Devotions for the Holy Souls, Prayers of Intercession for the Holy Souls** with Fr. Benedict Groeschel, and Fr. John Grigus of Marytown.*

(10/95)
Making Jesus and His Mother Happy
By Br. Craig Driscoll

Dear Children,

It's October, the month of the Holy Rosary. You can pray the Rosary anywhere- in your room, in the car, or outside while walking.

Do you know where the BEST place to pray the Rosary is? Can you guess? Try. Give up? In church! That's because Jesus lives inside His little house we call the tabernacle. He really lives there. Years ago tabernacles were called "Sacrament Houses" and once in Ireland I saw one with a tall, pointed roof!

He's really there.

Sometimes the priest puts Jesus in what is called a monstrance so that people can see Him. Some churches have Perpetual Adoration. This means people adore Jesus day and night in the monstrance. (No, not the same people; they take turns.)

So during October really try to go to church and pray a Rosary. You'll make Jesus and His Mother very happy.

Until next time, may Our Blessed Mother bless you.

Fr. Slavko speaking to pilgrims

(9/95)
Prayer for Blessing and Healing

This prayer for blessing and healing is said by Father Slavko Barbaric, O.F.M., at St. James Church, Medjugorje:

"Jesus, thank you for this time of prayer. Thank you for Your Presence. Thank you for the time You are spending with us. Now, we ask You to bless us and protect us. Protect Your work in us. Heal our wounds...our souls...heal our love, faith and hope. Heal our spirit of prayer. Heal us from every fear, every negative feeling. Make us holy. Sweet Jesus, take away all that is not holy in us. Bless us and heal us. Thy will be done. Heal our bodies with Your Merciful Hand. Touch every wound we have sustained. We present to You our sufferings for the salvation of the world. Jesus, please heal our families, all relationships between husbands and wives, between parents and children, between young and old. Heal our families and protect the family life, the holiness of our marriages. Protect, oh Jesus, the right to life, the unborn in our families; protect them, oh Jesus. Heal our families; make them holy. We thank You, Jesus. Protect and bless Your Church and keep it holy. Heal Your Church and make it a witness of Your Love and of Your Mercy in this world. Make her a witness and voice for peace. Heal and protect our Church. Heal the world on a spiritual level; protect it from Satan. Do not allow any destruction. Jesus, we ask You to heal all who have asked in Your name. Protect them- be with them to heal them. We believe, oh Jesus, that You have merciful love. Speak one word and our soul and body, our families, our church and the world shall be healed. Jesus, protect us and bless us. You who are Most Holy in the name of the Father, and of the Son, and of the Holy Spirit. Amen."

Editor's note: A psychologist by profession and versed in many languages, Fr. Slavko originally came to Medjugorje to try to discredit the visionaries, but ended up becoming their spiritual director. He was the author of many books on prayer and fasting. He also founded an orphanage called Mother's Village. Fr. Slavko passed away on 11/24/00. The next day Our Lady said in Her monthly message that Fr. Slavko was in Heaven and was interceding for us

(4/95)
Divine Mercy
By Joan Wieszczyk

Medjugorje is known to be an Oasis of Peace. It is no wonder that pilgrims spend hours praying. In Medjugorje they experience a school of prayer. Peace in oneself comes from prayer.

Some have forgotten how to say the Rosary, pray the Stations of the Cross, recite the Act of Contrition, partake in the prayers of the Mass. It is in Medjugorje that they learn how to pray. Included in all these prayers is the Chaplet of Divine Mercy. When I was in Medjugorje, we as a group prayed this prayer together in the Adoration Chapel.

The Divine Mercy prayers were made known by Sister Maria Faustina (Helen Kowalska). During the years 1930-1938, the message of Mercy was given to her. Our Lord appeared to her and revealed the devotion to the Mercy of God. Jesus also revealed to her the ways to ask for mercy on the strength of His Passion.

Today, many of us include this powerful prayer in our daily recitations and meditations. It is known as the Chaplet of Divine Mercy. The time between 3 and 4 o'clock is called the Hour of Mercy. It is at that hour when most of us recite the Chaplet of Divine Mercy.

Jesus told Blessed Faustina that He desired that the first Sunday after Easter be known as the Feast of Mercy. This feast is to be preceded by a novena, which is to begin on Good Friday. The novena should consist of novena prayers and the Chaplet of Divine Mercy.

It was on March 7, 1992, that Sister Maria Faustina was made venerable. Venerable means the first step of 3 degrees to becoming a saint. The process for her beatification began in 1966. It was through the efforts of our present Pope John Paul II. At the time he was still a Cardinal... Cardinal Karol Wojtyla.

If you want to know more about the life of Blessed Faustina Kowalska, you may read her diary, *Divine Mercy – In My Soul*, available from Marian Helpers, Stockbridge, MA 01263.

Formula for Reciting the Chaplet of Divine Mercy:
Using your Rosary beads-
1. Pray one Our Father
   One Hail Mary then the Apostles' Creed. (I believe in God...)
2. On the Our Father beads, say: "Eternal Father, I offer You the Body and Blood, Soul and Divinity of Your dearly beloved

Son, Our Lord Jesus Christ, in atonement for our sins and those of the whole world."

3. On the Hail Mary beads, say: "For the sake of His sorrowful Passion, have mercy on us and on the whole world."

4. End with repeating 3 times this final prayer: "Holy God, Holy Mighty One, Holy Immortal One, have mercy on us and on the whole world."

(2/91)
Importance of Fasting
By Fr. James Peterson

To people in America, one of the most startling aspects of Our Lady's messages at Medjugorje was Her insistence on the importance of fasting.

I don't say Her insistence on fasting. Mary's dealing with the seers is never demanding. When She comes to them She does not require an account of how they have fulfilled Her requests; She does not reprove them. She doesn't take them for granted. They are free. She thanks them for their time, for their generosity.

But She has told them that it is important for everyone to fast twice a week. People who are too sick or too old are not to fast. Their sickness in itself is enough for them to offer. But others should know it is an important discipline for their own growth and a form of prayer and reparation closely related to world peace.

For many of us, to hear any insistence on the importance of fasting is astounding. "Fasting? I thought that was a medieval holdover that we were rid of. And Lent? We don't want to be legalists. We're not sure anymore what is the difference between fasting and abstaining. We think one of them we are supposed to do on Ash Wednesday and Lenten Fridays. But does it bind under pain of serious sin? And who has the right to tell us what to do?"

Mary, the gentle, says bread and water are enough for Wednesday and Friday. She asks that we undertake it willingly and generously and without great scenes of fuss.

For a renewal of spiritual life, we ought to break from the domination of the senses: the constancy of junk food; the dissipation of wall-to-wall music; the fear of being silent and alone without distraction.

Ivan and Vicka say the most important part of the day is the Holy Mass. More than a visit from the Virgin Mary. Much more than the "entertainment" of the crowds.

The Mass is the highlight. Mary's teaching has brought them to that understanding.

In the spirit of Medjugorje, your own Lent should be a freely chosen time of self-discipline, of fasting, of prayer. A time of the primacy of the Mass.

(5/88)
The Our Father

In Medjugorje, not only is our Blessed Mother Mary appearing to the six visionaries (Mirjana, Ivanka, Ivan, Jakov, Marija, Vicka), but She also gives messages without visions (called locutions) to Jelena Vasilj and Marijana Vasilj , who were both ten at the time of the first locution in December, 1982.

This is the way Our Lady taught Jelena and Marijana to pray the Our Father:

OUR – Our Father! That is our Father. Why are you afraid of Him? Extend your hands to Him. Our Father – means: He gave Himself to you as a father. He gave you everything. Do you know that your father does everything for you, and how much more your heavenly Father?

FATHER – Whose father is that? Where is that Father?

WHO ART IN HEAVEN – Father, who are in Heaven, that means: Your earthly father loves you, but your heavenly Father loves you many times more than your father here. Your father becomes angry sometimes, but He doesn't. He only gives you love.

HALLOWED BE THY NAME – In return you must respect Him, for He gives everything to you and is Father to you; you must love Him. You must hallow and praise His name. That is the sign – hallowed be Thy name.

THY KINGDOM COME – That is the sign of our thanks to Jesus. Say to Him: "Jesus, we know nothing without Your Kingdom; we are weak without You. Our kingdom is a disaster. It is perishable, but Yours is not. Bring it to us."

THY WILL BE DONE – O Lord, let our kingdom go to ruins so that Yours becomes true. Let us realize that our kingdom will be ruined so that we immediately at the beginning allow Your will to be done.

ON EARTH AS IT IS IN HEAVEN - That is a sign, Lord, how the angels listen to You, how they respect You. Let us also be able to do that. Let our hearts be opened and enable our hearts to respect You as do the angels. Grant that everything on earth be done as holy as it is in Heaven.

GIVE US THIS DAY – Give us, Lord, bread and food for our soul. Give it to us now. Give it to us today. Give it to us always. Let that bread be food for our soul. Let that bread feed us. Let that bread hallow You. Let that bread be eternal.

OUR DAILY BREAD – Lord, we beg You for our bread. O Lord, let us be able to realize that we will not receive our daily bread without prayer.

AND FORGIVE US OUR TRESPASSES - And forgive us our trespasses. Forgive us, Lord, our trespasses! O, forgive us because we are not good because we are not faithful.

AS WE FORGIVE THOSE WHO TRESPASS AGAINST US - Forgive us because we will forgive those whose sins we were not able to forgive before. O Jesus, forgive us, we beg You! You pray that He forgives your sins as much as you forgive. That would be nothing. It is that which our heavenly Father is saying to you in that word.

AND LEAD US NOT INTO TEMPTATION – Lord, free us from difficult temptations. Lord, we are weak. O Lord, do not let those temptations be ruin for us.

BUT DELIVER US FROM EVIL – Lord, deliver us from evil. Let us feel only a grace in those temptations, only one step into life.

AMEN – Let it be done that way, Lord, and let Your will be done.

Statue on the grounds of the Oasis of Peace Community near Medjugorje

(2/94)
Be an Apostle of the Rosary
By Fr. James Peterson

Recently, I was reading an account of St. Dominic's preaching in the great church of Notre Dame in Paris.

He was already well known to many Parisians because of reports they had heard of his preaching and of his tremendous effectiveness in dealing with heretics. He didn't depend on persuasion nearly as much as he depended on God's grace, and on the intercession of Our Lady to bring torrents of grace into the lives of people with dried up souls.

In wonderful ways, he was the Apostle of the Rosary.

He knew that the faculty of the University of Paris would be there; it was still fashionable for intellectual and professional people to go to church.

He had worked hard on his sermon – not to impress them, but to be able to meet them on their level.

As he was saying his Rosary before the service – a final preparation – Mary came to him and said that the sermon was a good sermon, but that She didn't want him to use it. She wanted him to explain the Rosary as he would explain it to children.

So he told them of Our Lady's instruction; then he started in simple language to explain how to say the Rosary. He didn't say, "There are leaflets at the back of the church." He didn't say, "I assume you know the mysteries." He didn't say, "You know the Our Father and the Hail Mary." He explained them word by word in simple language.

And the power of God was at work.

It would be good for all who take seriously the messages of Our Lady not to stop at encouraging people – or even deciding – on the daily Rosary for everyone. But to go on in individual reflection – or in group discussion – to deal simply with how to say the Rosary.

Not just why, but how.

It can be like starting over. As simply as school children and the young. Those are the ones to whom Mary comes.

(2/91)
Lent
By Joan Wieszczyk

It won't be long before we enter into the 40 days of Lent. In the meantime, many will gorge themselves with food and pleasure, knowing that they will soon try to practice self-sacrifice and control.

Lent is a time of prayer and fasting. Prayer seems much easier than fasting. That's probably because it has been instilled in us since childhood.

I know myself how difficult fasting is. For instance, on Wednesdays and Fridays, it seems that I automatically wake up hungry. Just the aroma of coffee, no matter where I'm at, teases my stomach. Of course, those are the days when I'm usually asked out for lunch or an evening snack with my friends. Nothing wrong with having a piece of pizza – that's bread! Maybe I could fast on another day. What other excuses can I find? So to avoid being hungry on these days, I had the habit of stuffing myself the night before with goodies just so I won't be hungry the next day. I kept asking myself, "Why is it that Wednesdays and Fridays seem longer than the other days?" I know I'll try to keep myself busy, but every now and then the thought of food appears.

Have you ever tried going grocery shopping on these days? Fridays are the days when all the "free samples" are given away. Try passing up the bakery when those "samples" seem to stare right at you. That's when I run out of the store and head off to the bank. Wouldn't you know they seem to be celebrating something, for it's "free cookies and coffee." Why not a Monday, Tuesday, or Thursday?

The evil one is out there to get me. He sure is trying hard to tempt me. By this time, I have to admit my stomach is growling. Could I be hungry? Bread and water do absolutely nothing to curb my appetite. Then a thought, "I'll go without food and wait till midnight. Then I'll satisfy my hunger. After all, I can't go to sleep on an empty stomach."

I must admit, this is how it was in my early days of fasting. Now, knowing what fasting is all about and what good comes out of it, I actually look forward to Wednesday and Friday. It proves to me that I have "will power." That is a gift to me from God. I pray that I get more and more of it. For with it, I can say "no" to food; and a greater impact is when I can say "no" to sin!

The time wasted on thinking about "self," food and hunger can be used in thanking and praising God. He has given so much to us, and it's time we thank Him. It was Our Lady of Medjugorje who told us that prayer and fasting go together. That's where I learned the importance of Lent.

Now I can handle it. Do you remember the saying of Jesus, "Unless you eat the flesh of the Son of Man and drink His blood, you have no life in you; for My flesh is genuine food and My blood is genuine drink?" During Lent, let Jesus be your food and drink. Receive Him often, so you don't go hungry. Ask for the will to fast and pray. Realize how much Jesus loves us. Read the Passion. Go with Mary daily to the cross. Don't hesitate in your mind to climb the mountain and pray the Stations. Above all, live the messages!

Don't wait any longer. Begin now. There is no Resurrection without the crucifixion. In other words, no Easter without Lent.

Make this Lent the best ever, so that when Easter Sunday comes, you can truly rejoice in the words of Jesus- "Peace be with you."

PEACE, PEACE, PEACE. What a joy to have this peace and love in our hearts and to be able to pass it on to others.

(10/91)
Mary's Prayer
By Fr. James Peterson

Recently I shared in a holy hour before the Blessed Sacrament. Our prayer included five decades of the Rosary.

Afterwards, a middle-aged woman, a young grandmother, spoke of the consolation she found in the Rosary, but mentioned that she could look back at a time twenty years ago when "we Catholics" were embarrassed about Mary, and never spoke of Her, and thought that the Rosary was quaint.

I lived through that period. Sadly, it's not over. Recently, when I was talking to a priest about Mary and Fatima and Medjugorje, he said he wasn't interested. He didn't deny them. But he said, "We don't need them; we have so much else."

By God's grace, we have the Holy Trinity and Christ among us. That is magnificent. That we are made aware of that magnificence is one of God's greatest gifts. But we need someone to lead us into the life of God.

That is the basic work of the Church; and Mary - who is part of the Church as well as Mother of the Church – is the means by which God gave Himself to us and continues to lead us to Himself. Time and again, I have dealt with people, even those who were "saved," who found that prayer to Mary opened their eyes and their hearts to the Church – to the sinfulness of their own lives, their need of the prayer of others, and then their responsibility to pray for others.

I have still – through a video – the image of Father Pio fingering his beads in the many Rosaries he said daily. And of Mother Teresa.

Or of Pope John Paul II, kneeling before a statue of Mary and saying his Rosary at Fatima.

Anyone who is too busy to say the Rosary each day is busier than the Pope. Anyone who has "more important" things to do needs to look over his or her priorities.

Those who are great in their own eyes don't make it. God uses the little ones. And the little ones who use the Rosary to come to Mary come to understand how "much else" we have in the Church – the poor, and the real presence of Christ.

(8/91)
What's in a Word
By Phyllis Saunders

MARY – The Mother of God, who is bringing the MESSAGE OF PEACE (MIR)

EXAMPLE – Living the messages from the heart, especially fasting on Wednesday and Friday

DEVOTION – Pray, Pray, Pray the Rosary. Read the Bible. Go to daily Mass, if possible.

JESUS – Our Savior and our Brother

UNITY – One with Jesus and Mary and the Communion of Saints

GOD – Putting God #1 in our lives

OBEDIENCE – Loyalty to the hierarchy of the Church, especially to the Holy Father, the Pope

RECONCILIATION – Confession at least once a month

JOURNEY – Following the path of holiness

ETERNITY – Everlasting happiness with the Trinity, Mary, Angels, and Saints

Pilgrims praying at one of the Stations of the Cross on Mt. Krizevac

(5/96)
Prayer
By Msgr. James Peterson

If you look back over the years of Mary's messages to and through the seers of Medjugorje, it is impressive how many of them are concerned with prayer.

She spent over a month teaching the young people how to say the Lord's Prayer. And in that, She was teaching them the need of priorities.

In prayer we don't rush into God's presence and say, "Help me." "Help our team to win." "Heal me – or someone I love – of cancer."

In an honest relationship, any human being who comes into God's presence needs first to look at God and to praise Him. The saints and angels sing, "Praise and honor and glory and thanksgiving and dominion to our God." Jesus just simplifies it. Say, "Hallowed be Thy name."

And ask for the fulfillment of His kingship on earth, the honest obedience that comes from turning one's will over to God.

Only then do we ask for anything. And we ask not for Cadillac's or cakes – but for bread. Mary warns the children not to be caught up in consumerism. But She says when you ask, ask for what is important. "Lead all souls to Heaven." What a prayer, what a request!

It overwhelms me. And it gives me great confidence about the power of prayer and the reason for it.

(10/96)
Keep in Touch
By Rev. Charles J. Schoenbaechler, C.R.

A few days ago I was called to offer Holy Mass on a cruise ship, so the people were all strangers – about 90. While I was preparing to offer the Mass, they were in the process of praying the Rosary. I noticed that only a very few were fingering their Rosary. It was conspicuous by its absence.

At homily time I told them something they had never heard before. It was also new to me. On the Feast of the Holy Rosary, during meditation, it was given to me. I told them that the Rosary was our Blessed Mother's cellular phone. And like the cellular phone, it is to be carried with us at all times, wherever we go, if it is to be of benefit to us. One never knows when it will be needed. It is the way our Blessed Mother uses to communicate with us as well as our way to communicate with Her.

Little children need their security, it may be an old rag, to be at peace. As children of Mary, the Rosary is our security. With it, Mary keeps in touch with us, and we keep in touch with Her. I offered the Rosary to one of the husbands present, but the wife said it was no use. He would not say it. I told her I did not ask him to pray it – only to carry it with him at all times. Then, in private, I told her to let me know when the miracle happens. Our sense of touch, just the touch of the Rosary, calms and protects us. It is something to hold on to. When I go down the steps I need something to hold on to. The sick and dying person says, "Hold my hand." Mary's Rosary is a cellular phone to touch and hold on to in this valley of tears. When I carry Her cellular Rosary, I can always be in touch with Her, and She is always in touch with me.

Our Blessed Mother was a thousand years ahead of the present day cellular phone!

The Medjugorje Star

Statue and Crucifix in the courtyard in front of St. James Church, Medjugorje

(10/95)
Let Me Dry Your Tears
By a Non-Catholic subscriber

If I promise to pray daily
The Rosary that you love,
Will it comfort you in some way?
Can I ease your grief somehow,
Can I dry your tears,
Can I make you this solemn vow?

You ask for very little
After all you have done.
You agreed to be the Mother
Of God's one and only Son.
You knew well the pain He would
Suffer, and you would feel it all.

When His Body, torn and bloody
With crown of thorns dug in,
You had to watch in silence
Knowing it was for my sin.
You had to watch His suffering
And His loss of dignity.

Most Immaculate Mother Mary
What grief you still withstand,
Not only for that time and place
But the pain is felt daily
As we sin in such disgrace.

Most Immaculate Mother Mary
Queen of Heaven, let me try
To amend some of the evil
That caused your Son to die.
Let me dry your tears of sorrow
Let me hold your hand in mine –
Let me lift the thorns that crowned Him
And return them to their vine.

Chapter 5:

The War

Our Lady comes to Medjugorje with a message of peace. Ten years after She first began to appear in Medjugorje, war came to the area. Generations of problems between the Croatians and Serbs and Muslims needed to be reconciled. In March of 1992, Bosnia-Herzegovnia with Croatians being the majority, voted for its independence. It was recognized by the United Nations in the same year of 1992. The fight started in the early 90's and the civil war brought them murder, concentration camps, and attempts to eliminate the Croatian race by ethnic cleansing,

There is much to be said about the effects of Our Lady's messages of peace, love and conversion - for if people would live these messages war would not exist. Will we ever learn?

Fr. Svetozar Kraljevic, O.F. M.

(5/92)
A Plea for Help

A recent quote from Fr. Svet: "If a war happens, let the people know in America that if we are to die, that here we died peacefully, we are not afraid at this moment, and that we will not be afraid. We could only gain, we have nothing to lose. But, if we die, then there will be many questions unanswered, and many will have to ask, and many will be challenged. And, like always in life, especially in the New Testament, those who did not do anything, or those who were called to do something will be asked for their responsibility, and our destiny will be a judgment against them. But anyway, we are at peace with it. We know those who would like to destroy us, like those 324 churches, will be the losers. We are not afraid or concerned about that. We are the most concerned for those who didn't do anything, and who just out of their naïve attitude or ignorance will be unfortunately judged also."

Editor's note: Fr. Svet, a Franciscan priest who speaks English, gives talks to the pilgrims groups, hears confessions in several languages, does counseling, runs the orphanage, and serves in any other capacity where needed. He has written a number of books about Medjugorje.

(5/92)
Escalation of the War
By Joan Wieszczyk

It was February 29th and March 1st, 1992, when Bosnia-Herzegovina (Medjugorje is included in this area) voted for its independence from Yugoslavia. The majority of those voting were Muslims and Croatians. It's the Serbs who want to remain within the same state as Serbia. They make up about 1/3 of the republic's population. They have the backing of the Yugoslavian Nation army and the weapons. It was Radovan Karadzic – a Serb leader who opposed the recognition of Bosnia-Herzegovina and threatened, "I am afraid that we could not avoid an inter-ethnic war."

Whatever it is – it is very nasty. As this issue of "The Spirit of Medjugorje" goes to press, the war has escalated. The situation in Medjugorje is very tense. The areas around Medjugorje are being pounded terribly. There is a lot of bloodshed. Grenades, bombs, you name it, they do it. Breaking into stores, homes, and setting houses afire. This goes on daily in Citluk.

Most of the people of Medjugorje (women and children) left. Ivanka and Vicka were still there. The people that didn't leave were in shelters. The men are guarding the village. Trenches have been dug and are occupied by the men of Medjugorje, both on the north sides of Apparition Hill, as well as between it and Mt. Krizevac. Evening Mass is held in the basement of the old rectory, which has been sand-bagged for protection. A lean-to type construction has been put up to protect the door from any damage if a shell were to fall in the courtyard outside the building. The Church of St. James is locked to protect individuals. (Within Mostar alone, there are over 10,000 hostile soldiers.) Fr. Philip in Medjugorje said that this is the first time in the history of the Parish of St. James that the Holy Mass was not celebrated in the church. The Blessed Sacrament was removed from the church and placed in the rectory basement! The basement of the rectory served as an air-raid shelter for the parish priests and sisters.

Migs have been circling Medjugorje. A helicopter at night (can be only Yugo-army since they are the only ones who have them) was circling over Medjugorje without lights on. Everyone believes they were filming the lay out of Medjugorje under good moonlight.

North of Medjugorje big explosions caused by bombs have been heard. An unexploded bomb was found on the edge of Citluk. The bombs are the cluster bombs which have been outlawed by the International Convention.

The northwest and southwest sectors of the city of Mostar were under bombardment from the northeast. The Franciscans were directed to leave Mostar under the direction of their provincial. The Cathedral in Mostar and also Fr. Tomislav's church have been hit. The Mostar airport was in flames and completely useless to the Serbians.

Most of Hercegovina is under attack at this printing time.

Fr. Svetozar and 20 sisters were still in the convent. They were unable to leave because of the events around them. Fr. Szetozar has administered the Last Rites of the Church to the sisters and they are at peace.

Sister Janja with Joan Wieszczyk

(5/92)
News from Sister Janja

On the 15th of April, the sisters went for Adoration of the Blessed Sacrament before Mass. The sisters wore their habits, though it is no longer safe to do so.

They no longer have any phone contact with Medjugorje. It is completely cut off and surrounded.

Last night General Periseic, commander of the Federal Army in Mostar, declared on the news that anyone opposing the army would be crushed and buried. Sister Janja said that they pray for him with love and for his children and all the children of their attackers, so that their lives will not be harmed by what their fathers do.

How was it with she and her sisters? "We are a little bit scared, of course, but not as much as we could be. Our consolation is in prayer and in unity with Jesus Christ. And the unity we feel with all of the Body of Christ strengthens us. We are concerned for what may now happen, but not afraid."

Editor's note: Sister Janja is a Franciscan nun who was living in Medjugorje in the early years, but was later sent to Mostar. Through the years she has tended to orphans and other people who have been displaced or otherwise affected by the war.

(7/92)
Fr. Jozo Visits America
By Carla Levis

Fr. Jozo Zovko and Fr. Phillip Pavich arrived in Washington, D.C. from Medjugorje on Wednesday, May 20, 1992. They came to heighten the awareness of the plight of one million, three hundred thousand refugees from Croatia and Bosnia-Herzegovina. The following is a report of the homily given by Fr. Jozo on Sunday, May 24, at the Basilica of the National Shrine of the Immaculate Conception.

At the beginning of the apparitions in Medjugorje, 10 years, 11 months ago, Fr. Jozo was directed by a voice, "Protect the children." That same voice told him, "Protect my people." That is the reason he left his monastery to come to England and America – to find the key to help his people.

In London, he met with diplomats and other influential people. They told him, "We cannot do anything more." In America, he met with politicians. Again, the same response. "We are sorry, we cannot help. We remember Viet Nam. We do not want another war." Fr. Jozo spoke to the politicians of the tens of thousands of people killed and buried in the parks, cadavers left in the street, thousands of people with no food for 20 days and no fresh water for 2 weeks. He told of millions of people who lost their homes and have nowhere to go. One politician commented, "Something is missing here. We have to pray to find a way to help these people. God will inspire us." Father Jozo responded, "We have found the key to the weapon. The weapon is prayer. The weapon is the Rosary."

In his homily at the Basilica, Fr. Jozo suggested that the Shrine of the Immaculate Conception, rather than the White House, be the symbol of America, from which peace and blessings flow. He said that the destiny of the world is in the hands of those who pray. It is necessary for America to be the land of Jesus and Our Lady. He spoke of ecumenism, bringing all people to peace and unity in Jesus' Church.

Americans should read the Bible to bless and sanctify the family. "Do not betray the Bible." He spoke of a time the President of the

U.S. put his hand on the Bible, saying that he would protect the peace. Fr. Jozo felt that he was not speaking the truth.

He said that the prophecy of Genesis is starting to come true. The Blessed Mother is fighting the war against Satan and sin. This is the fight against indifference, against atheism, against murder of the unborn. It is the fight against injustice and violence. When people do not know how to solve these problems, they should place themselves in the service of the Gospa. What people cannot do, God can. Our Lady says over and over, "My dear children, I invite you again to prayer and fasting to stop the war." This will be the "Miracle of the Century."

After a brief tour of the U.S., Fr. Jozo will return to Medjugorje. He will return to war and will accept whatever is in store for him, whether it will be life or death.

Since we cannot now go on a pilgrimage to Medjugorje, he invites us all to make a spiritual pilgrimage of prayer to Medjugorje and bring the key for peace. He cordially thanked the people for this encounter. "Thank you, America, for the New Beginning."

Mary's Newsroom

(7/92)
Medjugorje Relief Flight
March 9-March 16, 1992
By Joan Wieszczyk

It was in January of 1992 that I received a letter concerning a Medjugorje relief Flight- "Journey for Inner Peace" from James M. Hyland, Jr., President of ITS International Tours. A combined pilgrimage-one of aid to the needy and one of a spiritual uplift (inner peace).

I felt the need and wanted to help the tragically wounded country of Croatia and even those villagers in Medjugorje who perhaps needed the kind of medicine and medical supplies that we would bring. Previous to this invitation, many of us sent a substantial amount of money and even some clothing to the Croatian Relief Fund.

In this era of war, I wanted to answer the call of our Mother which was deeply imbedded in me. I wanted to travel to Medjugorje on this Relief Flight. I would not travel alone, so I prayed and asked for a partner. My request was granted. I said "yes" to Mary and began preparing for my trip. It was after I had purchased the needed medical supplies and sent in my payment when I received a letter condemning this very same relief flight. It stated that by traveling JAT Airlines, I would be aiding the enemy with the money I used to get to my destination. In addition, the letter said that the medical supplies were not needed in Medjugorje. I was very confused. The daily reports of the turmoil and war was enough to cope with. I didn't need any more worries. After a few phone calls, I prayed and asked myself, "Why would Fr. Svet send a letter encouraging us to come and bring 2 suitcases – one full of medicine for those who are in need of it? Why would Fr. Pavich, OFM, an assistant at St. James Church in Medjugorje, fax a copy listing the medicine to bring?" I didn't want to be wrapped up in any political affairs. All I wanted was to share my love for those people. I felt their need. Not only were the supplies needed, but our presence would make a big impact. Yes, it was risky to be traveling at this time. We all knew that. The only way was JAT. There was no other airline flying into Croatia.

As we traveled to and from Sarajevo to Medjugorje, I could see that this journey was special. A look at the people signified to us that we became a beam of light and a spark of hope to them. I saw what our "yes" to the Blessed Mother brought. It brought good out of evil. As usual, "She" was protecting us. "She" had it all…all 45 of us in Her mantle, and all the time we were with Her, She kept rewarding us with many blessings and graces.

Never, never doubt the Mother of God. If you are truly called, nothing can stop you. Not even war!!!

Please, let us all try to end this terrible situation by living the messages of Medjugorje. This is the wish of the Croatian people.

Bringing gifts to the children

(7/92)
Medjugorje Relief Flight
Encounter with Fr. Svetozar Kraljevic, OFM

Fr. Svetozar Kraljevic, OFM, thanks the American group of 45 pilgrims that traveled to Medjugorje in March of 1992.

Fr. Svet: "The people in Medjugorje and the priest feel that the more pilgrims that are present, the safer we are over here."

The people in the village are very, very happy to see us. The more people come, the safer they feel. The parish of Medjugorje kept saying, "Always let the pilgrims come."

It would be very inappropriate actually to have the place empty in the time of crisis like this.

Question: Fr., would you like us to tell the people in America to start up the pilgrimages?

Answer: I would like to say that.

Fr. Svetozar speaks to the pilgrims on the bus going to Medjugorje: I would like to assure you as much as words could say, that this pilgrimage, which I call a pilgrimage of love and support, is really something that is not your work or your decision. It is something God would like to do to those people. He would like to touch them. He has no other hands but yours. So God is using your hands... reaching the people He would like to encourage and bless and heal in a special way. I assure you, as much as words could say, that these (monetary) gifts that you gave to Fr. Benedict, to me, and to the parish of Medjugorje, will reach those desolate and the most needy. I assure you of that. So it really doesn't make that much difference if you gave it to Fr. Benedict, to me, or to anyone. It is just the work that God accomplishes in this special way.

This help is wonderful, but your presence is better. The one who gives money is wonderful, but the one who puts himself, like Jesus does, in the midst of that drama of human suffering and human destiny, gives the most!

These days that you spend with us, you don't only give money or the help which you bring, but you give yourself. You put yourself together with us on the cross of the life here these days. We thank you for that. That will be written into the book of the everlasting memory of God. And this is the way I see your pilgrimage. This is the way I see your coming here, your presence. I'm sure you represent the spirit of the Church. In a very special way, you represent the intention and will and love of the Holy Father for the church of Croatia which is suffering so much and so tremendously.

Some 270 churches were destroyed. Convents and monasteries were destroyed. More than 500 cultural, historical monuments destroyed, not to mention the hundreds of thousands of apartments and houses, factories and thousands of lives. The Holy Father has this wonderful love and concern and care. You are the wonderful expression of that concern and care of the Holy Father and the whole Church.

I thank you for that and may God bless you for all that. Enjoy your days and also may you find this pilgrimage easy like the flight and everything that's nice. When you find the troublesome moments, the difficulties, when you lose your bus, or when the bus comes late, or when you get a headache like some people do, when you get hungry and angry, this will be part of your pilgrimage.

Don't get disillusioned in any way. Anything good or bad which you might experience in this pilgrimage is a pilgrimage. There is nothing that could happen to you that is not part of it or should not be part of it. That's the deal you struck with God Himself deciding to come.

Wounds from the war

(11/92)
A Return to Medjugorje
By Valerie K. Peretti

On Thursday, September 10, 1992, I left for my 6th pilgrimage to Medjugorje. Each pilgrimage has added a new dimension, a special meaning to my life. This time the emphasis was on the war, the villagers, the refugees, the sick and the dying.

We embarked on our "mission" via Frankfurt, Germany, Vienna, Austria, Zagreb (formerly Yugoslavia) and finally made it to Split, where we boarded our chartered bus. At 11:23 PM Friday, September 11, the full moon was shining majestically on the mountains and the sea as we began our 3 hour drive down the winding road on our "Journey of Peace" into Medjugorje. It was difficult to imagine that there was war here. The towns nestled in the hills by the Adriatic Sea, touched by some fog, appeared to be jewels on the sea. I felt like the wise men journeying to Bethlehem following their star. We were following our Star of the Sea: Maris Stella – Our Lady. As we journeyed in this country, ravaged by war, we prayed the Rosary, led by our priest, Father Kevin Webster. On 3 occasions we were stopped by border patrols, checking the nature of our entry. On Saturday, September 12, 1992, at 1:00 AM we were finally in Medjugorje.

The village of Medjugorje has been impacted by the war. Many injured people are coming into the village, and refugees have been flooding into Medjugorje. We could hear the bombs and machine gun fire from nearby Ljubuski. We witnessed the fear in the people's faces. They have husbands, brothers, sons, grandsons in the war zones. There is no way of knowing in some cases if relatives or friends in Sarajevo and other ex-Yugoslav areas are alive or dead.

The streets of Medjugorje seem so bare compared to other times, with exception of some villagers, soldiers and priests. Children in groups of 5 or 6 were seen walking arm-in-arm praying their Rosaries. The church yard and confessionals were empty. Shops and restaurants were closed, due to the lack of pilgrims traveling during the war.

As we climbed Apparition Hill, we encountered Tony, a soldier, also his soldier brother from Medjugorje who, with their father and mother (she was climbing in her bare feet as a sacrifice to bring her sons back safely from the war), were climbing the hill to pray as a family before the two young men left for duty to the front line. I gave them each a prayer card with a picture of the Sacred Heart of Jesus. They kissed it and held it close to their hearts. Tony said he and his brother were preparing to leave with other soldiers in Medjugorje. They go to the front lines for 10 days, holding back the aggressors. After 10 days, another group relieves them and they return home. All the soldiers can be seen wearing Rosaries. Tony and his brother wore their Rosaries around their necks and their guns at their side. It is their faith that they will be protected. Not one soldier or civilian from Medjugorje has lost his life in the war since the fighting began on April 7, 1992, when Bosnia's Muslims and Croatians declared their independence. Tony went on to inform us that they have few pilgrims because of the war. Therefore, stores and restaurants have closed, and most of the villagers have had no income since March – right before the war began. We said our farewells, as Tony repeated, "Please pray for us." His father broke down and cried as they resumed their climb on Apparition Hill.

The deep seated faith of these people was conveyed as the villagers, alone and as family, climbed to pray. In deep meditation, they sought refuge on Apparition Hill where the Gospa first appeared to the six visionaries. Their religion, their strong sense of God, is so apparent as they prayed for peace and protection for the safe return of their young men.

A Croatian Mass was celebrated on Sunday, September 13, 1992, on Mt. Krizevac, in honor of the Triumph of the Cross. What a sight to behold! During this time of war, the Cross was surrounded by many soldiers (in uniform) with their families, villagers and refugees. It looked like all of Croatia turned out for the Mass, singing praises to Our Lord!

Television crews from Austria and Germany were also present. I could see the sadness in these people's hearts, which reflected in their eyes and on their faces and in their countenance as they gave homage to God. We could hear the bombing in the distance. How sad, a village full of peace, yet racked with the heartache of war!!

Soldiers on Mt. Krizevac

Soldiers and their guns everywhere. But these soldiers came not to kill, but to pray with their families; on their necks they wore their Rosaries - "their weapons," as Fr. Jozo has commented. Not one single life has been lost (so far) from Medjugorje...Our Lady is watching over and protecting them. Amid the BOOM! BOOM! BOOM! across the horizon, the Queen of Peace still reigns in Medjugorje.

On Sunday our group was present in the choir loft for the apparition. I felt so unworthy to be there. I took the most distant position in the back, in the corner. During the Rosary, when Ivan entered and knelt down, you could feel Our Lady's presence. Silence prevailed in the entire church. During Our Lady's appearance, in the choir loft, Nancy Louer who walked with crutches for ten years was cured !! I recalled earlier how I encountered her with her crutches, struggling the descent of Mt. Podbrdo. She had artificial hips, arthritis throughout her body, several disks removed, and was in constant pain. That evening during our group's gathering for prayer and conversation, Nancy walked normally without the aid of her crutches. She ran up and down the room, even tapped danced! Beaming with joy, she reported she "had no pain!" Nancy left her crutches in Medjugorje. This miracle was registered with Fr. Slavko. Her medical reports will be sent back to Medjugorje.

On Monday we visited with the visionary Vicka. She was well and began praying and speaking of the Blessed Mother's request for peace, communication with God, faith, prayer (especially the Rosary, Creed – the 7 Our Father's, 7 Hail Mary's, and 7 Glory Be's), Scripture reading, fasting on Wednesdays and Fridays (on bread and water if possible, or if not, some other means of fasting and self denial), frequently receiving the Holy Sacrament (with monthly confession and receiving Holy Communion as often as possible). Vicka says, "Our Lady wants us to love, to pray and make Jesus the total center of our lives."

We visited with Ivan in the afternoon. He availed himself to our numerous questions. He said Our Lady has been very sorrowful during Her daily appearances. She continues to say that war can be averted through prayer and fasting.

On Tuesday, after an early breakfast, we set out by bus for Fr. Jozo's monastery. He greeted us in the church yard. His countenance is sad. His eyes reflect the sadness of his people. He appeared much thinner (which I attributed to fasting and concern for his people). He stated that "the Blessed Mother is fighting the war against Satan and sin. The weapon is prayer. The weapon is the Rosary." Our Lady says over and over, "My dear children, I invite you again to prayer and fasting to stop the war."

Father Jozo showed us the damage the bombs did. He spoke of the killing of children, the raping of nuns and women, the bombings, the destruction of villages, of the millions of people who have lost their homes and have nowhere to go. Also the destruction of over 300 churches, the refugees, the tens of thousands of people killed in the parks, cadavers left in the streets and forests, which are now concentration camps, and the destruction of over 500 historical monuments, along with thousands of apartments, houses and factories. But he said, "Pray for the conversion of the enemy. Forgive the enemy and love the enemy." In spite of all the devastation, the Spirit of God still permeates their souls. He's asking, as Our Lady is requesting, to pray, forgive and to be love.

My thoughts turned to how many in America, if our women were raped, our children were killed, our homes ravaged or destroyed, would pray, forgive, love...

Outside the church, we viewed the sandbags stacked outside the monastery as was apparent at the various airports and in Medjugorje, in an attempt to ward off shelling.

Returning to Medjugorje, we had lunch, and bid our tearful farewells to our host families. We then set out for our overnight stay in Split. We slept and awakened early for our trip to the Split airport. While waiting for our flight to Zagreb, we prayed the Rosary. We flew from Zagreb to Vienna, Austria, where we remained overnight, and left for the United States.

Our journey was truly a lesson in humility. Mary has been appearing in Medjugorje for over 11 years now. She comes as the "Queen of Peace." Her messages have been the same for 11 years: To pray – to pray for peace. She says She's come to teach us to pray. As Our Lady, Queen of Peace, the people of Medjugorje and former Yugoslavia are requesting – Please...Pray, pray, pray.

Are we answering Her call?

Statue of Our Lady in front of St. James Church

(2/95)
Thanksgiving from Priests, Visionaries and Parishioners of Medjugorje
Love Without Borders

"Thank you for having responded to my call."

This is how every message of Our Lady from Medjugorje ends. By thanking us in advance for the response, which is often only partial, Our Lady is teaching us to be thankful; thankful for every good word, for very gift, for every assistance.

We from Medjugorje, Herzegovina, Bosnia, and Croatia have every reason to be thankful to Our Lady, because by inviting pilgrims to Medjugorje, She gave to us a gift of so many friends, who think about us from across the world, pray for us, care for us, help us. By Her daily apparitions, Our Lady was preparing us to endure the terror of this brutal war, which cannot be compared to anything in history. Our Lady prepared the world to be aware of us, to feel with us, to help us. At the very beginning of the war, our friends started on the pilgrimage with gifts for the needy. When the war was in full scale and the needs became greater, small trucks started to arrive, and soon the wheels were rolling from Italy, Germany, Austria, the

Netherlands, Belgium, France, England and Ireland. And soon after even from the continents across the ocean.

Prayer groups became main gathering places for humanitarian aid in Europe, and so were centers for peace on other continents. Many women manifested themselves in a special way as strong organizers for help as if they were waiting for their moment to show their ability.

Now hungry are being fed, naked are being clothed, sick are receiving medicine, the lame are getting prostheses...hospitals are being supplied with instruments, vehicles, plasma, bandages...some of the sick and refugees find shelter abroad. War always brings with itself new hardships, which often are unpredictable and unforeseen, but for which love always finds a solution.

Therefore, dear friends, friends of Our Lady and friends of Medjugorje, **thank you that you responded to Our Lady's call.** We can neither name all of you individually nor by your prayer groups; for this we would need whole books of paper. Be certain of this: **Your names are inscribed in the Book of Life.**

We beg you, continue to help us. May your love remain without borders, religious or national. "May your left hand know not what your right hand is doing." **Be assured that help which you are sending through us goes to the hungry.** As long as we have you, there will be no hunger in our lands.

Translated by the Sarcevic's

231

Appendix

January 25, 1988

"Dear children! Today again I am calling you to complete conversion, which is difficult for those who have not chosen God. God can give you everything that you seek from Him. But you seek God only when sicknesses, problems and difficulties come to you and you think that God is far from you and is not listening and does not hear your prayers. No, dear children, that is not the truth. When you are far from God, you cannot receive graces because you do not seek them with a firm faith. Day by day, I am praying for you, and I want to draw you ever more near to God, but I cannot if you don't want it. Therefore, dear children put your life in God's hands. I bless you all. Thank you for having responded to my call."

February 25, 1988

"Dear children! Today again I am calling you to prayer to complete surrender to God. You know that I love you and am coming here out of love so I could show you the path to peace and salvation for your souls. I want you to obey me and not permit Satan to seduce you. Dear children, Satan is very strong and, therefore, I ask you to dedicate your prayers to me so that those who are under his influence can be saved. Give witness by your life. Sacrifice your lives for the salvation of the world. I am with you, and I am grateful to you, but in heaven you shall receive the Father's reward which He has promised to you. Therefore, dear children, do not be afraid. If you pray, Satan cannot injure you even a little bit because you are God's children and He is watching over you. Pray and let the rosary always be in your hand as a sign to Satan that you belong to me. Thank you for having responded to my call."

March 25, 1988

"Dear children! Today also I am inviting you to a complete surrender to God. Dear children, you are not conscious of how God loves you with such a great love because He permits me to be with you so I can instruct you and help you to find the way of peace. This way, however, you cannot discover if you do not pray. Therefore, dear children, forsake everything and consecrate your time to God and God will bestow gifts upon you and bless you. Little children, don't forget that your life is fleeting like a spring flower which today is wondrously beautiful but tomorrow has vanished. Therefore, pray in such a way that your prayer, your surrender to God, may become like a road sign. That way, your witness will not only have value for yourselves but for all eternity. Thank you for having responded to my call."

April 25, 1988

"Dear children! God wants to make you holy. Therefore, through me He is inviting you to complete surrender. Let holy Mass be your life. Understand that the church is God's palace, the place in which I gather you and want to show you the way to God. Come and pray. Neither look at others nor slander them, but rather, let your life be a testimony on the way of holiness. Churches deserve respect and are set apart as holy because God, who became man, dwells in them day and night. Therefore, little children, believe and pray that the Father increase your faith, and then ask for whatever you need. I am with you and I am rejoicing because of your conversion and I am protecting you with my motherly mantle. Thank you for having responded to my call."

May 25, 1988

"Dear children! I am inviting you to a complete surrender to God. Pray, little children, that Satan may not carry you about like the branches in the wind. Be strong in God. I desire that through you the whole world may get to know the God of joy. By your life bear witness for God's joy. Do not be anxious nor worried. God himself will help you and show you the way. I desire that you love all men with my love. Only in that way can love reign over the world. Little children, you are mine. I love you and want you to surrender to me so that I can lead you to God. Never cease praying so that Satan cannot take advantage of you. Pray for the knowledge that you are mine. I bless you with blessings of joy. Thank you for having responded to my call."

June 25, 1988

"Dear children! I am calling you to that love which is loyal and pleasing to God. Little children, love bears everything bitter and difficult for the sake of Jesus who is love. Therefore, dear children, pray that God come to your aid, not however according to your desire, but according to His love. Surrender yourself to God so that He may hear you, console you and forgive everything inside you which is a hindrance on the way of love. In this way God can move your life, and you will grow in love. Dear children, glorify God with a hymn of love so that God's love may be able to grow in you day by day to its fullness. Thank you for having responded to my call."

July 25, 1988

"Dear children! Today I am calling you to a complete surrender to God. Everything you do and everything you possess give over to God so that He can take control in your life as the King of all that you possess. That way, through me, God can lead you into the depths of the spiritual life. Little children, do not be afraid, because I am with you even if you think there is no way out and that Satan is in control. I am bringing peace to you I am your mother, the Queen of Peace. I am blessing you with the blessings of joy so that for you God may be everything in your life. Thank you for having responded to my call."

August 25, 1988

"Dear children! Today I invite you all to rejoice in the life which God gives you. Little children, rejoice in God, the Creator, because He has created you so wonderfully. Pray that your life be joyful thanksgiving which flows out of your heart like a river of joy. Little children, give thanks unceasingly for all that you possess, for each little gift which God has given you, so that a joyful blessing always comes down from God upon your life. Thank you for having responded to my call."

September 25, 1988

"Dear children! Today I am inviting all of you, without exception, to the way of holiness in your life. God gave you the grace, the gift of holiness. Pray that you may, more and more, comprehend it, and in that way, you will be able, by your life, to bear witness for God. Dear children, I am blessing you and I intercede to God for you so that your way and your witness may be a complete one and a joy for God. Thank you for having responded to my call."

October 25, 1988

"Dear children! My invitation that you live the messages which I am giving you is a daily one, specially, little children, because I want to draw you closer to the Heart of Jesus. Therefore, little children, I am inviting you today to the prayer of consecration to Jesus, my dear Son, so that each of you may be His. And then I am inviting you to the consecration of my Immaculate Heart. I want you to consecrate yourselves as parents, as families and as parishioners so that all belong to God through my heart. Therefore, little children, pray that you comprehend the greatness of this message which I am giving you. I do not want anything for myself, rather all for the salvation of your soul. Satan is strong and therefore, you, little children, by constant prayer, press tightly against my motherly heart. Thank you for having responded to my call."

November 25, 1988

"Dear children! I call you to prayer, to have an encounter with God in prayer. God gives Himself to you, but He wants you to answer in your own freedom to his invitation. That is why little children during the day, find yourself a special time when you could pray in peace and humility, and have this meeting with God the creator. I am with you and I intercede for you in front of God, so watch in vigil, so that every encounter in prayer be the joy of your contact with God. Thank you for having responded to my call."

December 25, 1988

"Dear children! I call you to peace. Live it in your heart and all around you, so that all will know peace, peace that does not come from you but from God. Little children, today is a great day. Rejoice with me. Glorify the Nativity of Jesus through the peace that I give you. It is for this peace that I have come as your Mother, Queen of Peace. Today I give you my special blessing. Bring it to all creation, so that all creation will know peace. Thank you for having responded to my call."

January 25, 1989

"Dear children! Today I am calling you to the way of holiness. Pray that you may comprehend the beauty and the greatness of this way where God reveals himself to you in a special way. Pray that you may be open to everything that God does through you that in your life you may be enabled to give thanks to God and to rejoice over everything that He does through each individual. I give you my blessing. Thank you for having responded to my call."

February 25, 1989

"Dear children! Today I invite you to prayer of the heart. Throughout this season of grace I wish each of you to be united with Jesus, but without unceasing prayer you cannot experience the beauty and greatness of the grace which God is offering you. Therefore, little children, at all times fill your heart with even the smallest prayers. I am with you and unceasingly keep watch over every heart which is given to me. Thank you for having responded to my call."

March 25, 1989

"Dear children! I am calling you to a complete surrender to God. I am calling you to great joy and peace which only God can give. I am with you and I intercede for you every day before God. I call you, little children, to listen to me and to live the messages that I am giving you. Already for years you are invited to holiness but you are still far away. I am blessing you. Thank you for having responded to my call."

April 25, 1989

"Dear children! I am calling you to a complete surrender to God. Let everything that you possess be in the hands of God. Only in that way shall you have joy in your heart. Little children, rejoice in everything that you have. Give thanks to God because everything is God's gift to you. That way in your life you shall be able to give thanks for everything and discover God in everything even in the smallest flower. Thank you for having responded to my call."

May 25, 1989

"Dear children! I invite you now to be open to God. See, children, how nature is opening herself and is giving life and fruits. In the same way I invite you to live with God and to surrender completely to him. Children, I am with you and I want to introduce you continuously to the joy of life. I desire that everyone may discover the joy and love which can be found only in God and which only God can give. God doesn't want anything from you only your surrender. Therefore, children, decide seriously for God because everything else passes away. Only God doesn't pass away. Pray to be able to discover the greatness and joy of life which God gives you. Thank you for having responded to my call."

June 25, 1989

"Dear children! Today I am calling you to live the messages I have been giving you during the past eight years. This is the time of grace and I desire the grace of God be great for every single one of you. I am blessing you and I love you with a special love. Thank you for having responded to call."

July 25, 1989

"Dear children! Today I am calling you to renew your hearts. Open yourselves to God and surrender to him all your difficulties and crosses so, God may turn everything into joy. Little children, you cannot open yourselves to God if you do not pray. Therefore, from today, decide to consecrate a time in the day only for an encounter with God in silence. In that way you will be able, with God, to witness my presence here. Little children, I do not wish to force you. Rather freely give God your time, like children of God. Thank you for having responded to my call."

August 25, 1989

"Dear children! I call you to prayer. By means of prayer, little children, you obtain joy and peace. Through prayer you are richer in the mercy of God. Therefore, little children, let prayer be the life of each one of you. Especially I call you to pray so that all those who are far away from God may be converted. Then our hearts shall be richer because God will rule in the hearts of all men. Therefore, little children, pray, pray, pray! Let prayers begin to rule in the whole world. Thank you for having responded to my call."

September 25, 1989

"Dear children! Today I invite you to give thanks to God for all the gifts you have discovered in the course of your life and even for the least gift that you have perceived. I give thanks with you and want all of you to experience the joy of these gifts. And I want God to be everything for each one of you. And then, little children, you can grow continuously on the way of holiness. Thank you for responding to my call."

October 25, 1989

"Dear children! Today also I am inviting you to prayer. I am always inviting you, but you are still far away. Therefore, from today, decide seriously to dedicate time to God. I am with you and I wish to teach you to pray with the heart. In prayer with the heart you shall encounter God. Therefore, little children, pray, pray, pray! Thank you for having responded to my call."

November 25, 1989

"Dear children! I am inviting you for years by these messages which I am giving you. Little children, by means of the messages I wish to make a very beautiful mosaic in your hearts, so I may be able to present each one of you to God like the original image. Therefore, little children, I desire that your decisions be free before God, because He has given you freedom. Therefore pray, so that, free from any influence of Satan, we may decide only for God. I am praying for you before God and I am seeking your surrender to God. Thank you for responding to my call."

December 25, 1989

"Dear children! Today I bless you in a special way with my motherly blessing and I am interceding for you before God that He gives you the gift of conversion of the heart. For years I am calling you and exhorting you to a deep spiritual life in simplicity, but you are so cold. Therefore, little children, I ask you to accept and live the messages with seriousness, so that your soul will not be sad when I will no longer be with you, and when I will no longer lead you like insecure children in their first steps. Therefore, little children, every day read the messages that I have given you and transform them into life. I love you and therefore I am calling you all to the way of salvation with God. Thank you for having responded to my call."

January 25, 1990

"Dear children! Today I invite you to decide for God once again and to choose Him before everything and above everything, so that He may work miracles in your life and that day by day your life may become joy with Him. Therefore, little children, pray and do not permit Satan to work in your life through misunderstandings, the non-understanding and non-acceptance of one another. Pray that you may be able to comprehend the greatness and the beauty of the gift of life. Thank you for having responded to my call."

February 25, 1990

"Dear children! I invite you to surrender to God. In this season I specially want you to renounce all the things to which you are attached but which are hurting your spiritual life. Therefore, little children, decide completely for God, and do not allow Satan to come into your life through those things that hurt both you and your spiritual life. Little children, God is offering Himself to you in fullness, and you can discover and recognize Him only in prayer. Therefore make a decision for prayer. Thank you for having responded to call."

March 25, 1990

"Dear children! I am with you even if you are not conscious of it. I want to protect you from everything that Satan offers you and through which he wants to destroy you. As I bore Jesus in my womb, so also, dear children, do I wish to bear you into holiness. God wants to save you and sends you messages through men, nature, and so many things which can only help you to understand that you must change the direction of your life. Therefore, little children, understand also the greatness of the gift which God is giving you through me, so that I may protect you with my mantle and lead you to the joy of life. Thank you for having responded to my call."

April 25, 1990

"Dear children! Today I invite you to accept with seriousness and to live the messages which I am giving you. I am with you and I desire, dear children, that each one of you be ever closer to my heart. Therefore, little children, pray and seek the will of God in your everyday life. I desire that each one of you discover the way of holiness and grow in it until eternity. I will pray for you and intercede for you before God that you understand the greatness of this gift which God is giving me that I can be with you. Thank you for having responded to my call."

May 25, 1990

"Dear children! I invite you to decide with seriousness to live this novena. Consecrate the time to prayer and to sacrifice. I am with you and I desire to help you to grow in renunciation and mortification, that you may be able to understand the beauty of the life of people who go on giving themselves to me in special way. Dear children, God blesses you day after day and desires a change of your life. Therefore, pray that you may have the strength to change your life. Thank you for having responded to my call."

June 25, 1990

"Dear children! Today I desire to thank you for all your sacrifices and for all your prayers. I am blessing you with my special motherly blessing. I invite you all to decide for God, so that from day to day you will discover His will in prayer. I desire, dear children, to call all of you to a full conversion so that joy will be in your hearts. I am happy that you are here today in such great numbers. Thank you for having responded to my call."

July 25, 1990

"Dear children! Today I invite you to peace. I have come here as the Queen of Peace and I desire to enrich you with my motherly peace. Dear children, I love you and I desire to bring all of you to the peace which only God gives and which enriches every heart. I invite you to become carriers and witnesses of my peace to this unpeaceful world. Let peace reign in the whole world which is without peace and longs for peace. I bless you with my motherly blessing. Thank you for having responded to my call."

August 25, 1990

"Dear children! I desire to invite you to take with seriousness and put into practice the messages which I am giving you. You know, little children, that I am with you and I desire to lead you along the same path to heaven, which is beautiful for those who discover it in prayer. Therefore, little children, do not forget that those messages which I am giving you have to be put into your everyday life in order that you might be able to say: "There, I have taken the messages and tried to live them." Dear children, I am protecting you before the heavenly Father by my own prayers. Thank you for having responded to my call."

September 25, 1990

"Dear children! I invite you to pray with the heart in order that your prayer may be a conversation with God. I desire each one of you to dedicate more time to God. Satan is strong and wants to destroy and deceive you in many ways. Therefore, dear children, pray every day that your life will be good for yourselves and for all those you meet. I am with you and I am protecting you even though Satan wishes to destroy my plans and to hinder the desires which the Heavenly Father wants to realize here. Thank you for having responded to my call."

October 25, 1990

"Dear children! Today I call you to pray in a special way that you offer up sacrifices and good deeds for peace in the world. Satan is strong and with all his strength, desires to destroy the peace which comes from God. Therefore, dear children, pray in a special way with me for peace. I am with you and I desire to help you with my prayers and I desire to guide you on the path of peace. I bless you with my motherly blessing. Do not forget to live the messages of peace. Thank you for having responded to my call."

November 25, 1990

"Dear children! Today I invite you to do works of mercy with love and out of love for me and for your and my brothers and sisters. Dear children, all that you do for others, do it with great joy and humility towards God. I am with you and day after day I offer your sacrifices and prayers to God for the salvation of the world. Thank you for having responded to my call."

December 25, 1990

"Dear children! Today I invite you in a special way to pray for peace. Dear children, without peace you cannot experience the birth of the little Jesus neither today nor in your daily lives. Therefore, pray the Lord of Peace that He may protect you with His mantle and that He may help you to comprehend the greatness and the importance of peace in your heart. In this way you shall be able to spread peace from your heart throughout the whole world. I am with you and I intercede for you before God. Pray, because Satan wants to destroy my plans of peace. Be reconciled with one another and by means of your lives help peace reign in the whole earth. Thank you for having responded to my call."

January 25, 1991

"Dear children! Today, like never before, I invite you to prayer. Let your prayer be a prayer for peace. Satan is strong and desires to destroy not only human life, but also nature and the planet on which you live. Therefore, dear children, pray that through prayer you can protect yourselves with God's blessing of peace. God has sent me among you so that I may help you. If you so wish, grasp for the rosary. Even the rosary alone can work miracles in the world and in your lives. I bless you and I remain with you for as long as it is God's will. Thank you for not betraying my presence here and I thank you because your response is serving the good and the peace."

February 25, 1991

"Dear children! Today, I invite you to decide for God, because distance from God is the fruit of the lack of peace in your hearts. God is only peace. Therefore, approach Him through your personal prayer and then live peace in your hearts and in this way peace will flow from your hearts like a river into the whole world. Do not talk about peace, but make peace. I am blessing each of you and each good decision of yours. Thank you for having responded to my call."

March 25, 1991

"Dear children! Again today I invite you to live the passion of Jesus in prayer, and in union with Him. Decide to give more time to God who gave you these days of grace. Therefore, dear children, pray and in a special way renew the love for Jesus in your hearts. I am with you and I accompany you with my blessing and my prayers. Thank you for having responded to my call."

April 25, 1991

"Dear children! Today I invite you all so that your prayer be prayer with the heart. Let each of you find time for prayer so that in prayer you discover God. I do not desire you to talk about prayer, but

245

to pray. Let your every day be filled with prayer of gratitude to God for life and for all that you have. I do not desire your life to pass by in words but that you glorify God with deeds. I am with you and I am grateful to God for every moment spent with you. Thank you for having responded to my call."

May 25,1991

"Dear Children! Today I invite all of you who have heard my message of peace to realize it with seriousness and with love in your life. There are many who think that they are doing a lot by talking about the messages, but do not live them. Dear children, I invite you to life and to change all the negative in you, so that it all turns into the positive and life. Dear children, I am with you and I desire to help each of you to live and by living, to witness the good news. I am here, dear children, to help you and to lead you to heaven, and in heaven is the joy through which you can already live heaven now. Thank you for having responded to my call!"

June 25,1991

"Dear children! Today on this great day which you have given to me, I desire to bless all of you and to say: these days while I am with you are days of grace. I desire to teach you and help you to walk the way of holiness. There are many people who do not desire to understand my messages and to accept with seriousness what I am saying. But you I therefore call and ask that by your lives and by your daily living you witness my presence. If you pray, God will help you to discover the true reason for my coming. Therefore, little children, pray and read the Sacred Scriptures so that through my coming you discover the message in Sacred Scripture for you. Thank you for having responded to my call."

July 25, 1991

"Dear Children! Today I invite you to pray for peace. At this time peace is being threatened in a special way, and I am seeking from you to renew fasting and prayer in your families. Dear children, I desire you to grasp the seriousness of the situation and that much of what will happen depends on your prayers and you are praying a little bit. Dear children, I am with you and I am inviting you to begin to pray and fast seriously as in the first days of my coming. Thank you for having responded to my call."

August 25, 1991

"Dear Children! Today also I invite you to prayer, now as never before when my plan has begun to be realized. Satan is strong and wants to sweep away plans of peace and joy and make you think that my Son is not strong in his decisions. Therefore, I call all of you, dear children to pray and fast still more firmly. I invite you to realize through the secrets I began in Fatima may be fulfilled. I call you, dear children, to grasp the importance of my coming and the seriousness of the situation. I want to save all souls and present them to God. Therefore, let us pray that everything I have begun be fully realized. Thank you for having responded to my call."

September 25, 1991

"Dear children! Today in a special way I invite you all to prayer and renunciation. For now as never before Satan wants to show the world his shameful face by which he wants to seduce as many people as possible onto the way of death and sin. Therefore, dear children, help my Immaculate Heart to triumph in the sinful world. I beseech all of you to offer prayers and sacrifices for my intentions so I can present them to God for what is most necessary. Forget your desires, dear children, and pray for what God desires, and not for what you desire. Thank you for having responded to my call."

October 25, 1991

"Dear children! Pray! Pray! Pray!"

November 25, 1991

"Dear Children! This time also I am inviting you to prayer. Pray that you might be able to comprehend what God desires to tell you through my presence and through the messages I am giving you. I desire to draw you ever closer to Jesus and to His wounded heart that you might be able to comprehend the immeasurable love which gave itself for each one of you. Therefore, dear children, pray that from your heart would flow a fountain of love to every person both to the one who hates you and to the one who despises you. That way you will be able through Jesus' love to overcome all the misery in this world of sorrows, which is without hope for those who do not know Jesus. I am with you and I love you with the immeasurable love of Jesus. Thank you for all your sacrifices and prayers. Pray so I might be able to help you still more. Your prayers are necessary to me. Thank you for having responded to my call."

December 25, 1991

"Dear children! Today in a special way I bring the little Jesus to you, that He may bless you with His blessing of peace and love. Dear children, do not forget that this is a grace which many people neither understand nor accept. Therefore, you who have said that you are mine, and seek my help, give all of yourself. First of all, give your love and example in your families. You say that Christmas is a family feast. Therefore, dear children, put God in the first place in your families, so that He may give you peace and may protect you not only from war, but also in peace protect you from every satanic attack. When God is with you, you have everything. But when you do not want Him, then you are miserable and lost, and you do not know on whose side you are. Therefore, dear children, decide for God. Then you will get everything. Thank you for having responded to my call."

January 25, 1992

"Dear Children! Today, I am inviting you to a renewal of prayer in your families so that way every family will become a joy to my son Jesus. Therefore, dear children, pray and seek more time for Jesus and then you will be able to understand and accept everything, even the most difficult sicknesses and crosses. I am with you and I desire to take you into my heart and protect you, but you have not yet decided. Therefore, dear children, I am seeking for you to pray, so through prayer you would allow me to help you. Pray, my dear little children, so prayer becomes your daily bread. Thank you for having responded to my call."

February 25, 1992

"Dear children! Today I invite you to draw still closer to God through prayer. Only that way will I be able to help you and to protect you from every attack of Satan. I am with you and I intercede for you with God, that He protect you. But I need your prayers and your - "Yes." You get lost easily in material and human things, and forget that God is your greatest friend. Therefore, my dear little children, draw close to God so He may protect you and guard you from every evil. Thank you for having responded to my call!"

March 25, 1992

"Dear children! Today as never before I invite you to live my messages and to put them into practice in your life. I have come to you to help you and, therefore, I invite you to change your life because you have taken a path of misery, a path of ruin. When I told you: convert, pray, fast, be reconciled, you took these messages superficially. You started to live them and then you stopped, because it was difficult for you. No, dear children, when something is good, you have to persevere in the good and not think: God does not see me, He is not listening, He is not helping. And so you have gone away from God and from me because of your miserable interest. I wanted to create of you an oasis of peace, love and goodness. God wanted you, with your love and with His help, to do miracles and, thus, give an example. Therefore, here is what I say to you: Satan is playing with you and with your souls and I cannot help you because you are far away from my heart. Therefore, pray, live my messages and then you will see the miracles of God's love in your everyday life. Thank you for having responded to my call."

April 25, 1992

"Dear children! Today also I invite you to prayer. Only by prayer and fasting can war be stopped. Therefore, my dear little children, pray and by your life give witness that you are mine and that you belong to me, because Satan wishes in these turbulent days to seduce as many souls as possible. Therefore, I invite you to decide for God and He will protect you and show you what you should do and which path to take. I invite all those who have said "yes" to me to renew their consecration to my Son Jesus and to His Heart and to me so we can take you more intensely as instruments of peace in this unpeaceful world. Medjugorje is a sign to all of you and a call to pray and live the days of grace that God is giving you. Therefore, dear children, accept the call to prayer with seriousness. I am with you and your suffering is also mine. Thank you for having responded to my call."

May 25, 1992

"Dear children! Today also I invite you to prayer, so that through prayer you come still nearer to God. I am with you and I desire to lead you on the path to salvation that Jesus gives you. From day to day, I am nearer to you although you are not aware of it and you do not want to admit that you are only linked to me in a small way with your few prayers. When trials and problems arise, you say, "O God! O Mother! Where are you?" As for me, I only wait for your "Yes" to present to Jesus for Him to fill you with His grace. That is why, once more, please accept my call and start to pray in a new way until prayer becomes joy to you. Then you will discover that God is all-powerful in your daily life. I am with you and I am waiting for you. Thank you for having responded to my call."

June 25, 1992

"Dear children! Today I am happy, even if in my heart there is still a little sadness for all those who have started on this path and then have left it. My presence here is to take you on a new path, the path to salvation. This is why I call you, day after day to conversion. But if you do not pray, you cannot say that you are on the way to being converted. I pray for you and I intercede to God for peace; first peace in your hearts and also peace around you, so that God may be your peace. Thank you for having responded to my call."

July 25, 1992

"Dear children! Today also I invite you to prayer, a prayer of joy so that in these sad days no one amongst you may feel sadness in prayer, but a joyful meeting with God His Creator. Pray, little children, to be able to come closer to me and to feel through prayer what it is I desire from you. I am with you and each day I bless you with my maternal blessing so that Our Lord may fill you abundantly with His grace for your daily life. Give thanks to God for the grace of my being able to be with you because I assure you it is a great grace. Thank you for having responded to my call."

August 25, 1992

"Dear children! Today I desire to tell you that I love you. I love you with my maternal love and I invite you to open yourselves completely to me so that, through each one of you, I can convert and save this world which is full of sin and bad things. That is why, my dear little children, you should open yourselves completely to me so that I may carry you always further toward the marvelous love of God the Creator who reveals Himself to you from day to day. I am with you and I wish to reveal to you and show you the God who loves you. Thank you for having responded to my call."

September 25, 1992

"Dear children! Today again I would like to say to you that I am with you also in these troubled days during which Satan wishes to destroy all that my Son Jesus and I are building. He desires especially to destroy your souls. He wants to take you away as far as possible from the Christian life and from the commandments that the Church calls you to live. Satan wishes to destroy everything that is holy in you and around you. This is why, little children, pray, pray, pray to be able to grasp all that God is giving you through my coming. Thank you for having responded to my call."

October 25, 1992

"Dear children! I invite you to prayer now when Satan is strong and wishes to make as many souls as possible his own. Pray, dear children, and have more trust in me because I am here in order to help you and to guide you on a new path toward a new life. Therefore, dear little children, listen and live what I tell you because it is important for you when I shall not be with you any longer that you remember my words and all that I told you. I call you to begin to change your life from the beginning and that you decide for conversion not with words but with your life. Thank you for having responded to my call."

November 25, 1992

"Dear Children! Today, more than ever, I am calling you to pray. May your life become a continuous prayer. Without love you cannot pray. That is why I am calling you to love God, the Creator of your lives, above everything else. Then you will come to know God and will love Him in everything as He loves you. Dear children, it is a grace that I am with you. That is why you should accept and live my messages for your own good. I love you and that is why I am with you, in order to teach you and to lead you to a new life of conversion and renunciation. Only in this way will you discover God and all that which now seems so far away from you. Therefore, my dear children, pray. Thank you for having responded to my call."

December 25, 1992

"Dear children! I desire to place all of you under my mantle and protect you from all satanic attacks. Today is a day of peace, but in the whole world there is a great lack of peace. That is why I call you all to build a new world of peace with me through prayer. This I cannot do without you, and this is why I call all of you with my motherly love and God will do the rest. So, open yourselves to God's plan and to His designs to be able to cooperate with Him for peace and for everything that is good. Do not forget that your life does not belong to you, but is a gift with which you must bring joy to others and lead them to eternal life. May the tenderness of the little Jesus always accompany you. Thank you for having responded to my call."

January 25, 1993

"Dear children! Today I call you to accept and live my messages with seriousness. These days are the days when you need to decide for God, for peace and for the good. May every hatred and jealousy disappear from your life and your thoughts, and may there only dwell love for God and for your neighbor. Thus, and only thus shall you be able to discern the signs of the time. I am with you and I guide you into a new time, a time which God gives you as grace so that you may get to know him more. Thank you for having responded to my call."

February 25, 1993

"Dear children! Today I bless you with my motherly blessing and I invite you all to conversion. I wish that each of you decide for a change of life and that each of you works more in the Church not through words and thoughts but through example, so that your life may be a joyful testimony for Jesus. You cannot say that you are converted, because your life must become a daily conversion. In order to understand what you have to do, little children, pray and God will give you what you completely have to do, and where you have to change. I am with you and place you all under my mantle. Thank you for having responded to my call."

March 25, 1993

"Dear children! Today like never I call you to pray for peace, for peace in your hearts, peace in your families and peace in the whole world, because Satan wants war, wants lack of peace, wants to destroy all which is good. Therefore, dear children, pray, pray, pray. Thank you for having responded to my call."

April 25, 1993

"Dear children! Today I invite you all to awaken your hearts to love. Go into nature and look how nature is awakening and it will be a help to you to open your hearts to the love of God, the Creator. I desire you to awaken love in your families so that where there is unrest and hatred, love will reign and when there is love in your hearts then there is also prayer. And, dear children, do not forget that I am with you and I am helping you with my prayer that God may give you the strength to love. I bless and love you with my motherly love. Thank you for having responded to my call."

May 25, 1993

"Dear children! Today I invite you to open yourselves to God by means of prayer so the Holy Spirit may begin to work miracles in you and through you. I am with you and I intercede before God for each one of you because, dear children, each one of you is important in my plan of salvation. I invite you to be carriers of good and peace. God can give you peace only if you convert and pray. Therefore, my dear little children, pray, pray, pray and do that which the Holy Spirit inspires you. Thank you for having responded to my call."

June 25, 1993

"Dear children! Today I also rejoice at your presence here. I bless you with my motherly blessing and intercede for each one of you before God. I call you anew to live my messages and to put them into life and practice. I am with you and bless all of you day by day. Dear children, these are special times and, therefore, I am with you to love and protect you; to protect your hearts from Satan and to bring you all closer to the heart of my Son, Jesus. Thank you for having responded to my call."

July 25, 1993

"Dear children! I thank you for your prayers and for the love you show toward me. I invite you to decide to pray for my intentions. Dear children, offer novenas, making sacrifices wherein you feel the most bound. I want your life to be bound to me. I am your Mother, little children, and I do not want Satan to deceive you for He wants to lead you the wrong way, but he cannot if you do not permit him. Therefore, little children, renew prayer in your hearts, and then you will understand my call and my live desire to help you. Thank you for having responded to my call."

August 25, 1993

"Dear children! I want you to understand that I am your Mother, that I want to help you and call you to prayer. Only by prayer can you understand and accept my messages and practice them in your life. Read Sacred Scripture, live it, and pray to understand the signs of the times. This is a special time, therefore, I am with you to draw you close to my heart and the heart of my Son, Jesus. Dear little children, I want you to be children of the light and not of the darkness. Therefore, live what I am telling you. Thank you for having responded to my call."

September 25, 1993

"Dear children! I am your Mother and I invite you to come closer to God through prayer because only He is your peace, your savior. Therefore, little children, do not seek comfort in material things, but rather seek God. I am praying for you and I intercede before God for each individual. I am looking for your prayers that you accept me and accept my messages as in the first days of the apparitions and only then when you open your hearts and pray will miracles happen. Thank you for having responded to my call."

October 25, 1993

"Dear children! These years I have been calling you to pray, to live what I am telling you, but you are living my messages a little. You talk, but do not live, that is why little children, this war is lasting so long. I invite you to open yourselves to God and in your hearts to live with God, living the good and giving witness to my messages. I love you and wish to protect you from every evil, but you do not desire it. Dear children, I cannot help you if you do not live God's commandments, if you do not live the Mass, if you do not give up sin. I invite you to be apostles of love and goodness. In this world of unrest give witness to God and God's love, and God will bless you and give you what you seek from Him. Thank you for having responded to my call."

November 25, 1993

"Dear children! I invite you in this time like never before to prepare for the coming of Jesus. Let little Jesus reign in your hearts and only then when Jesus is your friend will you be happy. It will not be difficult for you either to pray or offer sacrifices or to witness Jesus' greatness in your life because He will give you strength and joy in this time. I am close to you by my intercession and prayer and I love and bless all of you. Thank you for having responded to my call."

December 25, 1993

"Dear children! Today I rejoice with the little Jesus and I desire that Jesus' joy may enter into every heart. Little children, with the message I give you a blessing with my son Jesus, so that in every heart peace may reign. I love you, little children, and I invite all of you to come closer to me by means of prayer. You talk and talk but do not pray. Therefore, little children, decide for prayer. Only in this way will you be happy and God will give you what you seek from Him. Thank you for having responded to my call."

January 25,1994

"Dear children! You are all my children. I love you. But, little children, you must not forget that without prayer you cannot be close to me. In these times Satan wants to create disorder in your hearts and in your families. Little children, do not give in. You should not allow him to lead you and your life. I love you and intercede before God for you. Little children, pray. Thank you for having responded to my call."

February 25, 1994

"Dear children! Today I thank you for your prayers. All of you have helped me so that this war may end as soon as possible. I am close to you and I pray for each one of you and I beg you: pray, pray, pray. Only through prayer can we defeat evil and protect all that Satan wants to destroy in your lives. I am your Mother and I love you all equally, and I intercede for you before God. Thank you for having responded to my call."

March 25, 1994

"Dear children! Today I rejoice with you and I invite you to open yourselves to me, and become an instrument in my hands for the salvation of the world. I desire, little children, that all of you who have felt the odor of holiness through these messages which I am

257

giving you to carry, to carry it into this world, hungry for God and God's love. I thank you all for having responded in such a number and I bless you all with my motherly blessing. Thank you for having responded to my call."

April 25, 1994

"Dear children! Today I invite you to decide to pray according to my intention. Little children, I invite each one of you to help my plan to be realized through this parish. Now I invite you in a special way, little children, to decide to go along the way of holiness. Only this way will you be close to me. I love you and I desire to conduct you all with me to Paradise. But, if you do not pray and if you are not humble and obedient to the messages which I am giving you, I cannot help you. Thank you for having responded to my call."

May 25, 1994

"Dear children! I invite you all to have more trust in me and to live my messages more deeply. I am with you and I intercede before God for you but also I wait for your hearts to open up to my messages. Rejoice because God loves you and gives you the possibility to convert every day and to believe more in God the Creator. Thank you having responded to my call."

June 25, 1994

"Dear children! Today I rejoice in my heart in seeing you all present here. I bless you and I call you all to decide to live my messages which I give you here. I desire, little children, to guide you all to Jesus because He is your salvation. Therefore, little children, the more you pray the more you will be mine and of my Son, Jesus. I bless you all with my motherly blessing and I thank you for having responded to my call."

July 25, 1994

"Dear children! Today I invite you to decide to give time patiently for prayer. Little children, you cannot say you are mine and that you have experienced conversion through my messages if you are not ready to give time to God every day. I am close to you and I bless you all. Little children, do not forget that if you do not pray you are not close to me, nor are you close to the Holy Spirit who leads you along the path to holiness. Thank you for having responded to my call."

August 25, 1994

"Dear children! Today I am united with you in prayer in a special way, praying for the gift of the presence of my most beloved son in your home country. Pray, little children, for the health of my most beloved son, who suffers, and whom I have chosen for these times. I pray and intercede before my Son, Jesus, so that the dream that your fathers had may be fulfilled. Pray, little children, in a special way, because Satan is strong and wants to destroy hope in your heart. I bless you. Thank you for having responded to my call."

September 25, 1994

"Dear children! I rejoice with you and I invite you to prayer. Little children, pray for my intention. Your prayers are necessary to me, through which I desire to bring you closer to God. He is your salvation. God sends me to help you and to guide you towards paradise, which is your goal. Therefore, little children, pray, pray, pray. Thank you for having responded to my call."

October 25, 1994

"Dear children! I am with you and I rejoice today because the Most High has granted me to be with you and to teach you and to guide you on the path of perfection. Little children, I wish you to be a beautiful bouquet of flowers which I wish to present to God for the day of All Saints. I invite you to open yourselves and to live, taking the saints as an example. Mother Church has chosen them, that they may be an impulse for your daily life. Thank you for having responded to my call!"

November 25, 1994

"Dear children! Today I call you to prayer. I am with you and I love you all. I am your Mother and I wish that your hearts be similar to my heart. Little children, without prayer you cannot live and say that you are mine. Prayer is joy. Prayer is what the human heart desires. Therefore, get closer, little children, to my Immaculate Heart and you will discover God. Thank you for having responded to my call."

December 25, 1994

"Dear children! Today I rejoice with you and I am praying with you for peace: peace in your hearts, peace in your families, peace in your desires, peace in the whole world. May the King of Peace bless you today and give you peace. I bless you and I carry each one of you in my heart. Thank you for having responded to my call."

January 25, 1995

"Dear children! I invite you to open the door of your heart to Jesus as the flower opens itself to the sun. Jesus desires to fill your hearts with peace and joy. You cannot, little children, realize peace if you are not at peace with Jesus. Therefore, I invite you to confession so Jesus may be your truth and peace. So, little children, pray to have the strength to realize what I am telling you. I am with you and I love you. Thank you for having responded to my call."

February 25, 1995

"Dear children! Today I invite you to become missionaries of my messages, which I am giving here through this place that is dear to me. God has allowed me to stay this long with you and therefore, little children, I invite you to live with love the messages I give and to transmit them to the whole world, so that a river of love flows to people who are full of hatred and without peace. I invite you, little children, to become peace where there is no peace and light where there is darkness, so that each heart accepts the light and the way of salvation. Thank you for having responded to my call."

March 25, 1995

"Dear Children! Today I invite you to live the peace in your hearts and families. There is no peace, little children, where there is no prayer and there is no love, where there is no faith. Therefore, little children, I invite you all, to decide again today for conversion. I am close to you and I invite you all, little children, into my embrace to help you, but you do not want and in this way, Satan is tempting you, and in the smallest thing, your faith disappears. This is why little children, pray and through prayer, you will have blessing and peace. Thank you for having responded to my call."

April 25, 1995

"Dear children! Today I call you to love. Little children, without love you can neither live with God nor with brother. Therefore, I call all of you to open your hearts to the love of God that is so great and open to each one of you. God, out of love for man, has sent me among you to show you the path of salvation, the path of love. If you do not first love God, then you will neither be able to love neighbor nor the one you hate. Therefore, little children, pray and through prayer you will discover love. Thank you for having responded to my call."

May 25, 1995

"Dear Children! I invite you, little children, to help me through your prayers so that as many hearts as possible come close to my Immaculate Heart. Satan is strong and with all his forces wants to bring closer the most people possible to himself and to sin. That is why he is on the prowl to snatch more every moment. I beg you, little children, pray and help me to help you. I am your mother and I love you and that is why I wish to help you. Thank you for having responded to my call."

June 25, 1995

"Dear Children! Today I am happy to see you in such great numbers, that you have responded and have come to live my messages. I invite you, little children, to be my joyful carriers of peace in this troubled world. Pray for peace so that as soon as possible a time of peace, which my heart waits impatiently for, may reign. I am near to you, little children, and intercede for every one of you before the Most High. I bless you with my motherly blessing. Thank you for having responded to my call."

July 25, 1995

"Dear children! Today I invite you to prayer because only in prayer can you understand my coming here. The Holy Spirit will enlighten you to understand that you must convert. Little children, I wish to make of you a most beautiful bouquet prepared for eternity but you do not accept the way of conversion, the way of salvation that I am offering you through these apparitions. Little children, pray, convert your hearts and come closer to me. May good overcome evil. I love you and bless you. Thank you for having responded to my call."

August 25, 1995

"Dear children! Today I invite you to prayer. Let prayer be life for you. A family cannot say that it is in peace if it does not pray. Therefore, let your morning begin with morning prayer, and the evening end with thanksgiving. Little children, I am with you, and I love you and I bless you and I wish for every one of you to be in my embrace. You cannot be in my embrace if you are not ready to pray every day. Thank you for having responded to my call."

September 25, 1995

"Dear Children! Today I invite you to fall in love with the Most Holy Sacrament of the Altar. Adore Him, little children, in your Parishes and in this way you will be united with the entire world. Jesus will become your friend and you will not talk of Him like someone whom you barely know. Unity with Him will be a joy for you and you will become witnesses to the love of Jesus that He has for every creature. Little children, when you adore Jesus you are also close to me. Thank you for having responded to my call."

October 25, 1995

"Dear Children! Today I invite you to go into nature because there you will meet God the Creator. Today I invite you, little children, to thank God for all that He gives you. In thanking Him you will discover the Most High and all the goods that surround you. Little children, God is great and His love for every creature is great. Therefore, pray to be able to understand the love and goodness of God. In the goodness and the love of God the Creator, I also am with you as a gift. Thank you for having responded to my call."

November 25, 1995

"Dear Children! Today I invite you that each of you begin again to love, in the first place, God who saved and redeemed each of you, and then brothers and sisters in your proximity. Without love, little children, you cannot grow in holiness and cannot do good deeds. Therefore, little children, pray without ceasing that God reveals His love to you. I have invited all of you to unite yourselves with me and to love. Today I am with you and invite you to discover love in your hearts and in the families. For God to live in your hearts, you must love. Thank you for having responded to my call."

December 25, 1995

"Dear Children! Today I also rejoice with you and I bring you little Jesus, so that He may bless you. I invite you, dear children, so that your life may be united with Him. Jesus is the King of Peace and only He can give you the peace that you seek. I am with you and I present you to Jesus in a special way, now in this new time in which one should decide for Him. This time is the time of grace. Thank you for having responded to my call."

January 25, 1996

"Dear Children! Today I invite you to decide for peace. Pray that God give you the true peace. Live peace in your hearts and you will understand, dear children, that peace is the gift of God. Dear children, without love you cannot live peace. The fruit of peace is love and the fruit of love is forgiveness. I am with you and I invite all of you, little children, that before all else forgive in the family and then you will be able to forgive others. Thank you for having responded to my call."

February 25, 1996

"Dear children! Today I invite you to conversion. This is the most important message that I have given you here. Little children, I wish that each of you become a carrier of my messages. I invite you, little children, to live the messages that I have given you over these years. This time is a time of grace. Especially now, when the Church also is inviting you to prayer and conversion. I also, little children, invite you to live my messages that I have given you during the time since I appear here. Thank you for having responded to my call."

March 25, 1996

"Dear children! I invite you to decide again to love God above all else. In this time when due to the spirit of consumerism one forgets what it means to love and to cherish true values, I invite you again, little children, to put God in the first place in your life. Do not let Satan attract you through material things but, little children, decide for God who is freedom and love. Choose life and not death of the soul, little children, and in this time when you meditate upon the suffering and death of Jesus I invite you to decide for life which blossomed through the Resurrection, and that your life may be renewed today through conversion that shall lead you to eternal life. Thank you for having responded to my call."

April 25, 1996

"Dear children! Today I invite you again to put prayer in the first place in your families. Little children, when God is in the first place, then you will, in all that you do, seek the will of God. In this way your daily conversion will become easier. Little children, seek with humility that which is not in order in your hearts, and you shall understand what you have to do. Conversion will become a daily duty that you will do with joy. Little children, I am with you, I bless you all and I invite you to become my witnesses by prayer and personal conversion. Thank you for having responded to my call."

May 25, 1996

"Dear children! Today I wish to thank you for all your prayers and sacrifices that you, during this month which is consecrated to me, have offered to me. Little children, I also wish that you all become active during this time that is through me connected to heaven in a special way. Pray in order to understand that you all, through your life and your example, ought to collaborate in the work of salvation. Little children, I wish that all people convert and see me and my son, Jesus, in you. I will intercede for you and help you to become the light. In helping the other, your soul will also find salvation. Thank you for having responded to my call."

June 25, 1996

"Dear children! Today I thank you for all the sacrifices you have offered me these days. Little children, I invite you to open yourselves to me and to decide for conversion. Your hearts, little children, are still not completely open to me and therefore, I invite you again to open to prayer so that in prayer the Holy Spirit will help you, that your hearts become of flesh and not of stone. Little children, thank you for having responded to my call and for having decided to walk with me toward holiness."

July 25, 1996

"Dear children! Today I invite you to decide every day for God. Little children, you speak much about God, but you witness little with your life. Therefore, little children, decide for conversion, that your life may be true before God, so that in the truth of your life you witness the beauty God gave you. Little children, I invite you again to decide for prayer because through prayer, you will be able to live the conversion. Each one of you shall become in the simplicity, similar to a child which is open to the love of the Father. Thank you for having responded to my call."

August 25, 1996

"Dear children! Listen, because I wish to speak to you and to invite you to have more faith and trust in God, who loves you immeasurably. Little children, you do not know how to live in the grace of God, that is why I call you all anew, to carry the word of God in your heart and in thoughts. Little children, place the Sacred Scripture in a visible place in your family, and read and live it. Teach your children, because if you are not an example to them, children depart into godlessness. Reflect and pray and then God will be born in your heart and your heart will be joyous. Thank you for having for responded to my call."

September 25, 1996

"Dear children! Today I invite you to offer your crosses and suffering for my intentions. Little children, I am your mother and I wish to help you by seeking for you the grace from God. Little children, offer your sufferings as a gift to God so they become a most beautiful flower of joy. That is why, little children, pray that you may understand that suffering can become joy and the cross the way of joy. Thank you for having for responded to my call."

October 25, 1996

"Dear children! Today I invite you to open yourselves to God the Creator, so that He changes you. Little children, you are dear to me. I love you all and I call you to be closer to me and that your love towards my Immaculate Heart be more fervent. I wish to renew you and lead you with my Heart to the Heart of Jesus, which still today suffers for you and calls you to conversion and renewal. Through you, I wish to renew the world. Comprehend, little children, that you are today the salt of the earth and the light of the world. Little children, I invite you and I love you and in a special way implore: Convert! Thank you for having responded to my call."

November 25, 1996

"Dear children! Today, again, I invite you to pray, so that through prayer, fasting and small sacrifices you may prepare yourselves for the coming of Jesus. May this time, little children, be a time of grace for you. Use every moment and do good, for only in this way will you feel the birth of Jesus in your hearts. If with your life you give an example and become a sign of God's love, joy will prevail in the hearts of men. Thank you for having responded to my call."

December 25, 1996

"Dear children! Today I am with you in a special way, holding little Jesus in my lap and I invite you, little children, to open yourselves to His call. He calls you to joy. Little children, joyfully live the messages of the Gospel, which I am repeating in the time since I am with you. Little children, I am your Mother and I desire to reveal to you the God of love and the God of peace. I do not desire for your life to be in sadness but that it be realized in joy for eternity, according to the Gospel. Only in this way will your life have meaning. Thank you for having responded to my call."

January 25, 1997

"Dear children! I invite you to reflect about your future. You are creating a new world without God, only with your own strength and that is why you are unsatisfied and without joy in the heart. This time is my time and that is why, little children, I invite you again to pray. When you find unity with God, you will feel hunger for the word of God and your heart, little children, will overflow with joy. You will witness God's love wherever you are. I bless you and I repeat to you that I am with you to help you. Thank you for having responded to my call."

February 25, 1997

"Dear children! Today I invite you in a special way to open yourselves to God the Creator and to become active. I invite you, little children, to see at this time who needs your spiritual or material help. By your example, little children, you will be the extended hands of God, which humanity is seeking. Only in this way will you understand, that you are called to witness and to become joyful carriers of God's word and of His love. Thank you for having responded to my call."

March 25, 1997

"Dear children! Today, in a special way, I invite you to take the cross in the hands and to meditate on the wounds of Jesus. Ask of Jesus to heal your wounds, which you, dear children, during your life sustained because of your sins or the sins of your parents. Only in this way, dear children, you will understand that the world is in need of healing of faith in God the Creator. By Jesus' passion and death on the cross, you will understand that only through prayer you, too, can become true apostles of faith; when, in simplicity and prayer, you live faith which is a gift. Thank you for having responded to my call."

April 25, 1997

"Dear children! Today I call you to have your life be connected with God the Creator, because only in this way will your life have meaning and you will comprehend that God is love. God sends me to you out of love, that I may help you to comprehend that without Him there is no future or joy and, above all, there is no eternal salvation. Little children, I call you to leave sin and to accept prayer at all times, that you may in prayer come to know the meaning of your life. God gives Himself to him who seeks Him. Thank you for having responded to my call."

May 25, 1997

"Dear children! Today I invite you to glorify God and for the Name of God to be holy in your hearts and in your life. Little children, when you are in the holiness of God, He is with you and gives you peace and joy which come from God only through prayer. That is why, little children, renew prayer in your families and your heart will glorify the holy Name of God and heaven will reign in your heart. I am close to you and I intercede for you before God. Thank you for having responded to my call."

June 25, 1997

"Dear children! Today I am with you in a special way and I bring you my motherly blessing of peace. I pray for you and I intercede for you before God, so that you may comprehend that each of you is a carrier of peace. You cannot have peace if your heart is not at peace with God. That is why, little children, pray, pray, pray, because prayer is the foundation of your peace. Open your heart and give time to God so that He will be your friend. When true friendship with God is realized, no storm can destroy it. Thank you for having responded to my call."

July 25, 1997

"Dear children! Today I invite you to respond to my call to prayer. I desire, dear children, that during this time you find a corner for personal prayer. I desire to lead you towards prayer with the heart. Only in this way will you comprehend that your life is empty without prayer. You will discover the meaning of your life when you discover God in prayer. That is why, little children, open the door of your heart and you will comprehend that prayer is joy without which you cannot live. Thank you for having responded to my call."

August 25, 1997

"Dear children! God gives me this time as a gift to you, so that I may instruct and lead you on the path of salvation. Dear children, now you do not comprehend this grace, but soon a time will come when you will lament for these messages. That is why, little children, live all of the words which I have given you through this time of grace and renew prayer, until prayer becomes a joy for you. Especially, I call all those who have consecrated themselves to my Immaculate Heart to become an example to others. I call all priests and religious brothers and sisters to pray the rosary and to teach others to pray. The rosary, little children, is especially dear to me. Through the rosary open your heart to me and I am able to help you. Thank you for having responded to my call."

September 25, 1997

"Dear children! Today I call you to comprehend that without love you cannot comprehend that God needs to be in the first place in your life. That is why, little children, I call you all to love, not with a human but with God's love. In this way, your life will be more beautiful and without an interest. You will comprehend that God gives Himself to you in the simplest way out of love. Little children, so that you may comprehend my words which I give you out of love, pray, pray, pray and you will be able to accept others with love and to forgive all who have done evil to you. Respond with prayer; prayer is a fruit of love towards God the Creator. Thank you for having responded to my call."

October 25, 1997

"Dear children! Also today I am with you and I call all of you to renew yourselves by living my messages. Little children, may prayer be life for you and may you be an example to others. Little children, I desire for you to become carriers of peace and of God's joy to today's world without peace. That is why, little children, pray, pray, pray! I am with you and I bless you with my motherly peace. Thank you for having responded to my call."

November 25, 1997

"Dear children! Today I invite you to comprehend your Christian vocation. Little children, I led and am leading you through this time of grace, that you may become conscious of your Christian vocation. Holy martyrs died witnessing: I am a Christian and love God over everything. Little children, today also I invite you to rejoice and be joyful Christians, responsible and conscious that God called you in a special way to be joyfully extended hands toward those who do not believe, and that through the example of your life, they may receive faith and love for God. Therefore, pray, pray, pray that your heart may open and be sensitive for the Word of God. Thank you for having responded to my call."

December 25, 1997

"Dear children! Also today I rejoice with you and I call you to the good. I desire that each of you reflect and carry peace in your heart and say: I want to put God in the first place in my life. In this way, little children, each of you will become holy. Little children, tell everyone, I want the good for you and he will respond with the good and, little children, good will come to dwell in the heart of each man. Little children, tonight I bring to you the good of my Son who gave His life to save you. That is why, little children, rejoice and extend your hands to Jesus who is only good. Thank you for having responded to my call."

Epilogue

Many people have asked why I chose AuthorHouse to publish this book, so I have been inspired to share this amazing story.

About a year ago, my "cyber friend" Bunny Becker sent me a copy of a book published by her friend Carolyn Kenney. After I began work on this book, I asked Carolyn for some information about the company she had published with, "First Books" (now called AuthorHouse) and soon after, I was contacted by a representative. He kept in contact with me for a few months, and in December he offered me a sizable discount if I signed by December 31. I was not ready to go to print, and was not sure if I should accept this offer, even though it was very tempting. I always want to do God's will, so I prayed about this and asked God if I should accept this offer. Then I asked God to let me know if this was His will that I sign with AuthorHouse. I asked Him to give me a sign if it was His will. The sign I asked for was a penny. God began sending me pennies 5 years ago, when something traumatic happened in my life. It took me a while to figure out that the phrase on the penny, "In God we trust," was the reason I was receiving the pennies. (I could write a book on all my amazing penny stories.) So eventually a penny began to be my "special sign" from God, acknowledging His will for my life. In fact, when I got the inspiration for this book, I asked for a penny to discern whether it was His will, and within hours I got my penny.

So, on December 15, I asked for a penny. The next day in the mail I got a Christmas card from a couple who lives a thousand miles away from me. Inside the Christmas card was a penny attached to a paper with a poem entitled, **"Pennies from Heaven."** Also enclosed was an article about a statue of **Our Lady of Medjugorje** from a senior secular newspaper in Georgia. The words "Our Lady of Medjugorje" were circled. The people who sent this to me are not Catholic and did not know about my pennies. I began to shed tears as I realized God was answering my prayers and telling me to sign with AuthorHouse. Still a wee bit skeptical, I said, "Lord, I will know for absolute sure that You really want me to sign with them if this penny is a 2004 penny, the year I will be signing." Then I looked at the penny, and sure enough – it was a 2004 penny. The rest is history. God is good....all the time!

Additional Medjugorje Resources

To be "fed" monthly by Our Lady's messages to the world, you can subscribe to the monthly newsletter "The Spirit of Medjugorje" by sending a free will offering along with your name and address to P.O. Box 6614, Erie, PA 16512. It can also be read on-line at <u>www.birdsongatmidnight.com</u> We also offer an 8-page "beginner's guide" that can be distributed. The suggested donation for 25 copies is $6 to cover the printing and postage. It is also available on tape for a suggested donation of $3 to cover the cost of the tape and postage.

Hopefully this book has given you an introduction to Our Lady of Medjugorje and Her messages. For further information, we suggest you consult the hundreds of books and websites on Medjugorje. We present to you here favorites as determined by an informal survey with the members of the International Internet Medjugorje Prayer Group, which has ties to Ivan's prayer group in Medjugorje. The members determined the following to be their favorite books on Medjugorje in this order:

Visions of the Children - Janice Connell
Medjugorje the Message - Wayne Weible
Final Harvest - Wayne Weible
Medjugorje the Mission - Wayne Weible
Queen of the Cosmos - Janice Connel
Pilgrimage - Fr. Svetozar Kraljevic
Pray with the Heart- Fr. Slavko Barbaric
Medjugorje in the 90's - Sr. Emmanuel
Letters from Medjugorje - Wayne Weible
Medjugorje Day by Day - Fr. Richard Beyer

Suggested Medjugorje websites:
http://www.medjugorje.hr (The official Medjugorje website)
http://www.medjugorje.org (One of the most popular Medjugorje websites, has links to other sites too)

http://www.medjugorjeusa.org (This site was designed with the "doubting Thomas" in mind.)

http://www.childrenofmedjugorje.com (Excellent audio tapes by Sr. Emmanuel can be ordered on this site.)

Caution should be used in purchasing credible resources since there are some books and videos on the market that are "New Age" material. When in doubt seek advice from proper sources at the above websites.

About The Author

The author, who is a mathematics teacher by profession, received the gift of writing and editing on a pilgrimage to the village of Medjugorje in Bosnia-Herzegovina in 1998. A stranger walked up to her the first day there and told her she should be taking notes at the talks since she was a teacher. Since this man had no way of knowing that she was a teacher, she began taking notes at all the talks from that point on. When she came home, a lady from her parish gave her a copy of "The Spirit of Medjugorje" newsletter and told her to write up her testimony and send it to the editor. There were enough articles to last for months until her next pilgrimage the following year. She continued to write, and in two years became co-editor. Two years after that, the editor suffered a heart attack and the author had to take over the duties of editing the newsletter. In January of 2004, she was officially made editor. She has published a "beginner's guide" to Medjugorje for those who know little or nothing about Medjugorje. Over 14,000 have been distributed. "The Spirit of Medjugorje" monthly newsletter is distributed to 50 states and 33 foreign countries, and is published on the internet at www.birdsongatmidnight.com.

The author also has been published in the Catholic best-seller, *101 Inspirational Stories of the Rosary*.

She sent the story in this publication to Pope John Paul II and received a letter back from the Vatican saying the Pope thanked her for the story.

The author's mission in life is to spread the messages of Our Lady of Medjugorje to the world. Her articles have been used in many other publications, including ones in Canada, Australia, England, Poland, New Zealand, and Wales.

Printed in the United States
84713LV00003B/154-162/A